The Cricket World Cup

History, Highlights, Facts and Figures

by Faraz Sarwat

SCORE
MEDIA

My thanks to John Levy, Benjie Levy, David Errington,
Craig Malanka, Richard Guttman, Dan Diamond,
Allan Turowetz, James Sharman, Kristian Jack and
everyone at *Sports World* on The Score.

A special word of thanks to my sister Sabina,
without whom I would be lost.

This book is dedicated to the memory
of my grandfather
M. Parvez (1922-2005).

– F.S.

Published by Score Media, 370 King Street West, Suite 304, Toronto, Ontario M5V 1J9

ISBN 978-1-894801-07-2

Printed in Canada by National Printers, Ottawa, Ontario

Project Management: Dan Diamond and Associates, Inc., Toronto, Ontario

Cover Design: Brian Waddington; Creative Director: Sam Nasrawi

Photo Credits: see page 196

Trade sales and distribution in Canada by:
North 49 Books, 35 Prince Andrew Drive, Toronto, Ontario M3C 2H2
416/449-4000; Fax 416/449-9924

www.scoremedia.ca

The Cricket World Cup

History, Highlights,
Facts and Figures

TABLE OF CONTENTS

Andrew Flintoff (left) and Kevin Pietersen: More substance than style will be needed from the dynamic duo if England are to progress in the World Cup.

KEY TO ABBREVIATIONS

Ave – Average; **CT** – catches; **Econ**- economy rate; **HS** – highest score; I – innings; **LBW** – leg before wicket; **M** – matches; **M** (in scorecards) – minutes; **M** (in bowling section) – maidens; **NO** – not out; **NR** – no result; **O** – overs; **R**- runs; **SR** – strike rate; **ST** – stumpings; **W** – wickets; **4W** – 4 wickets in a match; **5W** – 5 wickets in a match; ***-** not out

The Cricket World Cup
History, Highlights,
Facts and Figures

INTRODUCTION

A SPORT UNLIKE ANY OTHER, a World Championship in cricket was unthinkable until the advent of One Day International (ODI) cricket. Impractical logistics coupled with the high possibility of a draw and hence no winner at the end of proceedings meant that the traditional form of the international game, the five-day Test match, was simply not conducive for staging a multi-nation championship. But after a crowd of more than 45,000 witnessed a 40 overs per side match arranged on the final day of a rained out Test match between England and Australia in 1971, a new international match format quickly evolved. ODI cricket finally allowed countries to battle it out for the right to be called the best in the world.

One-day cricket matches of limited overs and a single innings a side had been a part of the English domestic game since the 1960s, but the idea had never extended itself to international cricket until that first ODI between England

Michael Hussey is likely to be a key player for Australia as they defend their title as World Champions during the 2007 World Cup.

and Australia. With a viable format discovered, a World Championship was simply a matter of time. The first World Cup was held in 1975 and since then has taken place every four years. ODI cricket itself has continued to go from strength to strength with the World Cup being the most coveted trophy in the sport and the tournament being the third largest sporting event in the world after the Olympics and soccer's World Cup.

With the first three World Cups held during the summer in England, the longer days allowed for matches that were 60 overs per innings. ODIs outside of the World Cup varied in format, with matches being played that were 45, 50 or 55 overs per innings. The World Cup went to a standard 50 overs a side when the tournament hit the subcontinent for the first time in 1987.

In the late 1970s the Kerry Packer revolution in Australia introduced coloured clothing, floodlit day/night matches, white balls and black sightscreens to ODI cricket played in that country. These Packer-influenced innovations made their World Cup debut in the 1992 edition of the tournament, and are now a standard part of ODI cricket as a whole.

Besides the Test playing nations, the World Cup has also provided associate members of the International Cricket Council (ICC) the opportunity to play in the competition. Methods of selecting the non-Test playing participants have ranged from the purely arbitrary in the early days, to a process whereby ranking in the ICC Trophy (which is a competition for the non-Test teams) determines participation in the World Cup. Initially only the winner of the ICC Trophy was invited to the World Cup, but in 1996 the practice of inviting the top three teams was introduced. The 2007 World Cup has expanded the idea further and for the first time the top five teams from the 2005 edition of the ICC Trophy will be competing alongside the established cricketing countries for the sport's biggest prize.

Sri Lanka, Zimbabwe and Bangladesh all competed in the World Cup prior to gaining Test status and their encouraging performances in the competition certainly accelerated their progress to full international honours. Other non-Test teams to have competed in the World Cup are East Africa, Canada, the Netherlands, the United Arab Emirates, Kenya, Scotland and Namibia. The 2007 World Cup will see the tournament debuts of Ireland and Bermuda.

The West Indies, winners of the first two World Cups finally have their chance in 2007 to play host to the cricketing world. With 16 teams participating, it will be the biggest

World Cup in history. For the first time the tournament will have four pools, with two teams qualifying out of each pool for the second round, known as the Super Eights. The top four teams after that round will qualify for the semi-finals, leading to the final match to be played at the Kensington Oval in Bridgetown, Barbados on April 28, 2007.

The World Cup has grown by leaps and bounds since 1975 when the entire tournament consisted of just 15 matches. In contrast, the 2007 World Cup will require 51 matches to determine the winner. But whether it has been a short tournament or a long one, there has always been gripping cricket – no shortage of drama, tension, heroics, compelling debuts or memorable farewells here.

The World Cup continues to be the ultimate showcase for this most noble of sports.

– Faraz Sarwat
Toronto, 2007

ICC Cricket World Cup
West Indies • 2007
SCHEDULE OF MATCHES

Group Stage

MARCH 2007

Tue 13   1st Match, Group D - West Indies v Pakistan
Sabina Park, Kingston, Jamaica

Wed 14 2nd Match, Group A - Australia v Scotland
Warner Park, Basseterre, St Kitts

Wed 14 3rd Match, Group C - Canada v Kenya
Beausejour Stadium, Gros Islet, St Lucia

Thu 15   4th Match, Group B - Bermuda v Sri Lanka
Queen's Park Oval, Port of Spain, Trinidad

Thu 15   5th Match, Group D - Ireland v Zimbabwe
Sabina Park, Kingston, Jamaica

Fri 16   6th Match, Group A - Netherlands v South Africa
Warner Park, Basseterre, St Kitts

Fri 16   7th Match, Group C - England v New Zealand
Beausejour Stadium, Gros Islet, St Lucia

Sat 17   8th Match, Group B - Bangladesh v India
Queen's Park Oval, Port of Spain, Trinidad

Sat 17   9th Match, Group D - Ireland v Pakistan
Sabina Park, Kingston, Jamaica

Sun 18   10th Match, Group A - Australia v Netherlands
Warner Park, Basseterre, St Kitts

Sun 18   11th Match, Group C - Canada v England
Beausejour Stadium, Gros Islet, St Lucia

Mon 19 12th Match, Group B - Bermuda v India
Queen's Park Oval, Port of Spain, Trinidad

Mon 19 13th Match, Group D - West Indies v Zimbabwe
Sabina Park, Kingston, Jamaica

Tue 20   14th Match, Group A - Scotland v South Africa
Warner Park, Basseterre, St Kitts

Tue 20   15th Match, Group C - Kenya v New Zealand
Beausejour Stadium, Gros Islet, St Lucia

Wed 21 16th Match, Group B - Bangladesh v Sri Lanka
Queen's Park Oval, Port of Spain, Trinidad

Wed 21 17th Match, Group D - Pakistan v Zimbabwe
Sabina Park, Kingston, Jamaica

Thu 22   18th Match, Group A - Netherlands v Scotland
Warner Park, Basseterre, St Kitts

ICC World Cup 2007 Schedule
continued

MARCH 2007 *continued*

Thu 22 **19th Match, Group C - Canada v New Zealand**
Beausejour Stadium, Gros Islet, St Lucia
Fri 23 **20th Match, Group B - India v Sri Lanka**
Queen's Park Oval, Port of Spain, Trinidad
Fri 23 **21st Match, Group D - Ireland v West Indies**
Sabina Park, Kingston, Jamaica
Sat 24 **22nd Match, Group A - Australia v South Africa**
Warner Park, Basseterre, St Kitts
Sat 24 **23rd Match, Group C - England v Kenya**
Beausejour Stadium, Gros Islet, St Lucia
Sun 25 **24th Match, Group B - Bangladesh v Bermuda**
Queen's Park Oval, Port of Spain, Trinidad

Second Stage – Super Eight

Tue 27 **25th Match, Super Eights - D2 v A1**
Sir Vivian Richards Stadium, St Peter's, Antigua
Wed 28 **26th Match, Super Eights - A2 v B1**
Providence Stadium, Guyana
Thu 29 **27th Match, Super Eights - D2 v C1**
Sir Vivian Richards Stadium, St Peter's, Antigua
Fri 30 **28th Match, Super Eights - D1 v C2**
Providence Stadium, Guyana
Sat 31 **29th Match, Super Eights - A1 v B2**
Sir Vivian Richards Stadium, St Peter's, Antigua

APRIL 2007
Sun 1 **30th Match, Super Eights - D2 v C1**
Providence Stadium, Guyana
Mon 2 **31th Match, Super Eights - B2 v C1**
Sir Vivian Richards Stadium, St Peter's, Antigua
Tue 3 **32th Match, Super Eights - D1 v A2**
Providence Stadium, Guyana
Wed 4 **33th Match, Super Eights - C2 v B1**
Sir Vivian Richards Stadium, St Peter's, Antigua
Sat 7 **34th Match, Super Eights - B2 v A2**
Providence Stadium, Guyana

*APRIL **2007*** *continued*

Sun 8   35th Match, Super Eights - A1 v C2
Sir Vivian Richards Stadium, St Peter's, Antigua
Mon 9   36th Match, Super Eights - D1 v C1
Providence Stadium, Guyana
Tue 10   37th Match, Super Eights - D2 v A2
National Cricket Stadium, St George's, Grenada
Wed 11   38th Match, Super Eights - C2 v B2
Kensington Oval, Bridgetown, Barbados
Thu 12   39th Match, Super Eights - B1 v C1
National Cricket Stadium, St George's, Grenada
Fri 13   40th Match, Super Eights - A1 v D1
Kensington Oval, Bridgetown, Barbados
Sat 14   41th Match, Super Eights - A2 v C1
National Cricket Stadium, St George's, Grenada
Sun 15   42th Match, Super Eights - B2 v D1
Kensington Oval, Bridgetown, Barbados
Mon 16   43th Match, Super Eights - A1 v B1
National Cricket Stadium, St George's, Grenada
Tue 17   44th Match, Super Eights - A2 v C2
Kensington Oval, Bridgetown, Barbados
Wed 18   45th Match, Super Eights - D1 v B1
National Cricket Stadium, St George's, Grenada
Thu 19   46th Match, Super Eights - D2 v B2
Kensington Oval, Bridgetown, Barbados
Fri 20   47th Match, Super Eights - A1 v C1
National Cricket Stadium, St George's, Grenada
Sat 21   48th Match, Super Eights - D2 v C2
Kensington Oval, Bridgetown, Barbados

Semi-Final Round

Tue 24   1st Semi Final - 2 v 3
Sabina Park, Kingston, Jamaica
Wed 25   2nd Semi Final - 1 v 4
Beausejour Stadium, Gros Islet, St Lucia

Final

Sat 28   Final - TBC v TBC
Kensington Oval, Bridgetown, Barbados

The West Indies captain Clive Lloyd receives the inaugural World Cup from Prince Philip, Duke of Edinburgh, at Lord's, London, June 21, 1975.

The Cricket World Cup

History

1975

WORLD CUP 1975 • ENGLAND
Official Title: The Prudential World Cup
Winners: West Indies
Group A: England, New Zealand, India, East Africa
Group B: Australia, West Indies, Pakistan, Sri Lanka
June 7, 1975- June 21, 1975

The inaugural Cricket World Cup in1975 was a success by any stretch of the imagination. It was held in England, the country of the sport's birth, with the final being played at the historic Lord's cricket ground in London, between two powerful teams, the better of which rightfully emerged victorious. The fact that matches were largely played in bright sunshine, without any time lost to English summer rain, adds to the romance of how successful and auspicious cricket's first World Cup was, and how it set the template for future editions of the tournament.

One Day International (ODI) cricket was still in its infancy at the time and the first match of the tournament between England and India was only the 19th ODI ever played. Innings were 60 overs each, with bowlers limited to 12 overs apiece. There were only 15 matches played in the entire tournament, but the 1975 World Cup produced several noteworthy moments, from Sunil Gavaskar's notorious 36 not out, to the ODI debuts of legendary cricketers like Viv Richards and Javed Miandad. The 1975 World Cup also had two matches that continue to be remembered among the greatest ODIs ever played, the epic battle between the West Indies and Pakistan at Edgbaston, Birmingham and the final itself, between the West Indies and Australia.

The eight teams participating in the tournament were divided into two groups where each team played the other members of its group once and the top two teams from each group qualified for the semi-final. Both groups had a no-hoper, with East Africa (a motley collection of amateur cricketers from Tanzania, Uganda, Zambia and Kenya) playing the part in Group A and Sri Lanka (who did not have Test status at the time) playing the part in Group B.

In retrospect, it seems obvious that the West Indies under Clive Lloyd would go through the tournament undefeated, but even though they were the favourites, this 1975 West Indies team was yet to acquire the tag of invincible, as a post World Cup tour of Australia where the West Indies lost 5 of the 6 Tests would tellingly reveal. Indeed, hosts England, finalists Australia and Pakistan who, like the West Indies, were an outfit with plenty of English county professionals, were all seen as having a decent chance at winning the trophy. Lloyd himself has suggested that it was only after his team's nail-biting win against Pakistan that he was convinced that his side would be crowned World Champions. The fact that the West Indies did have challengers only made the inaugural tournament all the more gripping.

1st Semi-final • 1975
England v Australia
Headingley, Leeds

The Ashes rivals met in the first semi-final of the first World Cup. A match that everyone expected to be intense turned into something of a shocker on a Headingley wicket that offered generous assistance to swing bowlers. Australia won the toss and inserted England on the seamer's paradise, where unheralded left-arm medium-pacer Gary Gilmour proved to be more than a handful for England's batsmen.

Incredibly, the semi-final was Gilmour's first match of the tournament, and he made up for lost time. Bowling a tight line within the stumps, Gilmour troubled all of England's top batsmen who found it difficult to get him away for runs. In ideal pitch conditions for his type of bowling, Gilmour destroyed England's batting line-up. He bowled his full quota of 12 overs, six of which were maidens. Tony Greig went to an absolutely stunning catch taken by wicket-keeper Rod Marsh who flew to his right and caught the ball one-handed in front of the fielder stationed at first slip, but that was all the help that Gilmour would need. His tight line saw four batsmen, Dennis Amiss, Keith Fletcher, Frank Hayes and Alan Knott, adjudged LBW, while opener Barry Wood lost his off-stump to Gilmour. England were bundled out for an embarrassing 93 in 36.2 overs with Gary Gilmour taking 6-14 in his 12 overs, the first six-wicket haul in ODI history.

Australia then made heavy weather of knocking off the paltry total. John Snow and Mike Old also moved the ball prodigiously and it was left to Gary Gilmour (who else?) batting at number 8 to come out and make the top score of the match, a well-struck 28 not out off 28 deliveries, with five hits to the fence. Australia reached their target in the 28th over, for the loss of 6 wickets.

1st Semi-final • 1975
England v Australia
Headingley, Leeds • 18 June 1975 (60 overs per innings)
Toss: Australia
Umpires: WE Alley and DJ Constant

England innings (60 overs maximum)			R	M	B	4	6
DL Amiss	lbw	b Gilmour	2	11	7	0	0
B Wood		b Gilmour	6	29	19	1	0
KWR Fletcher	lbw	b Gilmour	8	59	45	0	0
AW Greig	c Marsh	b Gilmour	7	24	25	1	0
FC Hayes	lbw	b Gilmour	4	9	6	1	0
*MH Denness		b Walker	27	70	60	1	0
+APE Knott	lbw	b Gilmour	0	3	5	0	0
CM Old	c GS Chappell	b Walker	0	4	3	0	0
JA Snow	c Marsh	b Lillee	2	22	14	0	0
GG Arnold	not out		18	47	30	2	0
P Lever	lbw	b Walker	5	15	13	0	0
Extras	(lb 5, w 7, nb 2)		14				
Total	(all out, 36.2 overs)		93				

FoW: 1-2 (Amiss), 2-11 (Wood), 3-26 (Greig), 4-33 (Hayes), 5-35 (Fletcher), 6-36 (Knott), 7-37 (Old), 8-52 (Snow), 9-73 (Denness), 10-93 (Lever).

Bowling	O	M	R	W
Lillee	9	3	26	1
Gilmour	12	6	14	6
Walker	9.2	3	22	3
Thomson	6	0	17	0

Australia innings			R	M	B	4	6
A Turner	lbw	b Arnold	7	32	20	0	0
RB McCosker		b Old	15	65	50	0	0
*IM Chappell	lbw	b Snow	2	18	19	0	0
GS Chappell	lbw	b Snow	4	8	9	1	0
KD Walters	not out		20	60	43	2	0
R Edwards		b Old	0	2	3	0	0
+RW Marsh		b Old	5	7	8	0	0
GJ Gilmour	not out		28	44	28	5	0
Extras	(b 1, lb 6, nb 6)		13				
Total	(6 wickets, 28.4 overs)		94				

DNB: MHN Walker, DK Lillee, JR Thomson.

FoW: 1-17 (Turner), 2-24 (IM Chappell), 3-32 (GS Chappell), 4-32 (McCosker), 5-32 (Edwards), 6-39 (Marsh).

Bowling	O	M	R	W
Arnold	7.4	2	15	1
Snow	12	0	30	2
Old	7	2	29	3
Lever	2	0	7	0

Man of the Match: GJ Gilmour • Result: Australia won by 4 wickets

2nd Semi-final • 1975
New Zealand v West Indies
Kennington Oval, London

New Zealand's captain Glenn Turner had been in spectacular form in the 1975 World Cup, hitting two undefeated hundreds including one in the opening match of the tournament, a monumental 171 not out, that would remain the record for the highest score in ODI cricket for eight years. So when Turner and Geoff Howarth compiled 90 runs for the second wicket, after being put in by the West Indies at the Kennington Oval, hopes were that a big total beckoned. But when Turner fell to Andy Roberts for 36, with the score on 98, there appeared to be some panic in the ranks and wickets began to tumble with alarming regularity. The second-highest partnership of the innings was a mere 19 runs put on by Brian Hastings and wicket-keeper Ken Wadsworth. All of the West Indies bowlers were in good touch, with the left-arm fast bowler Bernard Julien taking the honours for his analysis of 12-5-27-4. From 98 for 1, New Zealand crashed to 158 all out in the 53rd over.

Roy Fredericks went early, but the matter was put to rest by a 125-run stand between Gordon Greenidge (55) and an in-form Alvin Kallicharan (72) who was fresh from having smashed Dennis Lillee for 35 runs in 10 balls, in the West Indies preceding match. In spite of losing some wickets themselves while going for a final flourish, the West Indies reached their target for the loss of five wickets, with almost 20 overs to spare.

2nd Semi-final • 1975
New Zealand v West Indies
Kennington Oval, London • 18 June 1975 (60 overs per innings)
Toss: West Indies
Umpires: WL Budd and AE Fagg

New Zealand innings (60 overs maximum)			R	B	4	6
*GM Turner	c Kanhai	b Roberts	36	74	3	0
JFM Morrison	lbw	b Julien	5	26	0	0
GP Howarth	c Murray	b Roberts	51	93	3	0
JM Parker		b Lloyd	3	12	0	0
BF Hastings	not out		24	57	4	0
+KJ Wadsworth	c Lloyd	b Julien	11	21	1	0
BJ McKechnie	lbw	b Julien	1	9	0	0
DR Hadlee	c Holder	b Julien	0	10	0	0
BL Cairns		b Holder	10	14	1	0
HJ Howarth		b Holder	0	1	0	0
RO Collinge		b Holder	2	4	0	0
Extras	(b 1, lb 5, w 2, nb 7)		15			
Total	(all out, 52.2 overs)		158			

FoW: 1-8 (Morrison), 2-98 (Turner), 3-105 (GP Howarth), 4-106 (Parker), 5-125 (Wadsworth), 6-133 (McKechnie), 7-139 (Hadlee), 8-155 (Cairns), 9-155 (HJ Howarth), 10-158 (Collinge).

Bowling	O	M	R	W
Julien	12	5	27	4
Roberts	11	3	18	2
Holder	8.2	0	30	3
Boyce	9	0	31	0
Lloyd	12	1	37	1

West Indies innings (target: 159 runs from 60 overs)			R	B	4	6
RC Fredericks	c Hastings	b Hadlee	6	14	0	0
CG Greenidge	lbw	b Collinge	55	95	9	1
AI Kallicharran	c & b Collinge		72	92	7	1
IVA Richards	lbw	b Collinge	5	10	1	0
RB Kanhai	not out		12	18	2	0
*CH Lloyd	c Hastings	b McKechnie	3	8	0	0
BD Julien	not out		4	5	1	0
Extras	(lb 1, nb 1)		2			
Total	(5 wickets, 40.1 overs)		159			

DNB: +DL Murray, KD Boyce, VA Holder, AME Roberts.

FoW: 1-8 (Fredericks), 2-133 (Kallicharran), 3-139 (Richards), 4-142 (Greenidge), 5-151 (Lloyd).

Bowling	O	M	R	W
Collinge	12	4	28	3
Hadlee	10	0	54	1
Cairns	6.1	2	23	0
McKechnie	8	0	37	1
HJ Howarth	4	0	15	0

Man of the Match: AI Kallicharran

Result: West Indies won by 5 wickets

The 1975 World Cup Final
Australia v West Indies
Lord's, London

The 1975 World Cup Final was played at Lord's on June 21, the longest day of the year. And for what was in store that day, it proved to be a wise date.

Having trounced England in the semi-final by unleashing the unknown man-in-form Gary Gilmour first upon the fresh pitch, and also knowing that on every occasion that the West Indies had won the toss they had chosen to bat second, Ian Chappell won the toss and duly inserted the West Indies.

The first bizarre incident of an eventful match happened when West Indies opener Roy Fredericks hooked a Dennis Lillee bouncer over the boundary, but in the process lost his footing and crashed into the stumps. The first wicket was down with only 12 runs on the board, but it meant that two batsmen in fine touch, Gordon Greenidge and Alvin Kallicharan were now at the crease. Kallicharan had savaged the Australian bowlers, particularly Lillee, when they had clashed earlier in the tournament and attempted to replicate that performance in the Final. Gilmour, who himself was coming off a good match, proved that the dodgy pitch at Headingley notwithstanding, he was going to continue to be a handful. He had the aggressive Kallicharan (12 off 18 balls with 2 fours) out caught behind by Rod Marsh.

Greenidge was uncharacteristically subdued in the face of some tight bowling and fell for 13 runs off a whopping 61 balls. At 50-3, the West Indies captain Clive Lloyd made his way to the crease and Dennis Lillee came back on to bowl. Lloyd smashed him for a six. It signalled the beginning of a majestic innings.

A strange partnership then ensued between Clive Lloyd and a 39-year-old Rohan Kanhai, who was playing the last match of his international career. Normally an aggressive batsman, Kanhai dropped anchor and left the scoring to Lloyd who smashed the Australian attack to all parts of the ground. The pair was together for 36 overs and put on 149 runs, no mean feat considering that there was a period where

Kanhai did not score for 11 overs. Lloyd was the first to go for a wonderful, scorching captain's innings of 102 off only 85 balls, which was studded with 12 fours and 2 sixes. Kanhai fell soon after for 55 off 105 balls, with 8 fours.

The West Indies eventually scored 291-8 off their 60 overs. Gary Gilmour again had a fine day, with bowling figures of 12-2-48-5; among his victims were the four danger men, Kallicharan, Lloyd, Kanhai and Viv Richards, as well as the wicket-keeper Deryk Murray, who was no mug with the bat.

Rick McCosker went early, but Alan Turner and captain Ian Chappell took Australia safely to 81 before Turner was run out by Viv Richards after a mix up with his skipper. That brought Australia's best batsman, Greg Chappell, to the crease. The Chappell brothers looked good playing together, stroking boundaries and

Gary Gilmour at the 1975 World Cup: 6-14 in the Semi-Final and 5-48 in the Final.

pinching singles, but their 34-runs partnership was undone while attempting a sharp run. It was Viv Richards again who took a shy at the stumps and caught Greg Chappell short of his ground.

Ian Chappell continued to play well, but with the West Indies fielding brilliantly, the Australians appeared unsure of whether to attempt runs or not. It was that kind of hesitation that accounted for Ian Chappell's wicket too. Unsure of a third run, Chappell saw that man gain – Richards – send a pinpoint throw to the bowler Lloyd who ran out his counterpart. Ian Chappell went for 62, reducing Australia to 162-4.

The rest of the Australian batsmen got starts, but no one went on to make a good score. By the time the last man Dennis Lillee came out to join his fast bowling partner Jeff Thomson at the batting crease in the 53rd over, the score line read a disappointing 233-9. Famously aggressive as bowlers, the two decided to apply the same strategy with the bat. They swung at everything and the scoreboard continued to tick away until a difficult but not impossible 21 runs were needed off the last two overs.

A no-ball from Vanburn Holder was hit by Thomson into the hands of Fredericks positioned at cover. The batsmen went for a run and Fredericks took a shy at the stumps, which missed and the batsmen then ran forn overthrows. Meanwhile, many in the crowd were not aware that a no-ball had been called and invaded the pitch to celebrate what they believed was the fall of the final wicket when Fredericks took the catch. In the mayhem, the ball was lost, but Lillee and Thomson continued to run like mad. The spectators were finally cleared off and even though the batsmen wanted more, the umpires only allowed for 3 runs to be added to the score.

There were nine balls left now and 18 runs to get. After swinging and missing at another ball from Holder, Thomson attempted to run for a bye, but was sent back by Lillee. It was too late. Even with Thomson diving to get back into his crease, he could not get there before Murray knocked off the bails.

With the match finishing at about 8:45 pm, it had been a long, hard day, but the West Indies emerged from it as the World Champions. The 1975 World Cup final truly was a fitting end to a wonderful tournament.

The 1975 World Cup Final
Australia v West Indies
Lord's, London • 21 June 1975 (60 overs per innings)
Toss: Australia
Umpires: HD Bird and TW Spencer

West Indies innings (60 overs maximum)			R	M	B	4	6
RC Fredericks	hit wicket	b Lillee	7	14	13	0	0
CG Greenidge	c Marsh	b Thomson	13	80	61	1	0
AI Kallicharran	c Marsh	b Gilmour	12	26	18	2	0
RB Kanhai		b Gilmour	55	156	105	8	0
*CH Lloyd	c Marsh	b Gilmour	102	108	85	12	2
IVA Richards		b Gilmour	5	12	11	1	0
KD Boyce	c GS Chappell	b Thomson	34	43	37	3	0
BD Julien	not out		26	54	37	1	0
+DL Murray	c & b Gilmour		14	11	10	1	1
VA Holder	not out		6	1	2	1	0
Extras	(lb 6, nb 11)		17				
Total	(8 wickets, 60 overs)		291				

DNB: AME Roberts.

FoW: 1-12 (Fredericks), 2-27 (Kallicharran), 3-50 (Greenidge), 4-199 (Lloyd), 5-206 (Kanhai), 6-209 (Richards), 7-261 (Boyce), 8-285 (Murray).

Bowling	O	M	R	W
Lillee	12	1	55	1
Gilmour	12	2	48	5
Thomson	12	1	44	2
Walker	12	1	71	0
GS Chappell	7	0	33	0
Walters	5	0	23	0

Australia innings (target: 292 runs from 60 overs)			R	M	B	4	6
A Turner	run out (Richards)		40	85	54	4	0
RB McCosker	c Kallicharran	b Boyce	7	29	24	1	0
*IM Chappell	run out (Richards/Lloyd)		62	125	93	6	0
GS Chappell	run out (Richards)		15	24	23	2	0
KD Walters		b Lloyd	35	52	51	5	0
+RW Marsh		b Boyce	11	34	24	0	0
R Edwards	c Fredericks	b Boyce	28	51	37	2	0
GJ Gilmour	c Kanhai	b Boyce	14	16	11	2	0
MHN Walker	run out (Holder)		7	10	9	1	0
JR Thomson	run out (Murray)		21	32	21	2	0
DK Lillee	not out		16	29	19	1	0
Extras	(b 2, lb 9, nb 7)		18				
Total	(all out, 58.4 overs)		274				

FoW: 1-25 (McCosker), 2-81 (Turner), 3-115 (GS Chappell), 4-162 (IM Chappell), 5-170 (Walters), 6-195 (Marsh), 7-221 (Gilmour), 8-231 (Edwards), 9-233 (Walker), 10-274 (Thomson).

Bowling	O	M	R	W
Julien	12	0	58	0
Roberts	11	1	45	0
Boyce	12	0	50	4
Holder	11.4	1	65	0
Lloyd	12	1	38	1

Man of the Match: CH Lloyd

Result: West Indies won the 1975 World Cup Final by 17 runs

1979

WORLD CUP 1979 • ENGLAND

Official Title: The Prudential World Cup
Winners: West Indies
Group A: West Indies, New Zealand, India, Sri Lanka
Group B: England, Australia, Pakistan, Canada
June 9, 1979- June 23, 1975

The 1979 World Cup was a virtual carbon copy of the inaugural event four years earlier. As in the 1975 edition, the tournament was held in England in early June for fifteen days and at the end of it all, West Indies captain Clive Lloyd held the trophy aloft at Lord's. As in the first World Cup, this edition also had two countries without Test status participating: Sri Lanka, who returned to the tournament, and Canada, who made their ODI debut.

By this time, the West Indies were firmly established as the premier force in world cricket and were out and out favourites to retain their title as World Champions. Clive Lloyd commanded a destructive batting line-up and then had an arsenal of four genuine fast bowlers, the vaunted quartet of Holding, Garner, Roberts and Croft, at his disposal. Everything went according to plan and the West Indies made their way through the tournament undefeated and largely untroubled.

The Australian Cricket Board was still at odds with its players over contracts signed with media baron Kerry Packer's World Series Cricket and did not select them for the World Cup. With the stakes so high, the West Indies and Pakistan, two other teams with Packer players, did not follow the Australian line. So while Australia were led by an undercooked Kim Hughes and missed out on the talent of players of the calibre of Dennis Lillee and Greg Chappell, the West Indies and Pakistan were both led by Packer players, Clive Lloyd and Asif Iqbal. What's more, they were able to call upon the considerable powers of stars such as Viv Richards and Imran Khan.

Gordon Greenidge was in great form in the 1979 World Cup, with scores of 106*, 65 and 73, before being run out for 9 in the Final.

Minnows Sri Lanka had a good time in the tournament, defeating India by 47 runs and marking the first instance in a World Cup of a non-Test team beating one of the big boys. But more than beating India, the Sri Lankans may have been pleased that their match with the West Indies was rained out and they escaped facing the fearsome pace battery. In the last World Cup, the genuine pace of Australia's Jeff Thomson had sent a couple of Sri Lankan players bloodied and bruised to the emergency room.

In the end, World Cup 1979 proved to be as successful a tournament as its predecessor. The two best teams in the tournament again faced each other in the final, and the superior team came out on top. The world was in order.

1st Semi-final • 1979
England v New Zealand
Old Trafford, Manchester

New Zealand had a decent pack of seamers led by the great Richard Hadlee, who was well supported by left-arm medium pacer Gary Troup, as well as Lance Cairns and Jeremy Coney. So when captain Mark Burgess won the toss, he inserted England in to bat at Old Trafford, hoping to take advantage of early morning conditions. The move was a good one and Hadlee soon removed England's opener and leading batsman Geoff Boycott for only 2.

Debutant Wayne Larkins was soon back in the pavilion too and England were 38-2. Captain Mike Brearley and Graham Gooch then settled into a 58-run partnership. But Brearley was caught behind off Coney and David Gower was run out in a mix-up with Gooch, which reduced England from a comfortable 96-2 to a troubling 98-4. Gooch and Botham, however, batted well together and took the score to 145 before Botham fell LBW to Cairns. Wickets continued to fall at regular intervals as the Kiwis kept things tight and broke England's partnerships before they could engage in any real adventurism. Still, Gooch managed to hit three sixes in his 84-ball 71 and Derek Randall hit a four and a six of his own as he scampered to 42 not out off 50 balls. England eventually ended their 60 overs with a score of 221-8, with Richard Hadlee's figures being an economical 12-4-32-1.

New Zealand began well in reply, putting on 47 for the 1st wicket before Bruce Edgar became the first of four New Zealanders to be adjudged LBW to four different bowlers. Other than Geoff Howarth, all of New Zealand's top order batsmen made it into double figures but were unable to capitalize. Top scorer John Wright (69 off 137 balls) and Mark Burgess were run out one after the other and once Glenn Turner went for 30, (162-6) it was always going to be difficult.

New Zealand finished a disappointing 212-9 in their 60 overs and remarkably the most economical 12 overs came from the unlikely pairing of Geoff Boycott, who bowled 9 overs for 24 and Graham Gooch, whose 3 overs cost only 8 runs.

1st Semi-final • 1979
England v New Zealand
Old Trafford, Manchester • 20 June 1979 (60 overs per innings)
Toss: New Zealand
Umpires: JG Langridge and KE Palmer • ODI Debut: W Larkins (Eng).

England innings (60 overs maximum)			R	M	B	4	6
*JM Brearley	c Lees	b Coney	53	114	115	3	0
G Boycott	c Howarth	b Hadlee	2	30	14	0	0
W Larkins	c Coney	b McKechnie	7	40	37	0	0
GA Gooch		b McKechnie	71	105	84	1	3
DI Gower	run out		1	2	1	0	0
IT Botham	lbw	b Cairns	21	31	30	2	0
DW Randall	not out		42	66	50	1	1
CM Old	c Lees	b Troup	0	2	2	0	0
+RW Taylor	run out		12	30	25	1	0
RGD Willis	not out		1	1	2	0	0
Extras	(lb 8, w 3)		11				
Total	(8 wickets, 60 overs)		221				

DNB: M Hendrick.

FoW: 1-13 (Boycott), 2-38 (Larkins), 3-96 (Brearley),4-98 (Gower), 5-145 (Botham),
6-177 (Gooch), 7-178 (Old), 8-219 (Taylor).

Bowling	O	M	R	W
Hadlee	12	4	32	1
Troup	12	1	38	1
Cairns	12	2	47	1
Coney	12	0	47	1
McKechnie	12	1	46	2

New Zealand innings (target: 222 runs from 60 overs)			R	M	B	4	6
JG Wright	run out		69	142	137	9	0
BA Edgar	lbw	b Old	17	58	38	1	0
GP Howarth	lbw	b Boycott	7	13	12	1	0
JV Coney	lbw	b Hendrick	11	56	39	0	0
GM Turner	lbw	b Willis	30	67	51	2	0
*MG Burgess	run out		10	28	13	0	0
RJ Hadlee	b Botham		15	44	32	0	0
+WK Lees	b Hendrick		23	33	20	0	1
BL Cairns	c Brearley	b Hendrick	14	5	6	1	1
BJ McKechnie	not out		4	13	9	0	0
GB Troup	not out		3	2	3	0	0
Extras	(b 5, w 4)		9				
Total	(9 wickets, 60 overs)		212				

FoW: 1-47 (Edgar), 2-58 (Howarth), 3-104 (Coney), 4-112 (Wright), 5-132 (Burgess),
6-162 (Turner), 7-180 (Hadlee), 8-195 (Cairns), 9-208 (Lees).

Bowling	O	M	R	W
Botham	12	3	42	1
Hendrick	12	0	55	3
Old	12	1	33	1
Boycott	9	1	24	1
Gooch	3	1	8	0
Willis	12	1	41	1

Man of the Match: GA Gooch

Result: England won by 9 runs

2nd Semi-final • 1979
Pakistan v West Indies
Kennington Oval, Londo

Asif Iqbal's decision to insert the West Indies backfired spectacularly when openers Gordon Greenidge and Desmond Haynes dug in to negate the potency of Pakistan's new ball pairing of Imran Khan and Sarfraz Nawaz. The West Indies openers put on 132 for the first wicket before Asif Iqbal had Greenidge (73 off 107 balls, 5 fours 1 six) edging to Wasim Bari behind the stumps.

The West Indies continued to accumulate runs and remained undisturbed by the fall of wickets. The gentle bowling of Majid Khan (12 overs for 26 runs) and Asif Iqbal (4-56 in 11 overs) kept things somewhat in check during the middle overs, but Sarfraz continued to leak runs going for 71 in his 12 overs. Collis King made merry with 34 off only 25 balls in a taste of what was to come in the final.

Set 294 runs to win, Pakistan lost Sadiq Mohammad for 2, caught behind off the bowling of Michael Holding. That dismissal, however, brought Zaheer Abbas to the crease and heralded the only real occasion where the West Indies were under any kind of pressure during the 1979 World Cup.

Majid Khan and Zaheer Abbas cut, pulled and drove with authority and their partnership brought back memories of the classic encounter between the two teams in the previous World Cup. However, any thoughts of an upset were put to rest by an inspired spell of bowling from Colin Croft who broke the back of Pakistan's middle-order. The 166-run partnership for the 2nd wicket came to an end when Zaheer Abbas (93 off 122 balls, 8 fours and 1 six) was caught by wicket-keeper Deryk Murray off Croft. From 176-1, Pakistan slipped to 187-4 with Croft also removing Majid Khan (81 off 124 balls, 7 fours) and then Javed Miandad, who was out LBW to his first ball.

The fight went out of Pakistan and the last five wickets fell to the off-spin of Viv Richards and the pace of Andy Roberts. Pakistan were bowled out for 250 in the 57th over and the West Indies had won by 43 runs.

2nd Semi-final • 1979
Pakistan v West Indies
Kennington Oval, London • 20 June 1979 (60 overs per innings)

Toss: Pakistan

Umpires: WL Budd and DJ Constant

West Indies innings (60 overs maximum)			R	M	B	4	6
CG Greenidge	c Wasim Bari	b Asif Iqbal	73	122	107	5	1
DL Haynes	c & b Asif Iqbal		65	155	115	4	0
IVA Richards		b Asif Iqbal	42	91	62	1	0
*CH Lloyd	c Mudassar Nazar	b Asif Iqbal	37	63	38	3	0
CL King	c sub	b Sarfraz Nawaz	34	37	25	3	0
AI Kallicharran		b Imran Khan	11	31	14	0	0
AME Roberts	not out		7	6	4	0	0
J Garner	not out		1	4	1	0	0
Extras	(b 1, lb 17, w 1, nb 4)		23				
Total	(6 wickets, 60 overs)		293				

DNB: +DL Murray, MA Holding, CEH Croft.

FoW: 1-132 (Greenidge), 2-165 (Haynes), 3-233 (Richards), 4-236 (Lloyd), 5-285 (Kallicharran), 6-285 (King).

Bowling	O	M	R	W
Imran Khan	9	1	43	1
Sarfraz Nawaz	12	1	71	1
Sikander Bakht	6	1	24	0
Mudassar Nazar	10	0	50	0
Majid Khan	12	2	26	0
Asif Iqbal	11	0	56	4

Pakistan innings (target: 294 runs from 60 overs)			R	M	B	4	6
Majid Khan	c Kallicharran	b Croft	81	175	124	7	0
Sadiq Mohammad	c Murray	b Holding	2	15	7	0	0
Zaheer Abbas	c Murray	b Croft	93	143	122	8	1
Haroon Rashid	run out		15	40	22	1	0
Javed Miandad	lbw	b Croft	0	1	1	0	0
*Asif Iqbal	c Holding	b Richards	17	15	20	1	0
Mudassar Nazar	c Kallicharran	b Richards	2	10	9	0	0
Imran Khan	c & b Richards		6	9	4	1	0
Sarfraz Nawaz	c Haynes	b Roberts	12	16	15	0	0
+Wasim Bari	c Murray	b Roberts	9	13	12	0	0
Sikander Bakht	not out		1	3	4	0	0
Extras	(lb 9, w 2, nb 1)		12				
Total	(all out, 56.2 overs)		250				

FoW: 1-10 (Sadiq Mohammad), 2-176 (Zaheer Abbas), 3-187 (Majid Khan), 4-187 (Javed Miandad), 5-208 (Haroon Rashid), 6-220 (Mudassar Nazar), 7-221 (Asif Iqbal), 8-228 (Imran Khan), 9-246 (Wasim Bari), 10-250 (Sarfraz Nawaz).

Bowling	O	M	R	W
Roberts	9.2	2	41	2
Holding	9	1	28	1
Croft	11	0	29	3
Garner	12	1	47	0
King	7	0	41	0
Richards	8	0	52	3

Man of the Match: CG Greenidge

Result: West Indies won by 43 runs

The 1979 World Cup Final
England v West Indies
Lord's, London

On June 23, 1979 Mike Brearley won the toss and sent the West Indies to bat in the World Cup final at Lord's. It promised to be a good contest, with both teams in terrific form. There were many in England who were cautiously optimistic that their team could put one over on the West Indies. And as the West Indies innings began to stutter, England's confidence grew.

Gordon Greenidge had been in excellent form, hitting one century and two half-centuries in his three previous matches. England were delighted then when they ran him out for only 9 and quickly dismissed his opening partner Desmond Haynes who nicked Chris Old to second slip as well. The West Indies were 36-2.

Viv Richards got the scoreboard moving along, but saw his partner Alvin Kallicharan bowled for 4 to leave the West Indies precariously placed at 55-3. The next man in was captain Clive Lloyd and although he looked good, striking two boundaries, he fell to a good return catch by Chris Old to be out for 13. Lloyd's dismissal left the West Indies at 99-4 and England felt that they now had one hand on the trophy. The hand however was wrenched off by perhaps the greatest displays of power hitting in a World Cup final.

Collis King joined Viv Richards at the crease and the two then set about rebuilding the innings with verve. King smashed the bowling with incredible power and the ferocity of his attack indicated disdain for England's bowlers. England continued to field well in the face of the onslaught, but there was really no stopping King and Richards – who remarkably was playing second fiddle. King was eventually caught on the boundary for 86 off a mere 66 balls. His innings included 10 fours and 3 sixes and in partnership with Richards, he had put on 139 runs in 21 overs.

Wickets began to tumble now, but it mattered little because Richards continued to bat well at the other end, completely owning the bowling and thrashing it to all parts of the ground. Richards' dominance was summed up with the final ball of the innings, which he picked up from off-stump and dispatched over the leg-side for a glorious six. Richards finished the day unbeaten on 138 off 157 balls with 11 fours and 3 sixes, with the West Indies making 286-9.

England began circumspectly, with Mike Brearley and Geoff Boycott opening the innings. Hoping to raise a good platform from where to launch an assault of their own seemed like a good plan, but England were far too slow, best indicated by the fact that Boycott only reached double figures in the 17th over. The opening partnership was a big one of 129 runs and it came to an end in the 38th over when Brearley (64 off 130 balls, 7 fours) was caught by King near the boundary after taking a swipe at Michael Holding.

The required run rate was more than 7 runs per over now. Two overs later, Boycott finally fell as well to Holding for a composed 57 off 105 balls. Graham Gooch (32 off 28 balls with 4 fours) attempted to increase the scoring rate, but there was too much for him to do in the face of such a lethal bowling attack. An excellent spell of bowling from Joel Garner (11-0-38-5) blew the rest away and the West Indies had won comprehensively by 92 runs. In spite of the ultimate margin of victory, it had been an absorbing day of cricket, thoroughly deserving of a World Cup final.

Viv Richards during his innings of 138*
in the 1979 World Cup Final

West Indies fans pour onto the field at Lord's after the West Indies beat England in the 1979 World Cup Final by 92 runs.

West Indies captain Clive Lloyd lifts the World Cup, watched by the defeated England team, June 23 1979.

The 1979 World Cup Final
England v West Indies
Lord's, London • 23 June 1979 (60-overs match) •
Toss: England
Umpires: HD Bird and BJ Meyer

West Indies innings (60 overs maximum)			R	M	B	4	6
CG Greenidge	run out (Randall)		9	31	31	0	0
DL Haynes	c Hendrick	b Old	20	49	27	3	0
IVA Richards	not out		138	207	157	11	3
AI Kallicharran		b Hendrick	4	19	17	0	0
*CH Lloyd	c & b Old		13	42	33	2	0
CL King	c Randall	b Edmonds	86	77	66	10	3
+DL Murray	c Gower	b Edmonds	5	12	9	1	0
AME Roberts	c Brearley	b Hendrick	0	8	7	0	0
J Garner	c Taylor	b Botham	0	4	5	0	0
MA Holding		b Botham	0	7	6	0	0
CEH Croft	not out		0	6	2	0	0
Extras	(b 1, lb 10)		11				
Total	(9 wickets, 60 overs)		286				

FoW: 1-22 (Greenidge), 2-36 (Haynes), 3-55 (Kallicharran), 4-99 (Lloyd), 5-238 (King),
6-252 (Murray), 7-258 (Roberts), 8-260 (Garner), 9-272 (Holding).

Bowling	O	M	R	W
Botham	12	2	44	2
Hendrick	12	2	50	2
Old	12	0	55	2
Boycott	6	0	38	0
Edmonds	12	2	40	2
Gooch	4	0	27	0
Larkins	2	0	21	0

England innings (target: 287 runs from 60 overs)			R	M	B	4	6
*JM Brearley	c King	b Holding	64	130	130	7	0
G Boycott	c Kallicharran	b Holding	57	137	105	3	0
DW Randall		b Croft	15	36	22	0	0
GA Gooch		b Garner	32	31	28	4	0
DI Gower		b Garner	0	6	4	0	0
IT Botham	c Richards	b Croft	4	7	3	0	0
W Larkins		b Garner	0	1	1	0	0
PH Edmonds	not out		5	14	8	0	0
CM Old		b Garner	0	4	2	0	0
+RW Taylor	c Murray	b Garner	0	1	1	0	0
M Hendrick		b Croft	0	4	5	0	0
Extras	(lb 12, w 2, nb 3)		17				
Total	(all out, 51 overs)		194				

FoW: 1-129 (Brearley), 2-135 (Boycott), 3-183 (Gooch), 4-183 (Gower), 5-186 (Randall), 6-186 (Larkins),
7-192 (Botham), 8-192 (Old), 9-194 (Taylor), 10-194 (Hendrick).

Bowling	O	M	R	W
Roberts	9	2	33	0
Holding	8	1	16	2
Croft	10	1	42	3
Garner	11	0	38	5
Richards	10	0	35	0
King	3	0	13	0

Man of the Match: IVA Richards
Result: West Indies won the 1979 World Cup by 92 runs

1983

WORLD CUP 1983 • ENGLAND

Official Title: The Prudential World Cup
Winners: India
Group A: England, New Zealand, Pakistan, Sri Lanka
Group B: Australia, West Indies, India, Zimbabwe
June 9, 1983- June 25, 1983

Like the previous two World Cups, the third edition of the tournament was played in England. Again there were eight teams, with Canada making way for Zimbabwe. Sri Lanka were now a Test playing country and so that left Zimbabwe as the only minnow in the competition, though one would not have known it by how well they played.

A minor change to the format meant that teams would now play the other members of their group twice, as opposed to once in previous tournaments. The mighty West Indies, again led by Clive Lloyd, were still the kings of the cricket world and were expected to retain the trophy without much fuss. It would not turn out that way.

India's win in the 1983 World Cup came as a shock to the cricket world, but anyone thinking that the win was a fluke would do well to remember their opening match of the tournament where India downed the defending champion West Indies by 34 runs. The key to India's success lay in the fact

*India's captain Kapil Dev raises the World Cup,
at Lord's, London, June 25, 1983*

that they jettisoned a spin-based bowling attack for bowlers who were better suited to English conditions. The likes of Madan Lal and Roger Binny were not quick, and in later years players of their ilk would be derided as "bits and pieces" men, but in a conducive environment, their bread-and-butter type seam bowling did the trick in the 1983 World Cup. Versatile all-rounders like Ravi Shastri and captain Kapil Dev, who could pretty much bat anywhere in the order, also gave India's batting line-up a sense of depth that would come in handy.

Much like the previous two tournaments, World Cup 1983 proved to be a roaring success. India's surprise win was a feel-good story that did wonders for the sport in South Asia and no doubt helped in bringing the tournament to the subcontinent four years later. It would be another 16 years before a captain would hoist the trophy on the Lord's balcony.

1st Semi-final • 1983
England v India
Old Trafford, Manchester

India's first trip to a World Cup semi-final proved to be a cakewalk over the hosts. An England middle-order comprising David Gower, Allan Lamb, Mike Gatting and Ian Botham – all capable of quick runs – meandered indifferently through the innings. Botham was the worst culprit, dawdling for 26 balls before being bowled by the off-spin of Kirti Azad. India's military medium men kept things tight and Kapil Dev brought himself back on to wind up the tail. England were all out for 213 which, given India's form in the tournament, was never going to be enough.

Needing only about 3.5 runs per over, India batted sensibly with the openers putting on 46 runs for the 1st wicket. Mohinder Amarnath came to bat at number three and thrived in the company of Yashpal Sharma. The pair put on 92 runs for the 3rd wicket, playing cautiously but hitting anything loose to the boundary. Victory was never in doubt and when Amarnath was run out for 42, Sharma was joined by the aggressive Sandeep Patil, who showed everyone how easy batting could be. Patil smashed his way to 51 off a mere 32 balls with 8 fours. India were home by 6 wickets, with 5 overs to spare.

1st Semi-final • 1983
England v India
Old Trafford, Manchester • 22 June 1983 (60 overs per innings)

Toss: England

Umpires: DGL Evans and DO Oslear

England innings (60 overs maximum)			R	B	4	6
G Fowler		b Binny	33	59	3	0
CJ Tavare	c Kirmani	b Binny	32	51	4	0
DI Gower	c Kirmani	b Amarnath	17	30	1	0
AJ Lamb	run out		29	58	1	0
MW Gatting		b Amarnath	18	46	1	0
IT Botham		b Azad	6	26	0	0
+IJ Gould	run out		13	36	0	0
VJ Marks		b Kapil Dev	8	18	0	0
GR Dilley	not out		20	26	2	0
PJW Allott	c Patil	b Kapil Dev	8	14	0	0
*RGD Willis		b Kapil Dev	0	2	0	0
Extras	(b 1, lb 17, w 7, nb 4)		29			
Total	(all out, 60 overs)		213			

FoW: 1-69 (Tavare), 2-84 (Fowler), 3-107 (Gower), 4-141 (Lamb), 5-150 (Gatting), 6-160 (Botham), 7-175 (Gould), 8-177 (Marks), 9-202 (Allott), 10-213 (Willis).

Bowling	O	M	R	W
Kapil Dev	11	1	35	3
Sandhu	8	1	36	0
Binny	12	1	43	2
Madan Lal	5	0	15	0
Azad	12	1	28	1
Amarnath	12	1	27	2

India innings (target: 214 runs from 60 overs)			R	B	4	6
SM Gavaskar	c Gould	b Allott	25	41	3	0
K Srikkanth	c Willis	b Botham	19	44	3	0
M Amarnath	run out		46	92	4	1
Yashpal Sharma	c Allott	b Willis	61	115	3	2
SM Patil	not out		51	32	8	0
*N Kapil Dev	not out		1	6	0	0
Extras	(b 5, lb 6, w 1, nb 2)		14			
Total	(4 wickets, 54.4 overs)		217			

DNB: KBJ Azad, RMH Binny, S Madan Lal, +SMH Kirmani, BS Sandhu

FoW: 1-46 (Srikkanth), 2-50 (Gavaskar), 3-142 (Amarnath), 4-205 (Yashpal Sharma).

Bowling	O	M	R	W
Willis	10.4	2	42	1
Dilley	11	0	43	0
Allott	10	3	40	1
Botham	11	4	40	1
Marks	12	1	38	0

Man of the Match: M Amarnath

Result: India won by 6 wickets

2nd Semi-final • 1983
Pakistan v West Indies
Kennington Oval, London

Imran Khan had been in peak form as a bowler when he suffered a shin fracture in 1982. Even with Imran not being able to bowl, the Pakistan Cricket Board retained him as captain of the side for the 1983 World Cup. Imran played the tournament as a batsman and did well, scoring a hundred and fifty along the way, but as one of the world's best bowlers, he was frustrated at not being a part of the attack. Missing their chief weapon could suffice in the group stage of the tournament, but in the semi-final, against the power of the West Indies, Pakistan had no hope of coming out alive.

Predictably, this match was never a contest and Pakistan gave the impression of simply being there to make up the numbers. Clive Lloyd won the toss and put Pakistan in to bat. Opener Mohsin Khan went about as

Malcolm Marshall bowling in the 1983 World Cup Semi-Final. Marshall took 3-28 in 12 overs as the West Indies beat Pakistan by 8 wickets.

if playing a Test innings, slowing the run rate to a crawl. Pakistan dragged themselves to 184-8 in 60 overs with Mohsin Khan the last man out for 70, made off 176 balls with a solitary boundary. Malcolm Marshall, coming on first change, bowled beautifully to finish with figures of 12-2-28-3.

The West Indies knocked off the required runs for the loss of only 2 wickets, in the 49th over – Viv Richards having clubbed his way to an unbeaten 80 with 11 fours and a six. It was the third time in a row that Pakistan were knocked out of the World Cup by the West Indies but the first time they went out without a semblance of a fight.

2nd Semi-final • 1983
Pakistan v West Indies
Kennington Oval, London • 22 June 1983 (60 overs per innings)
Toss: West Indies
Umpires: DJ Constant and AGT Whitehead

Pakistan innings (60 overs maximum)			R	B	4	6
Mohsin Khan		b Roberts	70	176	1	0
Mudassar Nazar	c & b Garner		11	39	0	0
Ijaz Faqih	c Dujon	b Holding	5	19	0	0
Zaheer Abbas		b Gomes	30	38	1	0
*Imran Khan	c Dujon	b Marshall	17	41	0	0
Wasim Raja	lbw	b Marshall	0	3	0	0
Shahid Mahboob	c Richards	b Marshall	6	10	0	0
Sarfraz Nawaz	c Holding	b Roberts	3	12	0	0
Abdul Qadir	not out		10	21	0	0
+Wasim Bari	not out		4	7	0	0
Extras	(b 6, lb 13, w 4, nb 5)		28			
Total	(8 wickets, 60 overs)		184			

DNB: Rashid Khan.

FoW: 1-23 (Mudassar Nazar), 2-34 (Ijaz Faqih), 3-88 (Zaheer Abbas), 4-139 (Imran Khan),
        5-139 (Wasim Raja), 6-159 (Shahid Mahboob), 7-164 (Sarfraz Nawaz), 8-171 (Mohsin Khan).

Bowling	O	M	R	W
Roberts	12	3	25	2
Garner	12	1	31	1
Marshall	12	2	28	3
Holding	12	1	25	1
Gomes	7	0	29	1
Richards	5	0	18	0

West Indies innings (target: 185 runs from 60 overs)			R	B	4	6
CG Greenidge	lbw	b Rashid Khan	17	38		
DL Haynes		b Abdul Qadir	29	58		
IVA Richards	not out		80	96	11	1
HA Gomes	not out		50	100	3	0
Extras	(b 2, lb 6, w 4)		12			
Total	(2 wickets, 48.4 overs)		188			

DNB: *CH Lloyd, SFAF Bacchus, +PJL Dujon, MD Marshall, AME Roberts, J Garner, MA Holding.

FoW: 1-34 (Greenidge), 2-56 (Haynes).

Bowling	O	M	R	W
Rashid Khan	12	2	32	1
Sarfraz Nawaz	8	0	23	0
Abdul Qadir	11	1	42	1
Shahid Mahboob	11	1	43	0
Wasim Raja	1	0	9	0
Zaheer Abbas	4.4	1	24	0
Mohsin Khan	1	0	3	0

Man of the Match: IVA Richards

Result: West Indies won by 8 wickets

The 1983 World Cup Final
India v West Indies
Lord's, London

The third World Cup final, played on June 25, 1983, turned out to be another classic. It still ranks as one of the greatest upsets in the history of ODI cricket, and certainly is the biggest upset in a World Cup final. Neither before nor since has a World Cup final pitted two teams together where one was thought to have no chance of winning. That India pulled it off, coming from behind with a committed and thoughtful performance, makes the match all the more remarkable.

As in the semi-final, Clive Lloyd won the toss and inserted the opposition. Things began slowly and when the first wicket fell in the 5th over, the score was only 2 runs, both courtesy of the departing Sunil Gavaskar. Mohinder Amarnath, fresh from his heroics in the semi-final, came out to join Krishnamachari Srikanth and the pair put on 57 for the 2nd wicket. Srikanth was in splendid touch, hitting the West Indies fearsome pace attack to all parts of the ground and looking great doing it. He was eventually dismissed by Malcolm Marshall, who rapped him on the pads. Srikanth's 38 contained 7 fours and a six off Andy Roberts.

After Srikanth's fireworks, Yashpal Sharma and Amarnath cautiously took the score up to 90 before Michael Holding got one through the latter's defences. This wicket triggered the slide and wickets began to fall with alarming regularity. Sharma and captain Kapil Dev both perished trying to hit sixes. It was left to the tail-enders to try to cobble together some sort of score. India's number 10 and 11 batsmen, Syed Kirmani (14) and Balwinder Sandhu (11 not out), put on 22 gutsy runs for the last wicket, during which Sandhu had to endure being knocked on the head by Marshall. India were all out for 183 in the 55th over. The West Indies could barely contain their glee.

The West Indies innings got off to a poor start when Sandhu nipped one back into Gordon Greenidge and bowled him for 1. But any joy for India was short-lived as the next man in was Viv Richards who promptly clattered Sandhu away for four.

Kapil Dev, who was hit for boundaries by Richards too, brought Madan Lal into the attack. The target for the West Indies in the semi-final against Pakistan had been an untroubling 185, and Richards had taken his team home by playing aggressively and stamping his authority all over the bowling attack. The situation in this match was virtually identical, with a victory target of 184 for the West Indies. Employing the same tactics as in the previous match, Richards launched into Madan Lal, creaming him for three fours in his first over.

Desmond Haynes carelessly hit Lal into the hands of Roger Binny and the next man in captain Clive Lloyd immediately pulled a muscle, necessitating Haynes to come back out as a runner. With the West Indies captain appearing hobbled, things took a turn for the worse when Richards, going for another shot of extravagant arrogance off Madan Lal, was caught near the boundary by Kapil Dev.

Kapil Dev was an inspirational figure during India's triumphant 1983 World Cup campaign. Among his personal highlights was a monumental innings of 175* versus Zimbabwe and figures of 5-43 against Australia.

Richards' dismissal galvanized India. With the West Indies 57-3 and the main threat back in the pavilion, India began to believe the impossible. Larry Gomes was dismissed cheaply and that seemed to affect the normally cool Lloyd. While caution and a slow rebuilding of the innings would have been the better route, the West Indies captain attempted to reassert his team's authority but, going for a cover drive, only managed to clip Roger Binny to the waiting Kapil Dev. The West Indies were 66-5 and then slipped to 76-6, before the next pair decided to bat sensibly.

A heap of wickets had fallen, but the West Indies still had 35 overs in which to make the required 108 runs at a required run rate that was barely over 3 runs per over. Wicket-keeper Jeff Dujon and Malcolm Marshall began inching the West Indies closer to their target. The pair had put on 43 runs for the 7th wicket when Dujon played on to an innocuous delivery from Amarnath.

With the score on 119 and only the bowlers left in the shed for the West Indies, victory was as good as India's. Kapil Dev and Amarnath swept them aside, bowling out the West Indies for 140 and registering a fantastic upset win.

In the immediate aftermath of the match, still flush with excitement, Kapil Dev could not hide his delight at coming out trumps over what he perceived was an arrogant West Indies side. The Indian captain mentioned how Viv Richards played as if the innings was scheduled for 30 overs instead of 60 overs, the unmistakable undertone being that India were simply waiting for the arrogance to get the better of Richards.

And so India broke the cycle of the West Indies' dominance of the World Cup. More significantly, the sound of Amarnath thudding the ball into Michael Holding's pad for that final wicket could also have very well been the heralding of the eventual shift of cricket's power base to South Asia.

The 1983 World Cup Final
India v West Indies

Lord's, London • 25 June 1983 (60 overs per innings)

Toss: West Indies

Umpires: HD Bird and BJ Meyer

India innings (60 overs maximum)			R	M	B	4	6
SM Gavaskar	c Dujon	b Roberts	2	14	12	0	0
K Srikkanth	lbw	b Marshall	38	82	57	7	1
M Amarnath		b Holding	26	108	80	3	0
Yashpal Sharma	c sub (AL Logie)	b Gomes	11	45	32	1	0
SM Patil	c Gomes	b Garner	27	48	29	0	1
*N Kapil Dev	c Holding	b Gomes	15	10	8	3	0
KBJ Azad	c Garner	b Roberts	0	3	3	0	0
RMH Binny	c Garner	b Roberts	2	9	8	0	0
S Madan Lal		b Marshall	17	31	27	0	1
+SMH Kirmani		b Holding	14	55	43	0	0
BS Sandhu	not out		11	42	30	1	0
Extras	(b 5, lb 5, w 9, nb 1)		20				
Total	(all out, 54.4 overs)		183				

FoW: 1-2 (Gavaskar), 2-59 (Srikkanth), 3-90 (Amarnath), 4-92 (Yashpal Sharma), 5-110 (Kapil Dev), 6-111 (Azad), 7-130 (Binny), 8-153 (Patil), 9-161 (Madan Lal), 10-183 (Kirmani).

Bowling	O	M	R	W
Roberts	10	3	32	3
Garner	12	4	24	1
Marshall	11	1	24	2
Holding	9.4	2	26	2
Gomes	11	1	49	2
Richards	1	0	8	0

West Indies innings (target: 184 runs from 60 overs)			R	M	B	4	6
CG Greenidge		b Sandhu	1	11	12	0	0
DL Haynes	c Binny	b Madan Lal	13	45	33	2	0
IVA Richards	c Kapil Dev	b Madan Lal	33	42	28	7	0
*CH Lloyd	c Kapil Dev	b Binny	8	32	17	1	0
HA Gomes	c Gavaskar	b Madan Lal	5	18	16	0	0
SFAF Bacchus	c Kirmani	b Sandhu	8	37	25	0	0
+PJL Dujon		b Amarnath	25	94	73	0	1
MD Marshall	c Gavaskar	b Amarnath	18	73	51	0	0
AME Roberts	lbw	b Kapil Dev	4	16	14	0	0
J Garner	not out		5	34	19	0	0
MA Holding	lbw	b Amarnath	6	28	24	0	0
Extras	(lb 4, w 10)		14				
Total	(all out, 52 overs)		140				

FoW: 1-5 (Greenidge), 2-50 (Haynes), 3-57 (Richards), 4-66 (Gomes), 5-66 (Lloyd), 6-76 (Bacchus), 7-119 (Dujon), 8-124 (Marshall), 9-126 (Roberts), 10-140 (Holding).

Bowling	O	M	R	W
Kapil Dev	11	4	21	1
Sandhu	9	1	32	2
Madan Lal	12	2	31	3
Binny	10	1	23	1
Amarnath	7	0	12	3
Azad	3	0	7	0

Man of the Match: M Amarnath

Result: India won the 1983 World Cup Final by 43 runs

1987

WORLD CUP 1987 •
INDIA and PAKISTAN

Official Title: The Reliance Cup
Winners: Australia
Pool A: Australia, New Zealand, India, Zimbabwe
Pool B: England, West Indies, Pakistan, Sri Lanka
October 8, 1987- November 8, 1987

In 1984, India and Pakistan had put in a joint bid to the ICC for the rights to host the 1987 World Cup. There had been some opposition from ICC member countries who believed that the tournament should only be held in England, but in the end the Indo-Pak bid was successful. The result was a wonderful tournament, with fan frenzy the likes of which had never been seen in cricket, running through the length and breadth of the subcontinent. It is in this World Cup that cricket's status as the undisputed commercial juggernaut of South Asia has its roots. Cricket players were seen in advertisements for everything from shoes to ice cream. Television was saturated with coverage from live games to highlight packages to cricket punditry shows. There was no getting away from the fever and with India and Pakistan both having strong teams, the people loved every second of it, waiting anxiously for the semi-final stage to begin.

ODI cricket had evolved from what it had been in 1983.

Teams approached the game differently than they did in the early days, where they just batted out their allotted overs without any real sense of purpose, when setting a target. Now strategizing had come into play, batting orders were shuffled with a game plan in mind. Matches were now a standard 50 overs, as opposed to the 60. Players were battle-hardened, having gained more experience of the format and accepted ODI cricket as a legitimate, and for some, a preferable form of the game. The World Cup had come at an ideal time.

India, the West Indies and England were all seen as having a shot at lifting the trophy, but Pakistan, led by Imran Khan who was now back to bowling at his best, were considered the heavy favourites. Imran had put together a powerful team, with the wily Javed Miandad as his vice-captain leading the batting stakes, followed by two talented batsmen in Rameez Raja and Saleem Malik, the latter of whom had stunned the cricket world earlier in the year by hammering 72 not out off 35 balls to win a match against the odds over India in Calcutta. Partnering Imran with the new ball was Wasim Akram. Then there was the leg-spinner Abdul Qadir, who was expected to cause havoc amongst batting line-ups. In home conditions for the whole tournament up to the semi-final, and then with the final being played at a lucky ground for Pakistan (the Eden Gardens in Calcutta), the World Cup was seen to be in the bag. Imran had already announced that he would retire after the tournament.

Kapil Dev's defending champions India were also in good shape, but curiously there were those in the Indian media who felt that India would have had a better chance of defending their title in England with the type of medium-pacers who won them the title in 1983. Any fears of India failing to reach the semi-final stage were allayed by the fact that they found themselves in the substantially weaker of the two pools, which they were expected to top without any trouble. India had a stellar batting line-up, with Sunil Gavaskar followed by the hard-hitting pair of Krishnamachari Srikanth and Navjot Sidhu, as well as batsmen of the class of Dilip

Vengsarkar and Mohammad Azharuddin. With Kapil Dev himself and Ravi Shastri in the mix too, India's batting looked secure enough to compensate for any shortcomings with the ball.

Flanked by his team, Australian captain Allan Border poses with the World Cup, after beating England in the Final by 7 runs at Eden Gardens, Calcutta, November 8, 1987.

The media outside of the sub-continent had either gone for the West Indies or Pakistan as favourites. It was as if so blinded by their aura that no one had been paying attention to the West Indies current form, which had been patchy coming off a tour Down Under, where England, Australia and Pakistan had all managed to beat them. Michael Holding and Joel Garner had retired earlier in the year, and missing Malcolm Marshall for the tournament as well as Gordon Greenidge, left the West Indies looking something considerably less than invincible.

England, on the other hand, looked a good and confident team, having won every ODI tournament before them that year, as well as defeating Pakistan in a bilateral 3 match ODI series at home. England's batting looked particularly impressive with captain Mike Gatting, Graham Gooch, Chris Broad and Allan Lamb all entering the tournament in good form.

New Zealand missing Richard Hadlee were a write off, as were the Australians who were seen as too dependent for runs on their dispirited captain Allan Border and the flashy Dean Jones. Young all-rounders Steve Waugh and Simon O'Donnell were not giving anyone sleepless nights. It's almost funny now.

1st Semi-final • 1987
Pakistan v Australia
Gaddafi Stadium, Lahore

Lahore's Gaddafi Stadium was bursting at the seams with an official crowd of 35,000 (unofficially several thousand more) turning out to see favourites Pakistan take on Australia. Unfortunately, expectations of a great match for the home side were gradually deflated from the start.

Australia won the toss and decided to bat on a pitch that looked like it would play low and slow later in the day. The strip seemed to be prepared for leg-spinner Abdul Qadir, who had been a handful for teams throughout the tournament. The Australians, considered weaker than England and the West Indies, were expected to have no answers to Qadir. But the Aussies had come prepared, reportedly spending time watching videos of the bowler before the crucial match.

Curiously, Imran decided to hold back Wasim Akram and opened the bowling with the medium-pace of another left-armer, Saleem Jaffer. Australia's opening batsmen Geoff Marsh and David Boon were in good form, with Marsh having hit a couple of centuries and Boon having made a clutch of fifties over the course of the competition. Buoyed by the prospect of not immediately having to face the more dangerous Akram, the pair settled in and picked easy runs off Jaffer. To make matters worse, when Akram did come into the attack, he sprayed the ball all over the place, often straying well outside off-stump and getting hit for boundaries.

That this was not going to be Pakistan's day became clearer when wicket-keeper Saleem Yousuf got hit on the mouth while keeping to Qadir and had to go off the field, surrendering the gloves to Javed Miandad. Off-spinner Tauseef Ahmed also dislocated his thumb while trying to hold on to a return catch, but manfully completed his quota of 10 overs.

After Australia had posted 73 runs for the 1st wicket in 18 overs, the platform was set for the next batsmen to play without too much pressure. Qadir bowled economically, but with the Australians having done their homework, failed to bring about the predicted destruction.

In the end it was left to Imran to try to wrest back the initiative. Bowling in front of his home crowd for what everyone believed was his last time, the captain returned with fine figures of 10-1-36-3. But Imran made one miscalculation and it proved to be a big one. Saleem Jaffer, who had been hit for 39 runs in his previous five overs, was entrusted to bowl the

Javed Miandad fighting in vain during his knock of 70 in the World Cup Semi-Final at the Gaddafi Stadium, Lahore November 4, 1987. Miandad put on 112 with Imran Khan for the 4th wicket, but Pakistan went down to Australia by 18 runs.

last over of the innings. Steve Waugh (32 off 28, 4 fours, 1 six) mercilessly dispatched him for 18 runs, lifting Australia to a commanding 267-8.

Pakistan's reply got off to a bad start when the in-form Rameez Raja was run out for only 1 and his opening partner, the perpetually out-of-form Mansoor Akhtar, was bowled by Craig McDermott for 9. Pakistan's other young batting star Saleem Malik fell after scoring 25 to leave Pakistan in deep trouble at 38-3. It prompted Imran Khan to push himself up the order to number five, and with Javed Miandad at the other end, the rebuilding work began.

With a long history together, Pakistan's captain and vice-captain knew each other's thinking well. Both were calm under pressure and understood the responsibility on their shoulders. If they didn't take Pakistan all the way there, no one else would. The pair batted sensibly, a partnership burgeoned and Allan Border remained focussed, well aware that one more wicket and Pakistan would be on the ropes. With the ball now keeping low, Border brought himself on to bowl. Imran, having put on 112 with Miandad, edged his counterpart to wicket-keeper Greg Dyer for 58, leaving Pakistan at 150-4.

Pakistan's lower order of Wasim Akram (20 off 13 balls, 2 sixes), Saleem Yousuf (21 off 15 balls) and Abdul Qadir (20 off 16) tried hard, but once Miandad was bowled for 70 to one that kept low from Bruce Reid, it was all over. Craig McDermott took 5-44 and Pakistan were dismissed for 249 in 49 overs. With one over to go and Pakistan 18 runs behind Australia, Saleem Jaffer was a sound mathematical choice for scapegoat.

1st Semi-final • 1987
Pakistan v Australia
Gaddafi Stadium, Lahore • 4 November 1987 (50 overs per innings)

Toss: Australia

Umpires: HD Bird (Eng) and DR Shepherd (Eng)

Australia innings (50 overs maximum)			R	M	B	4	6
GR Marsh	run out		31	78	57	2	0
DC Boon	st +Javed Miandad	b Saleem Malik	65	133	91	4	0
DM Jones		b Tauseef Ahmed	38	58	45	3	0
*AR Border	run out		18	43	22	2	0
MRJ Veletta		b Imran Khan	48	57	50	2	0
SR Waugh	not out		32	38	28	4	1
SP O'Donnell	run out		0	1	2	0	0
+GC Dyer		b Imran Khan	0	2	1	0	0
CJ McDermott		b Imran Khan	1	6	3	0	0
TBA May	not out		0	8	2	0	0
Extras	(b 1, lb 19, w 13, nb 1)		34				
Total	(8 wickets, 50 overs)		267				

DNB: BA Reid.

FoW: 1-73 (Marsh), 2-155 (Boon), 3-155 (Jones), 4-215 (Border), 5-236 (Veletta),
6-236 (O'Donnell), 7-241 (Dyer), 8-249 (McDermott).

Bowling	O	M	R	W
Imran Khan	10	1	36	3
Saleem Jaffar	6	0	57	0
Wasim Akram	10	0	54	0
Abdul Qadir	10	0	39	0
Tauseef Ahmed	10	1	39	1
Saleem Malik	4	0	22	1

Pakistan innings (target: 268 runs from 50 overs)			R	M	B	4	6
Rameez Raja	run out		1	2	1	0	0
Mansoor Akhtar		b McDermott	9	36	19	0	0
Saleem Malik	c McDermott	b Waugh	25	43	31	3	0
Javed Miandad		b Reid	70	149	103	4	0
*Imran Khan	c Dyer	b Border	58	98	84	4	0
Wasim Akram		b McDermott	20	16	13	0	2
Ijaz Ahmed	c Jones	b Reid	8	11	7	1	0
+Saleem Yousuf	c Dyer	b McDermott	21	23	15	2	0
Abdul Qadir	not out		20	23	16	2	0
Saleem Jaffar	c Dyer	b McDermott	0	7	2	0	0
Tauseef Ahmed	c Dyer	b McDermott	1	3	3	0	0
Extras	(lb 6, w 10)		16				
Total	(all out, 49 overs)		249				

FoW: 1-2 (Rameez Raja), 2-37 (Mansoor Akhtar), 3-38 (Saleem Malik), 4-150 (Imran Khan),
5-177 (Wasim Akram), 6-192 (Ijaz Ahmed), 7-212 (Javed Miandad), 8-236 (Saleem Yousuf),
9-247 (Saleem Jaffar), 10-249 (Tauseef Ahmed).

Bowling	O	M	R	W
McDermott	10	0	44	5
Reid	10	2	41	2
Waugh	9	1	51	1
O'Donnell	10	1	45	0
May	6	0	36	0
Border	4	0	26	1

Man of the Match: CJ McDermott

Result: Australia won by 18 runs

2nd Semi-final • 1987
India v England
Wankhede Stadium, Bombay

India entered this match in Bombay as firm favourites. In what was regarded as a duel between two batting sides, India clearly had the edge in spite of missing hometown hero Dilip Vengsarkar, unavailable for the match due to illness. Neither bowling attack was particularly impressive, but for what it was worth, India did have the best bowler on either side in the shape of their captain Kapil Dev, who won the toss and inserted England.

Runs were difficult to come by and after 10 overs England only had 20 on the board. Kapil brought on his spinners who found turn immediately. It proved to be the undoing of opener Tim Robinson, but Graham Gooch decided to counter the spin by playing the sweep shot. When Mike Gatting eventually came to bat, he followed suit and soon England had a good partnership going between the two men.

Gooch appeared married to the sweep shot, employing it whether the ball was pitched on the stumps, or outside of off, in which case he just put more power into the shot. The partnership with Gatting was worth 117. Maninder Singh eventually dismissed both men; Gatting first, bowled for 56, and then Gooch, caught deep in the field, for a masterful 115 scored off 136 balls with 11 fours.

Allan Lamb played a typically quick knock (32 off 29 balls), stealing singles and hitting the odd boundary and Kapil Dev came back for a fine spell, picking up two wickets and finishing with figures of 10-1-38-2. England had compiled a worthy total of 254-6 in 50 overs.

India should not have been troubled by this total and yet the openers appeared out of sorts. Despite demolishing New Zealand in their last pool match, both Krishnamachari Srikanth and Sunil Gavaskar appeared to be struggling with their timing. Gavaskar, in what would be his lat match for India, lost his off-stump to Phil DeFreitas for only 4. That brought Navjot Sidhu to the crease, a man who had been in great form during the tournament, having hit four half-centuries. Both Sidhu and Srikanth were big hitters of the ball, but neither looked particularly comfortable batting, even though Srikanth managed to hit four fours in his innings. Neil Foster dismissed both batsmen in a neat spell of bowling before either could do any real damage.

Chandrakant Pandit, in the side to replace the absent Vengsarkar, came to the wicket to play his first innings of the tournament and gave valuable support to Mohammad Azharuddin. Pandit had been scoring his runs at a good rate, and with Azharuddin had put on 48 runs for the 4th wicket before Foster had him LBW to a yorker.

With the score 131-4, Kapil Dev came out to bat and the runs started to flow. With Azharuddin well set at the other end, this looked to be the partnership that would bring India home. India were going along nicely when Kapil smashed spinner Eddie Hemmings over the legside for his third four. Mike Gatting moved himself into that previously vacant area and Hemmings bowled the same delivery to the Indian captain. Whether it was arrogance or carelessness, Kapil played the exact same shot and was caught by his counterpart, departing for 30 off only 22 balls and perhaps remembering his remarks about Viv Richards in the 1983 World Cup final. In any event, Kapil Dev's departure left India in a spot of bother at 168-5.

With 10 overs left, India had 5 wickets in hand and only needed 53 runs for victory with the solid pair of Azharuddin and Ravi Shastri at the crease. Typical of Indian cricket in that time period however, a secure and utterly winning position was thrown away. Azharuddin, who had

England have victory in their sights as India's top scorer, Mohammad Azharuddin falls LBW to Eddie Hemmings.

played beautifully for his 64 (74 balls, 7 fours), fell LBW to Hemmings and the next man in, wicket-keeper Kiran More, lobbed a return catch to England's other off-spinner John Emburey, for a duck. India had slumped to 205-7. With the pressure now on India, the lower order buckled. Shastri was the last man out, trying in vain to hit India out of trouble. The defending champions folded for 219 and lost by 35 runs. Kapil Dev paid for the debacle by being sacked as captain and was replaced by Dilip Vengsarkar.

2nd Semi-final • 1987
India v England
Wankhede Stadium, Bombay • 5 November 1987 (50 overs per innings)

Toss: India

Umpires: AR Crafter (Aus) and SJ Woodward (NZ)

England innings (50 overs maximum)			R	B	4	6
GA Gooch	c Srikkanth	b Maninder Singh	115	136	11	0
RT Robinson	st More	b Maninder Singh	13	36	2	0
CWJ Athey	c More	b Sharma	4	17	0	0
*MW Gatting		b Maninder Singh	56	62	5	0
AJ Lamb	not out		32	29	2	0
JE Emburey	lbw	b Kapil Dev	6	10	0	0
PAJ DeFreitas		b Kapil Dev	7	8	1	0
+PR Downton	not out		1	5	0	0
Extras	(b 1, lb 18, w 1)		20			
Total	(6 wickets, 50 overs)		254			

DNB: NA Foster, GC Small, EE Hemmings.

FoW: 1-40 (Robinson), 2-79 (Athey), 3-196 (Gatting), 4-203 (Gooch), 5-219 (Emburey), 6-231 (DeFreitas).

Bowling	O	M	R	W
Kapil Dev	10	1	38	2
Prabhakar	9	1	40	0
Maninder Singh	10	0	54	3
Sharma	9	0	41	1
Shastri	10	0	49	0
Azharuddin	2	0	13	0

India innings (target: 255 runs from 50 overs)			R	B	4	6
K Srikkanth		b Foster	31	55	4	0
SM Gavaskar		b DeFreitas	4	7	1	0
NS Sidhu	c Athey	b Foster	22	40	0	0
M Azharuddin	lbw	b Hemmings	64	74	7	0
CS Pandit	lbw	b Foster	24	30	3	0
*N Kapil Dev	c Gatting	b Hemmings	30	22	3	0
RJ Shastri	c Downton	b Hemmings	21	32	2	0
+KS More	c & b Emburey		0	5	0	0
M Prabhakar	c Downton	b Small	4	11	0	0
C Sharma	c Lamb	b Hemmings	0	1	0	0
Maninder Singh	not out		0	0	0	0
Extras	(b 1, lb 9, w 6, nb 3)		19			
Total	(all out, 45.3 overs)		219			

FoW: 1-7 (Gavaskar), 2-58 (Srikkanth), 3-73 (Sidhu), 4-121 (Pandit), 5-168 (Kapil Dev), 6-204 (Azharuddin),
7-205 (More), 8-218 (Prabhakar), 9-219 (Sharma), 10-219 (Shastri).

Bowling	O	M	R	W
DeFreitas	7	0	37	1
Small	6	0	22	1
Emburey	10	1	35	1
Foster	10	0	47	3
Hemmings	9.3	1	52	4
Gooch	3	0	16	0

Man of the Match: GA Gooch

Result: England won by 35 runs

The 1987 World Cup Final
Australia v England
Eden Gardens, Calcutta

Ashes rivals England and Australia met to decide the World Championship at the Eden Gardens, Calcutta on November 8, 1987. England were considered the favourites, having come out of the tougher pool and holding their nerve in a tense semi-final with India in Bombay. Moreover, England had been an excellent side in ODIs throughout the year with many trophies in the case to show for it. This however, was the big prize and England found themselves facing a surprise package in Allan Border's Australia, who had put in a thoroughly professional performance to knock out favourites Pakistan in their own semi-final.

Border won the toss and elected to bat. Geoff Marsh and David Boon, who had consistently given Australia a good platform, continued their fine work on this occasion too and raised 75 runs for the 1st wicket before Neil Foster slipped one past Marsh's defences. The 2nd wicket stand was even better, with Boon and Dean Jones taking the score to 151 before the latter fell to Hemmings.

With a decent total on the board and only two wickets down, Border got creative and sent Craig McDermott up the order. England knew that he had license to hit and Gatting got in on the chess game and threw the ball to Graham Gooch, who promptly dismissed McDermott for 14 off 8 balls. Normality resumed, and Border came out to bat himself.

When Boon fell for 75, the new man in Mike Veletta decided to have a go at England's bowlers, racing to an unbeaten 45 off only 31 balls with 6 fours. Australia ended their 50 overs at a comfortable 253-5.

England's reply got off to a poor start when opener Tim Robinson was out LBW first ball to McDermott. The next man in was Bill Athey and in the company of England's best player, Graham Gooch took England's score to 66. Simon O'Donnell, who had been bowling unthreateningly but tidily, then had the well-set Gooch LBW for 35. It was a big blow, but England refused to panic and the captain Mike Gatting continued to score freely with Athey.

Border was shrewd enough to know that if things continued this way, the game would soon drift decisively towards England. As he had done in Lahore to break the partnership between Imran Khan and Javed Miandad, Border brought himself on to bowl here too. Gatting took the ball, pitched on leg-stump and attempted a horrendous sweep shot that ballooned in the air and then lodged safely in the hands of wicket-keeper Greg Dyer. Just when Gatting looked like he was taking England to victory, he had thrown it away, out for 41 off 45 balls and leaving his team 135-3.

Athey continued to provide support to Allan Lamb, who in typical fashion had the scoreboard ticking. But sharp fielding from Steve Waugh saw Athey run out going for three. Border picked up another scalp, having wicket-keeper Paul Downton caught by O'Donnell and yet another run out saw John Emburey depart for 10. England had slumped to 218-6 with only the bowlers left to keep Lamb company.

In the recent past, this had been the kind of situation that brought out the best in Allan Lamb, but on this day he would fail, bowled by Steve Waugh for 45. Philip DeFreitas threw his bat around, including hitting McDermott for a towering six, but it was never going to be enough with all the batsmen already gone. England spiritedly scampered two runs off the last ball, but finished their 50 overs at 246-8, going down by the painfully thin margin of 7 runs.

After the way they played through the 1987 World Cup, Allan Border's men deserved to be World Champions. This triumph marked the rebirth of Australian cricket, which had been in the doldrums since the retirements of Dennis Lillee, Rod Marsh and Greg Chappell. The win also proved to be a stepping stone for previously underrated players like Steve Waugh and David Boon, who went on to become bonafide stars.

The 1987 World Cup Final
Australia v England
Eden Gardens, Calcutta • 8 November 1987 (50 overs per innings)

Toss: Australia

Umpires: RB Gupta and Mahboob Shah (Pak)

Australia innings (50 overs maximum)			R	M	B	4	6
DC Boon	c Downton	b Hemmings	75	159	125	7	0
GR Marsh		b Foster	24	71	49	3	0
DM Jones	c Athey	b Hemmings	33	75	57	1	1
CJ McDermott		b Gooch	14	6	8	2	0
*AR Border	run out (Robinson/Downton)		31	48	31	3	0
MRJ Veletta	not out		45	50	31	6	0
SR Waugh	not out		5	5	4	0	0
Extras	(b 1, lb 13, w 5, nb 7)		26				
Total	(5 wickets, 50 overs)		253				

DNB: SP O'Donnell, +GC Dyer, TBA May, BA Reid.

FoW: 1-75 (Marsh), 2-151 (Jones), 3-166 (McDermott), 4-168 (Boon), 5-241 (Border).

Bowling	O	M	R	W
DeFreitas	6	1	34	0
Small	6	0	33	0
Foster	10	0	38	1
Hemmings	10	1	48	2
Emburey	10	0	44	0
Gooch	8	1	42	1

England innings (target: 254 runs from 50 overs)			R	M	B	4	6
GA Gooch	lbw	b O'Donnell	35	74	57	4	0
RT Robinson	lbw	b McDermott	0	2	1	0	0
CWJ Athey	run out (Waugh/Reid)		58	126	103	2	0
*MW Gatting	c Dyer	b Border	41	55	45	3	1
AJ Lamb		b Waugh	45	56	55	4	0
+PR Downton	c O'Donnell	b Border	9	13	8	1	0
JE Emburey	run out (Boon/McDermott)		10	27	16	0	0
PAJ DeFreitas	c Reid	b Waugh	17	10	10	2	1
NA Foster	not out		7	12	6	0	0
GC Small	not out		3	6	3	0	0
Extras	(b 1, lb 14, w 2, nb 4)		21				
Total	(8 wickets, 50 overs)		246				

DNB: EE Hemmings.

FoW: 1-1 (Robinson), 2-66 (Gooch), 3-135 (Gatting), 4-170 (Athey), 5-188 (Downton),
      6-218 (Emburey), 7-220 (Lamb), 8-235 (DeFreitas).

Bowling	O	M	R	W
McDermott	10	1	51	1
Reid	10	0	43	0
Waugh	9	0	37	2
O'Donnell	10	1	35	1
May	4	0	27	0
Border	7	0	38	2

Man of the Match: DC Boon

Result: Australia won the 1987 World Cup Final by 7 runs

*Pakistan captain Imran Khan receives the World Cup,
Melbourne, March 25 1992.*

1992

WORLD CUP 1992 •
AUSTRALIA and NEW ZEALAND

Official Title: The Benson & Hedges World Cup
Winners: Pakistan
Participating teams: Australia, England,
South Africa, West Indies, New Zealand, India,
Pakistan, Sri Lanka and Zimbabwe
February 22, 1992- March 25, 1992

The 1992 World Cup was another great tournament, but was markedly different from its predecessors. For the first time the teams were not divided into two groups. The reason for this was that South Africa were back in the international fold after the sporting isolation of the Apartheid years. South Africa's virtual last-minute inclusion made it nine teams and the only logical solution to an odd number of teams was to have them all play each other. The top four teams were to go to the semi-final stage and the last team standing would surely have bragging rights as World Champions in a manner like no team before; with no begrudging of easy or difficult qualifying pools.

Coloured clothing and white balls were introduced to the World Cup in this tournament and some matches were to be day/night affairs played under floodlights. Australia were hot favourites to defend their title, but inexplicably made a hash of it. Co-hosts New Zealand, on the other hand, had a wonderful tournament. Led astutely by Martin Crowe, who would go on to be named player of the tournament, New

The captains pose with the 1992 World Cup in Sydney, prior to the start of the tournament. Back row, left to right: David Houghton (Zimbabwe), Kepler Wessels (South Africa), Mohammad Azharuddin (India), Richie Richardson (West Indies) and Aravinda de Silva (Sri Lanka). Front row, left to right: Martin Crowe (New Zealand), Allan Border (Australia), Graham Gooch (England) and Imran Khan (Pakistan).

Zealand impressed everyone with their innovation, particularly the use of spinner Dipak Patel as an opening bowler. New Zealand trounced all comers, losing only twice in the entire tournament; their last first-round match and then the semi-final, both to Pakistan.

All eyes were on South Africa, a team that a generation of cricket followers knew nothing about. Their captain Kepler Wessels, however was no stranger to Australians, having played Test cricket for Australia in the early 1980s and even representing them in the 1983 World Cup.

In spite of Australia's wobble, New Zealand's day in the sun and South Africa's return to international cricket, WorldCup 1992 will always be remembered for the triumph of Imran Khan's "cornered tigers." Pakistan were sitting just above Zimbabwe at the halfway stage of the tournament. Imran Khan, in his final World Cup campaign and with one eye on the cancer hospital he wished to build in his country, motivated his team out of the depths to do what at one stage looked nearly impossible. Imran Khan retired after the tournament, his legacy secure and his captaincy and motivational powers praised by all. Of course had Imran not retired immediately after winning the trophy, those leadership qualities would have been put to a stern test, seeing as how he infamously neglected to thank his team in his World Cup acceptance speech.

1st Semi-final • 1992
New Zealand v Pakistan
Eden Park, Auckland

A cliff-hanger of the highest order, Pakistan's semi-final win over New Zealand in Auckland is best remembered as the match that introduced Inzamam-ul-Haq to the world.

New Zealand had been in wonderful touch in the 1992 World Cup, winning everything until they faced a resurgent Pakistan in the last match of the tournament's first round. Pakistan's triumph in that game helped them squeak into the last semi-final berth and set up a rematch with New Zealand at Eden Park.

New Zealand captain Martin Crowe had a wonderful World Cup, earning plaudits for his innovative captaincy and sparkling batting form. New Zealand were the top team at the end of the first round, but were knocked out by Pakistan in a thriller of a Semi-Final. Crowe scored a tournament high 456 runs, at an astonishing average of 114.

New Zealand captain Martin Crowe won the toss and decided to bat. Mark Greatbatch opened the batting and was aggressive from the outset, smashing 2 sixes before Aaqib Javed bowled him for 17. John Wright and Andrew Jones were troubled and eventually dismissed by leg-spinner Mushtaq Ahmed, but Crowe and Ken Rutherford got the New Zealand innings back on track. Rutherford, having struck 5 fours and a six, fell for 50 off 68 balls. Unfazed, Crowe powered on. The Kiwi skipper was in devastating form, hitting boundaries at will before pulling his hamstring and eventually being run out by his runner. The injury meant that he would be unable to field during Pakistan's innings. Crowe's 83 ball, 91 contained 7 fours and 3 sixes and set up New Zealand for a final flourish that saw them reach a daunting 262-7 in their 50 overs.

Imran Khan's modus operandi in situations such as this had always been to preserve wickets and then attack the bowling in the final 10 overs or so. That plan was followed here too, but Pakistan appeared to be getting bogged down, leaving too much for the lower order to do in the face of a sharply increasing asking rate. Imran, batting at number three in the semi-final, did his best to lay a platform for the assault, which it seemed he intended to carry out himself having hit 2 sixes, but he fell for 44 after consuming 93 deliveries. With Saleem Malik getting out for 1, Pakistan were 140-4 in the 35th over and looking down the barrel. Enter Inzamam-ul-Haq.

The young batsman joined Javed Miandad at the crease and the veteran guided Inzamam through the innings, running him hard for tight singles. In between all that, Inzamam swished away mightily at the bowling, piercing the field with ease and leaving New Zealand's stand-in captain John Wright at a loss for answers. By the time Inzamam was run out, having scored a sizzling 60 off 37 balls, the playing field was levelled; Pakistan needing 36 runs from the last 30 balls. The cool head of Miandad at one end and the hitting of wicket-keeper Moin Khan at the other, saw Pakistan reach home with an over to spare. For the bitterly disappointed Auckland crowd, the match was no less than a heist, but Pakistan chose to see their win as destiny.

1st Semi-final • 1992
New Zealand v Pakistan
Eden Park, Auckland • 21 March 1992 (50 overs per innings)

Toss: New Zealand

Umpires: SA Bucknor (WI) and DR Shepherd (Eng) • Match Referee: PJP Burge (Aus)

New Zealand innings (50 overs maximum)			R	M	B	4	6
MJ Greatbatch		b Aaqib Javed	17	41	22	0	2
JG Wright	c Rameez Raja	b Mushtaq Ahmed	13	57	44	1	0
AH Jones	lbw	b Mushtaq Ahmed	21	60	53	2	0
*MD Crowe	run out		91	132	83	7	3
KR Rutherford	c Moin Khan	b Wasim Akram	50	68	68	5	1
CZ Harris	st Moin Khan	b Iqbal Sikander	13	15	12	1	0
+IDS Smith	not out		18	21	10	3	0
DN Patel	lbw	b Wasim Akram	8	10	6	1	0
GR Larsen	not out		8	7	6	1	0
Extras	(lb 11, w 8, nb 4)		23				
Total	(7 wickets, 50 overs)		262				

DNB: DK Morrison, W Watson.

FoW: 1-35 (Greatbatch), 2-39 (Wright), 3-87 (Jones), 4-194 (Rutherford),
5-214 (Harris), 6-221 (Crowe), 7-244 (Patel).

Bowling	O	M	R	W	
Wasim Akram	10	1	40	2	(4nb 2w)
Aaqib Javed	10	2	45	1	(2w)
Mushtaq Ahmed	10	0	40	2	
Imran Khan	10	0	59	0	(3w)
Iqbal Sikander	9	0	56	1	(1w)
Aamer Sohail	1	0	11	0	

Pakistan innings (target: 263 runs from 50 overs)			R	M	B	4	6
Aamer Sohail	c Jones	b Patel	14	26	20	1	0
Rameez Raja	c Morrison	b Watson	44	81	55	6	0
*Imran Khan	c Larsen	b Harris	44	98	93	1	2
Javed Miandad	not out		57	125	69	4	0
Saleem Malik	c sub	b Larsen	1	4	2	0	0
Inzamam-ul-Haq	run out		60	48	37	7	1
Wasim Akram		b Watson	9	12	8	1	0
+Moin Khan	not out		20	15	11	2	1
Extras	(b 4, lb 10, w 1)		15				
Total	(6 wickets, 49 overs)		264				

DNB: Mushtaq Ahmed, Iqbal Sikander, Aaqib Javed.

FoW: 1-30 (Aamer Sohail), 2-84 (Rameez Raja), 3-134 (Imran Khan), 4-140 (Saleem Malik),
5-227 (Inzamam-ul-Haq), 6-238 (Wasim Akram).

Bowling	O	M	R	W	
Patel	10	1	50	1	
Morrison	9	0	55	0	(1w)
Watson	10	2	39	2	(1nb)
Larsen	10	1	34	1	
Harris	10	0	72	1	

Man of the Match: Inzamam-ul-Haq

Result: Pakistan won by 4 wickets

2nd Semi-final • 1992
England v South Africa
Sydney Cricket Ground

A cruel game, this one. South Africa, newly returned to international cricket, had done remarkably well to get to the World Cup semi-final at the expense of teams such as the West Indies and hosts Australia. The South Africans had captured the imagination of cricket fans all over the world, if for no better reason than the novelty of having a team step back into the game after years away and immediately re-establishing itself as a force to be reckoned with. The Sydney Cricket Ground (SCG) looked forward to a historic semi-final match between England and South Africa, and a historic match is certainly what took place, albeit for all the wrong reasons.

South African skipper Kepler Wessels won the toss and asked England to bat. Ian Botham opened the batting and got the scoreboard ticking, but Graham Gooch edged Allan Donald to wicket-keeper Dave Richardson after scoring only 2 runs. Botham was looking good on 21 off 23 balls when he was bowled by medium pacer Meyrick Pringle to leave England 39-2. The South Africans were delighted to get two dangerous players early, but would have to wait for further success as Graeme Hick and Alec Stewart got stuck in for a 71-run partnership. Stewart and then Neil Fairbrother provided good support to Hick as he continued to score freely, eventually falling for 83 off 90 balls, with 9 fours. Some fine hitting in the final overs from Dermot Reeve (25 off 14 balls) and Chris Lewis (18 off 16 balls) saw England reach a challenging total of 252-6 in 45 overs, with 5 overs lost due to rain.

South Africa went about chasing the total in a positive manner, but any time a batsman looked set, England were able to snap up a wicket. Jonty Rhodes (43 off 38 balls) in particular looked to be taking the game away from England, but hit Gladstone Small to Chris Lewis to reduce South Africa to 206-6. Having dismissed all of South Africa's specialist batsmen, England may have felt the match was pocketed, but all-rounder Brian McMillan and Dave Richardson kept South Africa in the hunt, picking out gaps in the field and taking good singles. And then the rain came again.

There was one delivery left in the 42nd over when the players came off the field for 12 minutes with South Africa 22 runs behind England. Two overs were deemed to have been lost and a bizarre rule employed for rain-affected matches in the 1992 World Cup meant that South Africa's required target would come down by however many runs England had scored in their two worst overs. In this case, England's two worst overs had been maidens, which meant that South Africa's required total went down by zero. Instead of needing 22 runs off 13 balls, they now needed an impossible 22 runs off 1 ball.

The crowd booed the English win and South Africa were heartbroken. England captain Graham Gooch appeared a bit embarrassed to have won in this manner, but a trip to the World Cup final was richly deserved for a team that had played well throughout the tournament.

The scoreboard spells out the gloom for South Africa in their Semi-Final clash with England, at the Sydney Cricket Ground, March 22, 1992.

2nd Semi-final • 1992
England v South Africa
Sydney Cricket Ground (day/night) • 22 March 1992 (50 overs per innings)
Toss: South Africa
Umpires: BL Aldridge (NZ) and SG Randell • Match Referee: FJ Cameron (NZ)

England innings (45 overs maximum)			R	M	B	4	6
*GA Gooch	c Richardson	b Donald	2	15	9	0	0
IT Botham		b Pringle	21	38	23	3	0
+AJ Stewart	c Richardson	b McMillan	33	87	54	4	0
GA Hick	c Rhodes	b Snell	83	133	90	9	0
NH Fairbrother		b Pringle	28	64	50	1	0
AJ Lamb	c Richardson	b Donald	19	27	22	1	0
CC Lewis	not out		18	37	16	2	0
DA Reeve	not out		25	13	14	4	0
Extras	(b 1, lb 7, w 9, nb 6)		23				
Total	(6 wickets, 45 overs)		252				

DNB: PAJ DeFreitas, GC Small, RK Illingworth.

FoW: 1-20 (Gooch), 2-39 (Botham), 3-110 (Stewart), 4-183 (Fairbrother), 5-187 (Hick), 6-221 (Lamb).

Bowling	O	M	R	W	
Donald	10	0	69	2	(2nb 5w)
Pringle	9	2	36	2	(4nb 1w)
Snell	8	0	52	1	(2w)
McMillan	9	0	47	1	
Kuiper	5	0	26	0	
Cronje	4	0	14	0	

South Africa innings (target: 252 runs from 43 overs)			R	M	B	4	6
*KC Wessels	c Lewis	b Botham	17	17	21	1	0
AC Hudson	lbw	b Illingworth	46	78	52	6	0
PN Kirsten		b DeFreitas	11	30	26	0	0
AP Kuiper		b Illingworth	36	62	44	5	0
WJ Cronje	c Hick	b Small	24	72	45	1	0
JN Rhodes	c Lewis	b Small	43	61	38	3	0
BM McMillan	not out		21	41	21	0	0
+DJ Richardson	not out		13	19	10	1	0
Extras	(lb 17, w 4)		21				
Total	(6 wickets, 43 overs)		232				

DNB: RP Snell, MW Pringle, AA Donald

FoW: 1-26 (Wessels), 2-61 (Kirsten), 3-90 (Hudson), 4-131 (Kuiper), 5-176 (Cronje), 6-206 (Rhodes).

Bowling	O	M	R	W	
Botham	10	0	52	1	(3w)
Lewis	5	0	38	0	
DeFreitas	8	1	28	1	(1w)
Illingworth	10	1	46	2	
Small	10	1	51	2	

Man of the Match: GA Hick

Result: England won by 19 runs (revised target)

The 1992 World Cup Final
England v Pakistan
Melbourne Cricket Ground

The final of the 1992 World Cup was played between Pakistan and England on March 25th 1992 at the Melbourne Cricket Ground (MCG). It was Pakistan's first trip to the final, with England making their third appearance in five tournaments. Pakistan captain Imran Khan won the toss, and in bright sunshine decided to bat first.

Derek Pringle bowled a tight first spell, containing openers Rameez Raja (8 off 26 balls) and Aamer Sohail (4 off 19 balls) and eventually dismissing them. As in the semi-final, Imran Khan again batted at number three and was joined at the crease by his vice-captain Javed Miandad.

Imran Khan and Javed Miandad had played many innings in tandem and in their last match together the two veterans found themselves with the opportunity to make history. They had been in a similar situation before, the 1987 World Cup semi-final in Lahore, against Australia. They had put on a century stand there too, but it had not been enough. This time it would be.

The only cricketers to have played in every World Cup since 1975, both Imran and Miandad were restricted by health problems here – Imran with a shoulder injury and Javed with chronic stomach pain, and yet they soldiered on, putting on 139 runs for the 3rd wicket. They batted cautiously at first and then began to accelerate, entirely in keeping with a strategy that they had used for a number of years. Javed was out for 52 off 98 balls and Imran for 72 off 110 balls, but they set the stage for a stunning assault by Inzamam-ul-Haq (42 off 35 balls) and Wasim Akram (33 off 19 balls). Boundaries were hit to all parts of the ground and England appeared helpless in the field. Pringle (10-2-22-3) continued to bowl well, dismissing Inzamam with the penultimate ball of the innings, but Pakistan had rattled up 249 in their 50 overs and looked confident that they had done enough.

England's reply got off to a terrible start when Ian Botham edged Wasim Akram to wicket-keeper Moin Khan without having scored. The Pakistani pace attack kept pitching the ball up to the England batsmen and Alec Stewart was lucky to survive an appeal for caught behind off Akram. His luck did not last and he eventually nicked Aaqib Javed to Moin Khan.

Imran brought leg-spinner Mushtaq Ahmed on and he trapped Graeme Hick LBW with a beautiful googly. England captain Graham Gooch, whose sweep shot against spinners had been so effective in the 1987 World Cup semi-final against India, decided to try the method to get runs off Mushtaq, but only ended up lofting the ball to Aaqib Javed in the deep. As he left the field, Gooch turned back to have a wistful look. At 69-4, the writing was on the wall.

Allan Lamb and Neil Fairbrother undertook a mini-revival that Pakistan did not appear overly concerned by at first. However, as the runs started to accrue in earnest, Imran turned to his biggest gun. Wasim Akram was expected to return to the attack some time after the 40th over, but Imran brought him back earlier in the 35th over in an attempt to break the Lamb/Fairbrother partnership. It worked.

Wasim Akram's two-ball burst where he bowled Lamb and then Chris Lewis is the stuff of legend. Swinging the ball prodigiously, Akram reduced England from 141-4 to 141-6 in the space of two balls and it then became just a matter of time.

Imran Khan took England's last wicket with what would be the final ball of his career. Pakistan had won the 1992 World Cup in fairytale fashion, completing a memorable run through the tournament, where they lifted themselves from the cellar to the summit, under their captain's truly inspirational leadership.

England wicket-keeper Alec Stewart can only watch as Pakistan captain Imran Khan goes for a big hit during his 139 run partnership with Javed Miandad in the World Cup Final at Melbourne, March 25 1992.

Time to celebrate: The Pakistan dressing room after the team's World Cup triumph, March 25, 1992.

The 1992 World Cup Final
England v Pakistan
Melbourne Cricket Ground (day/night) • 25 March 1992 (50 overs per innings)
Toss: Pakistan
Umpires: BL Aldridge (NZ) and SA Bucknor (WI) • Match Referee: PJP Burge

Pakistan innings (50 overs maximum)			R	M	B	4	6
Aamer Sohail	c Stewart	b Pringle	4	20	19	0	0
Rameez Raja	lbw	b Pringle	8	36	26	1	0
*Imran Khan	c Illingworth	b Botham	72	159	110	5	1
Javed Miandad	c Botham	b Illingworth	58	125	98	4	0
Inzamam-ul-Haq		b Pringle	42	46	35	4	0
Wasim Akram	run out		33	21	19	4	0
Saleem Malik	not out		0	2	1	0	0
Extras	(lb 19, w 6, nb 7)		32				
Total	(6 wickets, 50 overs)		249				

DNB: Ijaz Ahmed, +Moin Khan, Mushtaq Ahmed, Aaqib Javed

FoW: 1-20 (Aamer Sohail), 2-24 (Rameez Raja), 3-163 (Javed Miandad), 4-197 (Imran Khan),
     5-249 (Inzamam-ul-Haq), 6-249 (Wasim Akram).

Bowling	O	M	R	W	
Pringle	10	2	22	3	(5nb 3w)
Lewis	10	2	52	0	(2nb 1w)
Botham	7	0	42	1	
DeFreitas	10	1	42	0	(1w)
Illingworth	10	0	50	1	
Reeve	3	0	22	0	(1w)

England innings (target: 250 runs from 50 overs)			R	M	B	4	6
*GA Gooch	c Aaqib Javed	b Mushtaq Ahmed	29	93	66	1	0
IT Botham	c Moin Khan	b Wasim Akram	0	12	6	0	0
+AJ Stewart	c Moin Khan	b Aaqib Javed	7	22	16	1	0
GA Hick	lbw	b Mushtaq Ahmed	17	49	36	1	0
NH Fairbrother	c Moin Khan	b Aaqib Javed	62	97	70	3	0
AJ Lamb		b Wasim Akram	31	54	41	2	0
CC Lewis		b Wasim Akram	0	6	1	0	0
DA Reeve	c Rameez Raja	b Mushtaq Ahmed	15	38	32	0	0
DR Pringle	not out		18	29	16	1	0
PAJ DeFreitas	run out		10	13	8	0	0
RK Illingworth	c Rameez Raja	b Imran Khan	14	9	11	2	0
Extras	(lb 5, w 13, nb 6)		24				
Total	(all out, 49.2 overs)		227				

FoW: 1-6 (Botham), 2-21 (Stewart), 3-59 (Hick), 4-69 (Gooch), 5-141 (Lamb), 6-141 (Lewis),
     7-180 (Fairbrother),8-183 (Reeve), 9-208 (DeFreitas), 10-227 (Illingworth).

Bowling	O	M	R	W	
Wasim Akram	10	0	49	3	(4nb 6w)
Aaqib Javed	10	2	27	2	(1nb 3w)
Mushtaq Ahmed	10	1	41	3	(1w)
Ijaz Ahmed	3	0	13	0	(2w)
Imran Khan	6.2	0	43	1	(1nb)
Aamer Sohail	10	0	49	0	(1w)

Man of the Match: Wasim Akram

Result: Pakistan won the 1992 World Cup Final by 22 runs

*Sri Lankan captain Arjuna Ranatunga receives the
World Cup from Pakistan's Prime Minister
Benazir Bhutto, Gaddafi Stadium Lahore,
March 17, 1996*

1996

WORLD CUP 1996 •
PAKISTAN, INDIA
and SRI LANKA

Official Title: The Wills World Cup
Winners: Sri Lanka
Group A: Australia, West Indies, India,
Sri Lanka, Zimbabwe, Kenya
Group B: England, South Africa, New Zealand,
Pakistan, Netherlands, UAE
February 14, 1996- March 17, 1996

After several absorbing World Cups, it was bound to happen sooner or later that one would not be up to scratch. This was it. The 1996 World Cup was an utter clunker, an ill-conceived behemoth of a tournament.

For the first time in its history, the World Cup expanded to include 12 teams. There were six teams in each of the two pools, with four (yes, *four*) of them qualifying for the second round, which was a knockout stage. The idea of a quarter-final was quite ridiculous, seeing as how one glance at the pool would tell you who wouldn't be qualifying. It was odd to see a hapless team like England, who were unable to beat a Test playing country in the tournament, padding up in a

England captain Mike Atherton wishing he played for a better team, Karachi, March 3, 1996.

quarter-final match. The format also put co-hosts Pakistan in a position where there was temptation to throw a game in order to get a cushy quarter-final slot at home instead of having to travel to India to play. In the end, Pakistan decided to put their best foot forward, went to India and got trampled in a teeming stadium in Bangalore.

Bomb blasts in Colombo meant that Australia and the West Indies refused to travel to Sri Lanka for their scheduled matches. Those games were forfeited in favour of Sri Lanka, who shot to the top of their group. Australia didn't care too much, as a quarter-final berth was going to be there for them anyway. The West Indies, however, had a bit of a scare when they lost to minnow Kenya. It would take a win over Australia in the first round to guarantee their passage to the next stage.

This is the tournament where Sri Lanka officially shook off the tag of minnow. Led by the veteran Arjuna Ranatunga, Sri Lanka had a decidedly elite-team feel to them heading into the tournament. Opener Sanath Jayasuriya, who went on to be named the player of the tournament, used the centre stage of the World Cup to cement his status as one of the most destructive batsmen in the history of ODI cricket. It is he who will forever be associated with the concept of attacking the bowling with all guns blazing in the first 15 overs of an innings.

In pre-tournament analysis, South Africa had been declared the favourites to win the 1996 World Cup. Their form justified the hype, as they finished the first round with five wins in five matches, only to be undone by a Brain Lara hundred in the quarter-final. A bad tournament was made worse by a semi-final that will live on in infamy.

1st Semi-final • 1996
India v Sri Lanka
Eden Gardens, Calcutta

Eden Gardens, Calcutta was packed with a crowd of more than 100,000 for the first semi-final of the 1996 World Cup. The home side had dispatched arch-rivals and defending champions Pakistan in the quarter-finals and hopes were high that Sri Lanka could be tamed too, in spite of India having lost to them in the first round.

India's captain Mohammad Azharuddin won the toss and put Sri Lanka in to bat to the surprise of many. It proved to be a master stroke. The Sri Lankan openers, Sanath Jayasuriya and Romesh Kaluwitharana, who had built up a reputation for tearing apart bowling attacks in the first 15 overs of the innings, were both back in the pavilion, courtesy of Javagal Srinath with only 1 run on the board. Aravinda de Silva, in the form of his life, came to bat at number four and dominated a 34-run partnership with Asanka Gurusinha who only contributed 1 run before becoming a fired-up Srinath's third victim of the morning.

Roshan Mahanama joined de Silva, who continued to unfurl boundaries with ease. The pair had put on 50 before Anil Kumble bowled de Silva for a silky 66 made off only 44 balls, with 14 fours. Mahanama also reached a half-century before retiring hurt. It was left to captain Arjuna Ranatunga and the lower order to cobble together runs and take Sri Lanka to 251-8 in their 50 overs.

Navjot Sidhu went early with the score on 8, but Sanjay Manjrekar blocked one end, allowing Sachin Tendulkar (65 off 88 balls with 9 fours) to go after the bowling. With the ball spinning sharply, Tendulkar's was a masterful innings, ended by a smart stumping from Kaluwitharana off the bowling of Jayasuriya. Azharuddin was out for a duck and right after that Jayasuriya got one past the defences of Manjrekar. From 98-1, India had slumped to 101-4.

Srinath, promoted ahead of Ajay Jadeja and wicket-keeper Nayan Mongia, lasted a mere six balls and when Jadeja did come out to bat, a rampant Jayasuriya bowled him for a duck too. Vinod Kambli, struggling himself with only 10 off 29 balls, could only watch from the other end as wickets continued to tumble.

Attendance reportedly topped 110,000 at Eden Gardens, Calcutta, on March 13, 1996 for India's World Cup Semi-Final clash with Sri Lanka.

At 120-8 in 34 overs, the crowd had seen enough. Fires were lit in the stands and all manner of debris rained down on the field, forcing the players to come off for a brief period. When they came out again, the crowd's behaviour picked up where it had left off and match referee Clive Lloyd (who knew a thing or two about tense World Cup games) awarded the match to a deserving Sri Lankan side. Aravinda de Silva was declared the man of the match, though Sanath Jayasuriya's 3-12 with the ball would have made a fine choice too.

1st Semi-final • 1996
India v Sri Lanka
Eden Gardens, Calcutta (day/night) • 13 March 1996 (50 overs per innings)
Toss: India
Umpires: RS Dunne (NZ) and CJ Mitchley (SA) • TV Umpire: Mahboob Shah (Pak)
Match Referee: CH Lloyd (WI)

Sri Lanka innings (50 overs maximum)			R	M	B	4	6
ST Jayasuriya	c Prasad	b Srinath	1	4	3	0	0
+RS Kaluwitharana	c Manjrekar	b Srinath	0	1	1	0	0
AP Gurusinha	c Kumble	b Srinath	1	29	16	0	0
PA de Silva		b Kumble	66	63	47	14	0
RS Mahanama	retired hurt		58	126	101	6	0
*A Ranatunga	lbw	b Tendulkar	35	72	42	4	0
HP Tillakaratne	c Tendulkar	b Prasad	32	51	43	1	0
HDPK Dharmasena		b Tendulkar	9	21	20	0	0
WPUJC Vaas	run out (Azharuddin)		23	19	16	3	0
GP Wickramasinghe	not out		4	10	9	0	0
M Muralitharan	not out		5	4	4	0	0
Extras	(b 1, lb 10, w 4, nb 2)		17				
Total	(8 wickets, 50 overs)		251				

FoW: 1-1 (Kaluwitharana), 2-1 (Jayasuriya), 3-35 (Gurusinha), 4-85 (de Silva), 5-168 (Ranatunga),
6-206 (Dharmasena), 7-236 (Tillakaratne), 8-244 (Vaas)

Bowling	O	M	R	W	
Srinath	7	1	34	3	
Kumble	10	0	51	1	(1w)
Prasad	8	0	50	1	(2nb, 2w)
Kapoor	10	0	40	0	
Jadeja	5	0	31	0	
Tendulkar	10	1	34	2	(1w)

India innings (target: 252 runs from 50 overs)			R	M	B	4	6
SR Tendulkar	st Kaluwitharana	b Jayasuriya	65	96	88	9	0
NS Sidhu	c Jayasuriya	b Vaas	3	7	8	0	0
SV Manjrekar		b Jayasuriya	25	105	48	1	0
*M Azharuddin	c & b Dharmasena		0	3	6	0	0
VG Kambli	not out		10	49	29	0	0
J Srinath	run out		6	8	6	1	0
A Jadeja		b Jayasuriya	0	9	11	0	0
+NR Mongia	c Jayasuriya	b de Silva	1	10	8	0	0
AR Kapoor	c de Silva	b Muralitharan	0	1	1	0	0
A Kumble	not out		0	1	0	0	0
Extras	(lb 5, w 5)		10				
Total	(8 wickets, 34.1 overs)		120				

DNB: BKV Prasad

FoW: 1-8 (Sidhu), 2-98 (Tendulkar), 3-99 (Azharuddin), 4-101 (Manjrekar),
5-110 (Srinath), 6-115 (Jadeja), 7-120 (Mongia), 8-120 (Kapoor)

Bowling	O	M	R	W	
Wickramasinghe	5	0	24	0	(2w)
Vaas	6	1	23	1	
Muralitharan	7.1	0	29	1	(1w)
Dharmasena	7	0	24	1	
Jayasuriya	7	1	12	3	(1w)
de Silva	2	0	3	1	(1w)

Man of the Match: PA de Silva

Result: Sri Lanka won by default

2nd Semi-final • 1996
Australia v West Indies
Punjab C.A. Stadium, Mohali, Chandigarh

This incredible match began with a wonderful display of fast bowling as Curtly Ambrose and Ian Bishop blew away the Australian top order. Mark Waugh (0), Mark Taylor (1), Ricky Ponting (0) and Steve Waugh (3) were all either bowled or LBW to the two West Indies' quicks. At 15-4, Australia looked to be dead in the water before Stuart Law and Michael Bevan carefully began to rebuild the innings.

The pair took the score to 153 before Law was run out for 72. Bevan then found some support in Ian Healy before getting out for 69 attempting to up the run rate. Australia finished their 50 overs having made 208-8. It was a good recovery, but still looked inadequate.

The West Indies began their run chase well. Wicket-keeper Courtney Brown, opening the innings with Shivnarine Chanderpaul, fell with the score on 25. Brian Lara came in and kept the scoreboard moving before being bowled by Steve Waugh for a run a ball, 45. The West Indies were now 93-2, but both Chanderpaul and captain Richie Richardson looked good at the crease and brought the score up to 165 before Glenn McGrath got in on the action and dismissed Chanderpaul. Still, with only 44 runs needed and 7 wickets in hand, the match was firmly in the West Indies' hands. And then they lost the plot.

Richardson could only watch in horror from the other end as batsman after batsman got out taking wild swipes at Shane Warne and McGrath. The last over began with the West Indies needing 10 runs and being down by nine wickets. Richardson hit Damien

Fleming's first ball for 4 and then went for a single, which saw Ambrose run out. The new man in was Courtney Walsh and he missed a straight one. The West Indies were all out for 202, with Richardson stranded at the other end, on 49. He chose to retire from cricket after this match.

The moment the West Indies crashed out of the World Cup Semi-Final: Last man Courtney Walsh is bowled first ball by Australia's Damien Fleming, Mohali, March 14, 1996.

2nd Semi-final • 1996
Australia v West Indies
Punjab C.A. Stadium, Mohali, Chandigarh (day/night) •
14 March 1996 (50 overs per innings)
Toss: Australia
Umpires: BC Cooray (SL) and S Venkataraghavan • TV Umpire: Khizer Hayat (PAK)
Match Referee: JR Reid (NZ)

Australia innings (50 overs maximum)			R	M	B	4	6
ME Waugh	lbw	b Ambrose	0	2	2	0	0
*MA Taylor		b Bishop	1	16	11	0	0
RT Ponting	lbw	b Ambrose	0	18	15	0	0
SR Waugh		b Bishop	3	22	18	0	0
SG Law	run out		72	152	105	5	0
MG Bevan	c Richardson	b Harper	69	146	110	4	1
+IA Healy	run out		31	36	28	2	0
PR Reiffel	run out		7	10	11	0	0
SK Warne	not out		6	10	6	0	0
Extras	(lb 11, w 5, nb 2)		18				
Total	(8 wickets, 50 overs)		207				

DNB: DW Fleming, GD McGrath

FoW: 1-0 (ME Waugh), 2-7 (Taylor), 3-8 (Ponting), 4-15 (SR Waugh), 5-153 (Law), 6-171 (Bevan), 7-186 (Reiffel), 8-207 (Healy)

B\owling	O	M	R	W	
Ambrose	10	1	26	2	(3w)
Bishop	10	1	35	2	(3nb, 1w)
Walsh	10	1	33	0	(1nb)
Gibson	2	0	13	0	(1nb)
Harper	9	0	47	1	
Adams	9	0	42	0	(1w)

West Indies innings (target: 208 runs from 50 overs)			R	M	B	4	6
S Chanderpaul	c Fleming	b McGrath	80	172	126	7	0
+CO Browne	c & b Warne		10	26	18	0	0
BC Lara		b SR Waugh	45	69	45	4	0
*RB Richardson	not out		49	123	83	4	0
RA Harper	lbw	b McGrath	2	8	5	0	0
OD Gibson	c Healy	b Warne	1	3	2	0	0
JC Adams	lbw	b Warne	2	10	11	0	0
KLT Arthurton	c Healy	b Fleming	0	5	4	0	0
IR Bishop	lbw	b Warne	3	2	3	0	0
CEL Ambrose	run out		2	4	2	0	0
CA Walsh		b Fleming	0	1	1	0	0
Extras	(lb 4, w 2, nb 2)		8				
Total	(all out, 49.3 overs)		202				

FoW: 1-25 (Browne), 2-93 (Lara), 3-165 (Chanderpaul), 4-173 (Harper), 5-178 (Gibson), 6-183 (Adams), 7-187 (Arthurton), 8-194 (Bishop), 9-202 (Ambrose), 10-202 (Walsh).

Bowling	O	M	R	W	
McGrath	10	2	30	2	(1nb)
Fleming	8.3	0	48	2	(1w)
Warne	9	0	36	4	(1w)
ME Waugh	4	0	16	0	
SR Waugh	7	0	30	1	
Reiffel	5	0	13	0	(2nb)
Bevan	4	1	12	0	
Law	2	0	13	0	

Man of the Match: SK Warne
Result: Australia won by 5 runs

The 1996 World Cup Final
Australia v Sri Lanka
Gaddafi Stadium, Lahore

Two teams in form and brimming with confidence arrived at Lahore's Gaddafi Stadium on March 17, 1996 to play the World Cup final.

Sri Lankan skipper Arjuna Ranatunga won the toss and bravely sent the Australians in to bat. His counterpart, Mark Taylor took the attack to the Sri Lankans while at the other end Mark Waugh was just starting to look good when he chipped Chaminda Vaas to Sanath Jayasuriya. This was a big wicket, with Waugh having hit three centuries in the tournament. On a track taking early turn, Ranatunga pulled off his medium-pacers and brought on his spinners. The result was that scoring became difficult and although many Australian batsmen got starts, they couldn't turn it into anything bigger.

Australia sluggishly made their way to 241-7 in 50 overs with Aravinda de Silva, Sri Lanka's main wicket taker with 3-42, including the wicket of Taylor for 74.

Fresh from their nail-biting triumph over the West Indies and with the track promising to offer assistance to Shane Warne, Australia were confident that they could defend their score. Things began well enough for Australia with Sri Lanka's explosive opening pair of Jayasuriya (9) and Kaluwitharana (6) again failing. Sri Lanka were 23-2, but that would be as close as they would come to any strife.

Asanka Gurusinha and Aravinda de Silva batted without any trouble and it simply became a matter of how many overs Sri Lanka would take to reach their target. Gurusinha eventually fell for 65 off 99 balls, with 6 fours and a six that was struck off Warne.

Ranatunga came to bat with Sri Lanka well placed at 148-3 and lent good support to de Silva who marched on towards a hundred. Sri Lanka reached their target in the 47th over, with de Silva scoring an elegant 107 that contained 13 fours. Ranatunga himself thumped 47 off 37 balls.

Sri Lanka had played in every World Cup but had only won four matches in total over the five previous tournaments. Now, they had gone undefeated through the tournament. The journey from minnow to the top of the cricket world was complete.

Umpire Steve Bucknor hangs on to a souvenir, while Australia's Shane Warne and Glenn McGrath look on in dismay, as Sri Lanka celebrate winning the World Cup, Lahore March 17, 1996.

The 1996 World Cup Final
Australia v Sri Lanka
Gaddafi Stadium, Lahore (day/night) • 17 March 1996 (50 overs per innings)
Toss: Sri Lanka
Umpires: SA Bucknor (WI) and DR Shepherd (Eng) • TV Umpire: CJ Mitchley (SA)
Match Referee: CH Lloyd (WI)

Australia innings (50 overs maximum)			R	M	B	4	6
*MA Taylor	c Jayasuriya	b de Silva	74	109	83	8	1
ME Waugh	c Jayasuriya	b Vaas	12	29	15	1	0
RT Ponting		b de Silva	45	90	73	2	0
SR Waugh	c de Silva	b Dharmasena	13	32	25	0	0
SK Warne	st Kaluwitharana	b Muralitharan	2	4	5	0	0
SG Law	c de Silva	b Jayasuriya	22	43	30	0	1
MG Bevan	not out		36	58	49	2	0
+IA Healy		b de Silva	2	2	3	0	0
PR Reiffel	not out		13	21	18	0	0
Extras	(lb 10, w 11, nb 1)		22				
Total	(7 wickets, 50 overs)		241				

DNB: DW Fleming, GD McGrath

FoW: 1-36 (ME Waugh), 2-137 (Taylor), 3-152 (Ponting), 4-156 (Warne),
        5-170 (SR Waugh), 6-202 (Law), 7-205 (Healy).

Bowling	O	M	R	W	
Wickramasinghe	7	0	38	0	(2w)
Vaas	6	1	30	1	
Muralitharan	10	0	31	1	(1w)
Dharmasena	10	0	47	1	(1nb)
Jayasuriya	8	0	43	1	(5w)
de Silva	9	0	42	3	(3w)

Sri Lanka innings (target: 242 runs from 50 overs)			R	M	B	4	6
ST Jayasuriya	run out		9	9	7	1	0
+RS Kaluwitharana	c Bevan	b Fleming	6	27	13	0	0
AP Gurusinha		b Reiffel	65	119	99	6	1
PA de Silva	not out		107	176	124	13	0
*A Ranatunga	not out		47	72	37	4	1
Extras	(b 1, lb 4, w 5, nb 1)		11				
Total	(3 wickets, 46.2 overs)		245				

DNB: HP Tillakaratne, RS Mahanama, HDPK Dharmasena, WPUJC Vaas, GP Wickramasinghe, M Muralitharan

FoW: 1-12 (Jayasuriya), 2-23 (Kaluwitharana), 3-148 (Gurusinha).

Bowling	O	M	R	W	
McGrath	8.2	1	28	0	
Fleming	6	0	43	1	(4w)
Warne	10	0	58	0	(1nb, 1w)
Reiffel	10	0	49	1	
ME Waugh	6	0	35	0	
SR Waugh	3	0	15	0	(1nb)
Bevan	3	0	12	0	

Man of the Match: PA de Silva

Result: Sri Lanka won the 1996 World Cup Final by 7 wickets

1999

WORLD CUP 1999 • ENGLAND
Official Title: The ICC World Cup
Winners: Australia
Group A: England, South Africa, India,
Sri Lanka, Zimbabwe, Kenya
Group B: Australia, West Indies, New Zealand,
Pakistan, Scotland, Bangladesh
May 14, 1999- June 20, 1999

Arguably the best World Cup of the lot, the 1999 edition was bursting at the seams with excellent matches. A number of good cricket players were elevated to star status during the competition, foremost among them Shoaib Akhtar and man of the tournament Lance Klusener. Meanwhile, established stars like Shane Warne and Sachin Tendulkar had the opportunity to remind the world why they were already great.

Hosts England aside, all of the Test playing countries fielded strong teams, including Zimbabwe – Sir Richard Hadlee even picked them as his dark horse to win the tournament. Depending on who you asked, Australia, South Africa or Pakistan were favourites to win the World Cup. All three made it to the semi-finals.

This World Cup, like the previous one, had 12 teams but

A fantastic Australian side poses with the World Cup at Lord's, London, June 20, 1999. Left to right: Adam Gilchrist, Glenn McGrath, Steve Waugh (captain), Damien Martyn, Tom Moody, Ricky Ponting, Shane Warne, Damien Fleming and a bit of Shane Lee.

the ridiculous quarter-final format was shelved and replaced with something called the Super Sixes. It meant that after playing each of their group members once, the top three teams in each group would qualify for the next round. With each win garnering two points, the twist was that only points earned over fellow group members also progressing to the Super Sixes would be carried over. The aim was to reward teams that played consistently well against decent opposition. The format came in for criticism by India who felt that the mountain of reaching the semi-final was virtually unscalable given that they had lost to fellow Super Six qualifiers South Africa and Zimbabwe in first-round matches and so did not have any points. Many had sympathy for this position until the Australians, who also failed to carry over any points to the Super Sixes, managed to win the tournament.

Sections of the English media derided the tournament as being a failure, but this was disingenuous and no doubt fuelled by their own team's embarrassing inability to climb out of the first round. The truth is that every game was a success. Along with thousands of visiting fans, multicultural Britain turned out in droves, full of colour and enthusiasm for the 1999 World Cup. Any time one of the South Asian teams was involved, ticket demands went through the roof. Even having hosted three World Cups prior to this, England had seen nothing approaching this level of frenzy.

There were a number of matches prior to the semi-finals that had fans glued to their seats. Australia had epic clashes with Pakistan (losing) and South Africa (winning), England went down to India at Edgbaston, with Indian support shockingly more plentiful (or at least louder) than their own.

In a highly anticipated match, India beat Pakistan, who also lost to Bangladesh in a match that had tongues wagging. Zimbabwe were already in on the giant killing, with wins over South Africa and India. In short, it was all gripping cricket and in the end there could be no griping about the identity of any of the semi-finalists. The final match of this grand tournament was an anticlimax, but the semi-final that got Australia to that final is perhaps the greatest game of ODI cricket ever played.

India's Rahul Dravid was in scintillating form in the 1999 World Cup, scoring 461 runs at an average of 65.85, with 2 hundreds and 3 fifties.

1st Semi-final • 1999
New Zealand v Pakistan
Old Trafford, Manchester

In an exciting tournament, this was a relatively dull semi-final where New Zealand never really bothered Pakistan. Shoaib Akhtar was recognized at this point as the fastest bowler in the world and any time he charged in to bowl, the crowd's anticipation of cartwheeling Kiwi stumps was palpable. Much to the delight of a packed Old Trafford, Shoaib the showman was able to bowl three of New Zealand's batsmen, although in the final analysis he conceded 55 runs off his 10 overs.

Stephen Fleming, Roger Twose and Chris Cairns all got into the 40s, but the batsman who had looked the best for New Zealand was opener Matt Horne, who made 35 before being bowled by a beauty from Abdul Razzaq. New Zealand set Pakistan 242 to win.

Saeed Anwar had looked in fine touch throughout the tournament, but kept getting out when well set before he could get a good score. Pakistan's media and fans were quite vocal about their concern for Anwar's form, something which seemed unnecessary. Anwar quieted the criticism by making a century in Pakistan's last match of the Super Six stage and here too set about making a big score.

His opening partner was the unknown Wajahatullah Wasti, picked for the World Cup ahead of the dashing Aamer Sohail who was rumoured to be unpopular with certain senior Pakistani players. Wasti would eventually be found to be out of his depth at the international level, but he did well in this match, playing a mix of good and streaky shots. More importantly the opener made sure that Pakistan did not lose any wickets. By the time Wasti was out for 84, Pakistan were just 48 runs away from their target, with the semi-final long over as a contest.

Geoff Allott, who had been the World Cup's best bowler, failed to make an impression on Pakistan's batsmen conceding 41 runs in his 9 overs and going wicketless. Saeed Anwar duly completed his second century of the 1999 World Cup and Pakistan went on to beat New Zealand by 9 wickets. Pakistan captain Wasim Akram's dream of emulating his mentor Imran Khan was now just one win away.

Pakistan's Shoaib Akhtar bowled with venom and guile throughout the World Cup, pictured here celebrating a wicket during the Semi-Final win over New Zealand at Old Trafford, Manchester, June 16, 1999.

1st Semi-final • 1999
New Zealand v Pakistan
Old Trafford, Manchester • 16 June 1999 (50 overs per innings)
Toss: New Zealand
Umpires: DB Hair (Aus) and P Willey • TV Umpire: DL Orchard (SA)
Match Referee: CW Smith (WI)

New Zealand innings (50 overs maximum)			R	M	B	4	6
MJ Horne		b Abdul Razzaq	35	67	48	5	0
NJ Astle		b Shoaib Akhtar	3	24	18	0	0
CD McMillan	c Moin Khan	b Wasim Akram	3	22	19	0	0
*SP Fleming		b Shoaib Akhtar	41	93	57	5	0
RG Twose	c Ijaz Ahmed	b Abdul Razzaq	46	101	83	3	0
CL Cairns	not out		44	77	48	3	0
CZ Harris		b Shoaib Akhtar	16	26	21	0	0
+AC Parore		b Wasim Akram	0	5	4	0	0
DJ Nash	not out		6	17	10	1	0
Extras	(b 4, lb 14, w 17, nb 12)		47				
Total	(7 wickets, 50 overs)		241				

DNB: GR Larsen, GI Allott

FoW: 1-20 (Astle, 5.3 ov), 2-38 (McMillan, 10.3 ov), 3-58 (Horne, 15.1 ov), 4-152 (Fleming, 33.5 ov),
5-176 (Twose, 39.3 ov), 6-209 (Harris, 45.4 ov), 7-211 (Parore, 46.4 ov).

Bowling	O	M	R	W	
Wasim Akram	10	0	45	2	(4nb, 7w)
Shoaib Akhtar	10	0	55	3	(2nb, 1w)
Abdul Razzaq	8	0	28	2	(1w)
Saqlain Mushtaq	8	0	36	0	(1w)
Azhar Mahmood	9	0	32	0	(3w)
Shahid Afridi	5	0	27	0	(2nb, 2w)

Pakistan innings (target: 242 runs from 50 overs)			R	M	B	4	6
Saeed Anwar	not out		113	193	148	9	0
Wajahatullah Wasti	c Fleming	b Cairns	84	166	123	10	1
Ijaz Ahmed	not out		28	25	21	4	1
Extras	(lb 3, w 7, nb 7)		17				
Total	(1 wicket, 47.3 overs)		242				

DNB: Inzamam-ul-Haq, Abdul Razzaq, Shahid Afridi, +Moin Khan, *Wasim Akram, Azhar Mahmood, Saqlain
Mushtaq, Shoaib Akhtar

FoW: 1-194 (Wajahatullah, 40.3 ov).

Bowling	O	M	R	W	
Allott	9	0	41	0	(1nb, 1w)
Nash	5	0	34	0	(2nb, 2w)
Larsen	10	0	40	0	(1nb)
Cairns	8	0	33	1	(3nb)
Harris	6	0	31	0	
Astle	7.3	0	41	0	(1w)
McMillan	2	0	19	0	(1w)

Man of the Match: Shoaib Akhtar

Result: Pakistan won by 9 wickets

2nd Semi-final • 1999
Australia v South Africa
Edgbaston, Birmingham

This is the match that many regard as the greatest ODI in the history of cricket. It was an incredible contest, with the pendulum swinging back and forth between the two sides right until the final ball of the match.

South African captain Hansie Cronje won the toss and put Australia in to bat. Success was immediate when Shaun Pollock dismissed Mark Waugh for a duck in the first over. Ricky Ponting and opener Adam Gilchrist got the score past 50 before Allan Donald removed Ponting and then Darren Lehmann in quick succession. Three overs later, Donald caught Gilchrist off Kallis. Australia had slumped to 68-4 in the 17th over and out came Steve Waugh.

When these two teams had clashed in the Super Sixes, Australia won after having their backs to the wall. They had looked dead and buried when Steve Waugh clawed Australia out of trouble and got them home. Now he had to do it all over again. Waugh was up to the task, taking on all of South Africa's bowlers and being well supported by Michael Bevan. The pair had added 90 runs to the total and Australia looked like they were pulling away from South Africa, but Pollock came back to dismiss the dangerous Steve Waugh (56 off 76 balls, 6 fours and 1 six) and then had Tom Moody LBW for a duck in the same over to leave Australia at 158-6.

Shane Warne and Bevan kept the scoreboard ticking with ones and twos in a good partnership of 49 runs, but

The pendulum swings once more: Shaun Pollock dismisses Australian captain Steve Waugh during the unforgettable Semi-Final clash between South Africa and Australia, at Edgbaston, Birmingham June 17, 1999.

from 207-6, Australia slipped to 207-9 with Donald and Pollock bringing the house down while bowling in tandem. Australia were eventually bowled out for a disappointing 213, with Michael Bevan's 65 being the top score. South Africa's star duo of Allan Donald (4-32) and Shaun Pollock (5-36) bowled beautifully against a powerful batting line-up and the team went in to bat full of confidence.

South Africa's openers Gary Kirsten and Herschelle Gibbs got South Africa off to a sound start. Gibbs in particular looked good in the early going, hitting both Damien Fleming and Glenn McGrath for four, and keeping South Africa ahead of the required run rate. Steve Waugh brought on Paul Reiffel, but Gibbs hit him for boundaries in his first two overs as well. Knowing the match could slip away here, Waugh in the 11th over introduced another bowling change in Shane Warne.

Warne's first over went for three runs, but in his next over he bowled what was possibly the best ball of the tournament. With Gibbs facing, Warne pitched a ball that looked in the air to be going away. It landed outside of leg stump and then spun in sharply to hit the stumps. Gibbs was stunned but had to walk off, out for a well-made 30 with 6 fours. South Africa were 48-1.

Shane Warne's next over swung the game Australia's way. The first ball accounted for Gary Kirsten, bowled while attempting to sweep a ball that spun appreciably into him and then two balls later, the South African captain Hansie Cronje fell, adjudged having edged the ball to Mark Waugh. South Africa were 53-3, which turned into 65-4 with Darryl Cullinan run out for 6 having dawdled around for 30 balls. South Africa looked dead, but Jacques Kallis and Jonty Rhodes gradually put them on the road to recovery.

Loose deliveries were hit for four, but otherwise the pair batted sensibly. There was no flash other than Rhodes hitting Mark Waugh for a six in the 40th over in an attempt to finally accelerate, and then another lofted drive off Reiffel in the next over which brought about his downfall for 43 off 55 balls.

Kallis and Pollock put on 30 for the 6th wicket and looked to be taking South Africa home. The threat of Shane Warne was coming to an end. He came on to bowl his last over and after Kallis took three from his first ball, Pollock smashed him for a six and a four. Kallis came back on strike after a single and Warne had the last laugh dismissing the burly all-rounder for 53, caught by Mark Waugh. In spite of the last-over mauling, Shane Warne's final analysis was a remarkable 10-4-29-4 and he had left South Africa in a spot of bother again at 175-6, after 45 overs, with a required run rate that had gone over 7 runs per over.

Pollock (20 off 14) was bowled by Fleming and then Boucher (5) by McGrath, but as long as Lance Klusener was at the crease, the South Africans held on to hope. Klusener had been a star for South Africa all tournament, coolly taking them to victory in key matches. Here too, he appeared unperturbed.

The penultimate over was a heart-stopper. Boucher was out to McGrath's second ball and Steve Elworthy was run out on the fourth to leave South Africa on the brink at 198-9. Klusener hit the fifth ball of the over with immense power. A flat hit over long leg, it went straight to the hands of Reiffel, but he couldn't hang on to it and only succeeded in pushing it over the boundary for six. If the fielder hadn't been there at all, the ball would not have carried for six. On the last ball of the over, Klusener took a single to retain strike.

Nine runs were now needed off the last over. Looking as cool as can be, Klusener smashed the first two balls of the over through the off-side for boundaries, with the Australians having no chance to cut off the shots. The scores were tied and with only 1 run needed, panic inexplicably set in with both Klusener and last man Allan Donald losing their heads. Donald was run out off the fourth ball of the over, setting off late for a run that Klusener had misjudged in the first place. The match ended in a dramatic tie, with Australia progressing to the final, based on a superior position in the Super Sixes.

2nd Semi-final • 1999
Australia v South Africa
Edgbaston, Birmingham • 17 June 1999 (50 overs per innings)
Toss: South Africa
Umpires: DR Shepherd and S Venkataraghavan (Ind) • TV Umpire: SA Bucknor (WI)
Match Referee: R Subba Row

Australia innings (50 overs maximum)			R	M	B	4	6
+AC Gilchrist	c Donald	b Kallis	20	70	39	1	1
ME Waugh	c Boucher	b Pollock	0	3	4	0	0
RT Ponting	c Kirsten	b Donald	37	49	48	3	1
DS Lehmann	c Boucher	b Donald	1	4	4	0	0
*SR Waugh	c Boucher	b Pollock	56	108	76	6	1
MG Bevan	c Boucher	b Pollock	65	151	101	6	0
TM Moody	lbw	b Pollock	0	2	3	0	0
SK Warne	c Cronje	b Pollock	18	36	24	1	0
PR Reiffel		b Donald	0	2	1	0	0
DW Fleming		b Donald	0	2	2	0	0
GD McGrath	not out		0	4	1	0	0
Extras	(b 1, lb 6, w 3, nb 6)		16				
Total	(all out, 49.2 overs)		213				

FoW: 1-3 (ME Waugh, 0.5 ov), 2-54 (Ponting, 13.1 ov), 3-58 (Lehmann, 13.6 ov), 4-68 (Gilchrist, 16.6 ov), 5-158 (SR Waugh, 39.3 ov), 6-158 (Moody, 39.6 ov), 7-207 (Warne, 47.6 ov), 8-207 (Reiffel, 48.1 ov), 9-207 (Fleming, 48.3 ov), 10-213 (Bevan, 49.2 ov).

Bowling	O	M	R	W	
Pollock	9.2	1	36	5	
Elworthy	10	0	59	0	(2nb, 1w)
Kallis	10	2	27	1	(1nb, 1w)
Donald	10	1	32	4	(1w)
Klusener	9	1	50	0	(3nb)
Cronje	1	0	2	0	

South Africa innings (target: 214 runs from 50 overs)			R	M	B	4	6
G Kirsten		b Warne	18	59	42	1	0
HH Gibbs		b Warne	30	51	36	6	0
DJ Cullinan	run out (Bevan)		6	39	30	0	0
*WJ Cronje	c ME Waugh	b Warne	0	2	2	0	0
JH Kallis	c SR Waugh	b Warne	53	119	92	3	0
JN Rhodes	c Bevan	b Reiffel	43	70	55	2	1
SM Pollock		b Fleming	20	27	14	1	1
L Klusener	not out		31	32	16	4	1
+MV Boucher		b McGrath	5	13	10	0	0
S Elworthy	run out (Reiffel/McGrath)		1	3	1	0	0
AA Donald	run out (ME Waugh/Fleming/Gilchrist)		0	7	0	0	0
Extras	(lb 1, w 5)		6				
Total	(all out, 49.4 overs)		213				

FoW: 1-48 (Gibbs, 12.2 ov), 2-53 (Kirsten, 14.1 ov), 3-53 (Cronje, 14.3 ov), 4-61 (Cullinan, 21.2 ov), 5-145 (Rhodes, 40.3 ov), 6-175 (Kallis, 44.5 ov), 7-183 (Pollock, 45.5 ov), 8-196 (Boucher, 48.2 ov), 9-198 (Elworthy, 48.4 ov), 10-213 (Donald, 49.4 ov).

Bowling	O	M	R	W	
McGrath	10	0	51	1	(1w)
Fleming	8.4	1	40	1	(3w)
Reiffel	8	0	28	1	
Warne	10	4	29	4	(1w)
ME Waugh	8	0	37	0	
Moody	5	0	27	0	

Man of the Match: SK Warne

Result: Match tied. Australia advance to the final.

The 1999 World Cup Final
Australia v Pakistan
Lord's, London

What should have been an epic ended in a farce, with Pakistan putting in a surprisingly feeble effort with the bat.

Wasim Akram won the toss and decided to bat. Wajahatullah Wasti was preferred to Shahid Afridi as opener and made 1 run off 14 balls before edging Glenn McGrath to the slips. Saeed Anwar then decided that he wanted to change the grip on his bat. After a delay of several minutes, with the grip having been fiddled with, Anwar resumed his innings and was bowled by Damien Fleming. Anwar had played several breezy innings in the tournament before throwing it all away, and this was a typical effort. The left-hander was gone for 15 off 17 balls, leaving Pakistan at 21-2.

A scratchy 22 from Ijaz Ahmed is all that Pakistan could muster by way of a top score. Wickets kept falling after every few runs, with all the Australian bowlers picking up a scalp or two. Shane Warne, fresh from his semi-final heroics, did the most damage with figures of 9-1-33-4. Pakistan crashed out for an appallingly low 132 in 39 overs.

Shoaib Akhtar came out breathing fire, hoping to blast out the Australians, but they were in peak form in this match. Once Gilchrist had the measure of Shoaib's speed, he cut loose on the bowler, hitting him for a six and a four off consecutive deliveries in the 6th over of the innings. Shoaib had gone for 23 runs in 3 overs and any thoughts of a Pakistani fightback were put on ice. Australia raced to the victory target in the 21st over, for the loss of only 2 wickets.

It was a comprehensive victory and turnaround for Steve Waugh's team which had struggled to even qualify for the Super Sixes. After losses to New Zealand and Pakistan in the first round, there had been no margin for error. A single defeat would have meant elimination and it is a testament to their mental toughness that the Australians did not falter in spite of being tested all the way to the final. At the end of the day there was no doubt that the best cricket team in the world had walked away with the 1999 World Cup.

Shane Warne during the World Cup Final against Pakistan, at Lord's, London, June 20, 1999. Warne was a key figure in Australia's successful World Cup campaign, with Man of the Match winning performances in both the Semi-Final (4-29 in 10 overs) and Final (4-33 in 9 overs).

The 1999 World Cup Final
Australia v Pakistan

Lord's, London • 20 June 1999 (50 overs per innings)
Toss: Pakistan
Umpires: SA Bucknor (WI) and DR Shepherd • TV Umpire: S Venkataraghavan (Ind)
Match Referee: RS Madugalle (SL)

Pakistan innings (50 overs maximum)			R	M	B	4	6
Saeed Anwar		b Fleming	15	26	17	3	0
Wajahatullah Wasti	c ME Waugh	b McGrath	1	20	14	0	0
Abdul Razzaq	c SR Waugh	b Moody	17	67	51	2	0
Ijaz Ahmed		b Warne	22	79	46	2	0
Inzamam-ul-Haq	c Gilchrist	b Reiffel	15	47	33	0	0
+Moin Khan	c Gilchrist	b Warne	6	16	12	0	0
Shahid Afridi	lbw	b Warne	13	22	16	2	0
Azhar Mahmood	c & b Moody		8	32	17	1	0
*Wasim Akram	c SR Waugh	b Warne	8	23	20	0	1
Saqlain Mushtaq	c Ponting	b McGrath	0	10	4	0	0
Shoaib Akhtar	not out		2	8	6	0	0
Extras	(lb 10, w 13, nb 2)		25				
Total	(all out, 39 overs)		132				

FoW: 1-21 (Wajahatullah, 4.4 ov), 2-21 (Saeed Anwar, 5.1 ov), 3-68 (Abdul Razzaq, 19.4 ov), 4-77 (Ijaz Ahmed, 23.4 ov), 5-91 (Moin Khan, 27.1 ov), 6-104 (Inzamam-ul-Haq, 30.1 ov), 7-113 (Shahid Afridi, 31.6 ov), 8-129 (Azhar Mahmood, 36.6 ov), 9-129 (Wasim Akram, 37.2 ov), 10-132 (Saqlain Mushtaq, 38.6 ov).

Bowling	O	M	R	W	
McGrath	9	3	13	2	
Fleming	6	0	30	1	(2nb, 4w)
Reiffel	10	1	29	1	(2w)
Moody	5	0	17	2	(1w)
Warne	9	1	33	4	(2w)

Australia innings (target: 133 runs from 50 overs)			R	M	B	4	6
ME Waugh	not out		37	95	52	4	0
+AC Gilchrist	c Inzamam-ul-Haq	b Saqlain Mushtaq	54	49	36	8	1
RT Ponting	c Moin Khan	b Wasim Akram	24	32	27	3	0
DS Lehmann	not out		13	12	9	2	0
Extras	(lb 1, w 1, nb 3)		5				
Total	(2 wickets, 20.1 overs)		133				

DNB: *SR Waugh, MG Bevan, TM Moody, SK Warne, PR Reiffel, DW Fleming, GD McGrath.

FoW: 1-75 (Gilchrist, 10.1 ov), 2-112 (Ponting, 17.4 ov).

Bowling	O	M	R	W	
Wasim Akram	8	1	41	1	(2nb, 1w)
Shoaib Akhtar	4	0	37	0	(1nb)
Abdul Razzaq	2	0	13	0	
Azhar Mahmood	2	0	20	0	
Saqlain Mushtaq	4.1	0	21	1	

Man of the Match: SK Warne

Result: Australia won the 1999 World Cup Final by 8 wickets

Australian captain Ricky Ponting poses with the World Cup, after his team's victory over India in the Final at the New Wanderers Stadium, Johannesburg, March 23, 2003.

2003

WORLD CUP 2003 • SOUTH AFRICA
Official Title: The ICC World Cup
Winners: Australia
Pool A: England, Australia, India, Pakistan,
Zimbabwe, Netherlands, Namibia
Pool B: South Africa, West Indies, New Zealand,
Sri Lanka, Bangladesh, Kenya, Canada
February 9, 2003- March 23, 2003

After the 1996 World Cup, the 2003 World Cup ranks as the second worst edition of the tournament. The number of countries participating swelled from 12 to 14, which prolonged the tournament and eroded interest. Granted, Canada with the heroic John Davison were fun to watch, but the rest of the minnows were largely uninteresting. Respect however, must be accorded to a likeable Kenyan side that made it to the semi-finals, on the back of the requisite giant killing that takes place in virtually every World Cup; Sri Lanka being the victims on this occasion. New Zealand refused to play their match in Kenya citing security concerns, and with Zimbabwe's morale as low as could be, Kenya had gathered enough points to go to the semi-finals, only to get a hiding from India.

A World Cup in which Kenya goes to the semi-finals and South Africa, the West Indies and Pakistan do not even make it to the Super Sixes is a World Cup that quite possibly has serious flaws. Nevertheless, the big teams got what they deserved. South Africa miscalculated on the Duckworth-Lewis equation. West Indies beat South Africa but lost to the other Test teams in the group, even getting manhandled by Canada for good measure. Pakistan selected big-name players who were past their prime and when they were not losing, they were fighting with each other. England were England, self-important, but not much else. The only saving grace for World Cup 2003 was that the two best teams in the tournament, Australia and India, did meet in the final. However, the gulf in class between them was all too apparent.

Australia entered the tournament as favourites to retain their title as World Champions and left undefeated. The only blight on an otherwise great tournament for Australia was that leg-spinner Shane Warne, who had played an integral role in Australia's previous World Cup success, had to leave the team after failing an internal doping test. Anyone who thought that Warne's loss would weaken Australia or impact their focus was dead wrong. Australia brushed off the loss and then steamrolled their opponents.

Pakistani and Indian players look on as their captains exchange pleasantries before their riveting World Cup match at Centurion on March 1, 2003 – the first ODI between the two teams in three years. Pakistan captain Waqar Younis would dismiss his counterpart Sourav Ganguly for a first ball duck later in the day, but it would be the Indian captain who had the last laugh with his team triumphing by 6 wickets.

1st Semi-final • 2003
Australia v Sri Lanka
St George's Park, Port Elizabeth

This match may have given Australia an initial scare. Chaminda Vaas, Aravinda de Silva and Muttiah Muralitharan all bowled with exceptional economy to put the clamps on Australia's scoring rate. Adam Gilchrist swished 22 off 20 balls, but everyone else in the early goings found runs hard to come by. Andrew Symonds held the innings together, making sure a collapse didn't happen. His 91 off 118 balls was a fantastic knock on a sluggish surface. Andy Bichel came in at the end and smashed a six to help Australia get past the 200-run mark.

Vaas took 3-34 in his 10 overs, while de Silva took 2-36 in his quota. Muralitharan was wicketless but conceded only 29 runs in his 10 overs.

Set 213 to win, Sri Lanka fancied their chances on a pitch where they felt that they would not have to worry about pace and bounce. However, things went south very quickly. After putting on 21 for the 1st wicket, Atapattu got a scorcher from Brett Lee measured at 99 miles per hour and was bowled. Jayasuriya, who had used the pace to his advantage to get his runs, erred in his shot selection, pulling Glenn McGrath to Symonds, to leave Sri Lanka 37-2. Wickets kept falling to the pace of Lee, and Bichel bowled a claustrophobic spell that had the Sri Lankans panicking.

At 51-5, the match already looked as good as over, but then Brad Hogg got involved too, with 2 quick wickets to put the result beyond any doubt. Once Sri Lanka were 76-7 there was no coming back even with the intervention of Duckworth-Lewis. Australia won by 48 runs, with Andy Bichel bowling a scarcely believable 10-4-18-0. On a pitch where batting was a nightmare, Symonds walked away with the man of the match award.

1st Semi-final • 2003
Australia v Sri Lanka
St George's Park, Port Elizabeth • 18 March 2003 (50 overs per innings)
Toss: Australia
Umpires: RE Koertzen and DR Shepherd (Eng) • TV Umpire: BF Bowden (NZ)
Match Referee: CH Lloyd (WI)

Australia innings (50 overs maximum)			R	M	B	4	6
+AC Gilchrist	c Sangakkara	b de Silva	22	25	20	2	1
ML Hayden	c Tillakaratne	b Vaas	20	53	38	2	0
*RT Ponting	c Jayasuriya	b Vaas	2	6	8	0	0
DS Lehmann		b Jayasuriya	36	101	66	2	0
A Symonds	not out		91	145	118	7	1
MG Bevan	c Sangakkara	b Jayasuriya	0	8	1	0	0
GB Hogg	st Sangakkara	b de Silva	8	19	19	0	0
IJ Harvey	c Sangakkara	b Vaas	7	13	10	0	0
AJ Bichel	not out		19	21	21	0	1
Extras	(lb 3, w 3, nb 1)		7				
Total	(7 wickets, 50 overs, 199 mins)		212				

DNB: B Lee, GD McGrath

FoW: 1-34 (Gilchrist, 5.2 ov), 2-37 (Ponting, 6.5 ov), 3-51 (Hayden, 12.2 ov), 4-144 (Lehmann, 34.6 ov), 5-144 (Bevan, 36.1 ov), 6-158 (Hogg, 40.3 ov), 7-175 (Harvey, 43.5 ov).

Bowling	O	M	R	W	
Vaas	10	1	34	3	(1nb, 1w)
Gunaratne	8	0	60	0	(1w)
de Silva	10	0	36	2	(1w)
Muralitharan	10	0	29	0	
Jayasuriya	10	0	42	2	
Arnold	2	0	8	0	

Sri Lanka innings (target: 172 runs from 38.1 overs)			R	M	B	4	6
MS Atapattu	b Lee	14	18	17	3	0	
*ST Jayasuriya	c Symonds	b McGrath	17	40	24	0	1
HP Tillakaratne	c Gilchrist	b Lee	3	27	15	0	0
DA Gunawardene	c Ponting	b Lee	1	14	4	0	0
PA de Silva	run out (Bichel)		11	20	16	2	0
+KC Sangakkara	not out		39	111	70	3	0
DPMD Jayawardene	c Gilchrist	b Hogg	5	14	8	1	0
RP Arnold	c Lee	b Hogg	3	29	27	0	0
WPUJC Vaas	not out		21	56	50	1	1
Extras	(b 4, lb 1, w 2, nb 2)		9				
Total	(7 wickets, 38.1 overs, 167 mins)		123				

DNB: M Muralitharan, PW Gunaratne

FoW: 1-21 (Atapattu, 3.6 ov), 2-37 (Jayasuriya, 8.5 ov), 3-37 (Tillakaratne, 9.3 ov), 4-43 (Gunawardene, 11.2 ov), 5-51 (de Silva, 13.1 ov), 6-60 (Jayawardene, 16.1 ov), 7-76 (Arnold, 24.2 ov).

Bowling	O	M	R	W	
McGrath	7	1	20	1	
Lee	8	0	35	3	(2nb, 2w)
Bichel	10	4	18	0	
Hogg	10	1	30	2	
Harvey	2.1	0	11	0	
Lehmann	1	0	4	0	

Man of the Match: A Symonds

Result: Australia won by 48 runs (D/L Method)

2nd Semi-final • 2003
India v Kenya
Kingsmead, Durban

Hard work and a nice bit of luck had got the Kenyans to the semi-final, but they were never expected to trouble a strong India that had only tripped up against Australia in the first round.

India batted first, and Sachin Tendulkar and Sourav Ganguly literally had a blast, putting on 103 for the 2nd wicket before Tendulkar was out for 83 at the end of the 38th over. Ganguly powered on to a splendid 111 off 114 balls with 5 fours and 5 sixes. India finished on 270-4 in their 50 overs.

As expected, a fired-up Indian seam attack proved to be too much for Kenya. Steve Tikolo (56) with the help of 2 sixes, did well to take a half-century off India, but it was never going to be enough. Kenya were bowled out in the 47th over and lost by 91 runs.

World Cup Semi-Final, Durban, March 20, 2003: Indian captain Sourav Ganguly smashes one of five sixes during his match-winning knock of 111 against Kenya.

2nd Semi-final • 2003
India v Kenya
Kingsmead, Durban (day/night) • 20 March 2003 (50 overs per innings)
Toss: India
Umpires: SA Bucknor (WI) and DJ Harper (Aus) • TV Umpire: SJA Taufel (Aus)
Match Referee: MJ Procter

India innings (50 overs maximum)			R	M	B	4	6
V Sehwag	c Odumbe	b Ongondo	33	81	56	3	0
SR Tendulkar	c DO Obuya	b Tikolo	83	166	101	5	1
*SC Ganguly	not out		111	140	114	5	5
M Kaif run out (CO Obuya)			15	35	20	0	0
Yuvraj Singh	c DO Obuya	b Odoyo	16	15	10	1	1
+R Dravid	not out		1	3	1	0	0
Extras	(w 9, nb 2)		11				
Total	(4 wickets, 50 overs, 222 mins)		270				

DNB: D Mongia, J Srinath, A Nehra, Z Khan, Harbhajan Singh

FoW: 1-74 (Sehwag, 18.3 ov), 2-177 (Tendulkar, 37.5 ov), 3-233 (Kaif, 45.5 ov), 4-267 (Yuvraj Singh, 49.3 ov).

Bowling	O	M	R	W	
Suji	10	1	62	0	
Odoyo	10	1	45	1	(2nb, 1w)
Ongondo	10	1	38	1	
Karim	4	0	25	0	(1w)
Tikolo	10	0	60	1	(2w)
CO Obuya	6	0	40	0	(1w)

Kenya innings (target: 271 runs from 50 overs)			R	M	B	4	6
+KO Otieno	c Dravid	b Srinath	15	66	43	1	0
RD Shah	lbw	b Khan	1	39	17	0	0
PJ Ongondo	c Khan	b Nehra	0	11	5	0	0
TM Odoyo	c Sehwag	b Nehra	7	22	15	0	0
*SO Tikolo		b Tendulkar	56	109	83	5	2
MO Odumbe	c Khan	b Yuvraj Singh	19	13	16	1	1
HS Modi	c Dravid	b Khan	9	26	25	0	0
DO Obuya	run out (Kaif/Harbhajan Singh)		3	26	23	0	0
CO Obuya	lbw	b Tendulkar	29	44	42	1	1
MA Suji		b Khan	1	13	8	0	0
AY Karim	not out		0	2	1	0	0
Extras	(b 16, lb 8, w 15)		39				
Total	(all out, 46.2 overs, 190 mins)		179				

FoW: 1-20 (Shah, 8.2 ov), 2-21 (Ongondo, 10.1 ov), 3-30 (Otieno, 13.1 ov), 4-36 (Odoyo, 14.3 ov), 5-63 (Odumbe, 18.4 ov), 6-92 (Modi, 26.4 ov), 7-104 (DO Obuya, 33.1 ov), 8-161 (Tikolo, 43.4 ov), 9-179 (CO Obuya, 45.4 ov), 10-179 (Suji, 46.2 ov).

Bowling	O	M	R	W	
Khan	9.2	2	14	3	(3w)
Srinath	7	1	1	1	(1w)
Nehra	5	1	1	2	(2w)
Harbhajan Singh	10	1	32	0	
Yuvraj Singh	6	0	43	1	
Sehwag	3	1	16	0	(1w)
Tendulkar	6	0	28	2	(3w)

Man of the Match: SC Ganguly

Result: India won by 91 runs

The 2003 World Cup Final
Australia v India
New Wanderers Stadium, Johannesburg

This match turned out to be as big a rout as the previous final. The Australians batted first in this one and put on a breathtaking display.

Matthew Hayden and Adam Gilchrist opened the batting and Zaheer Khan, the bowling for India. Zaheer appeared nervous, erring in his line and length and gave away 15 runs in his first over. Sensing fear, Gilchrist and Hayden went after the bowling. Eventually the two openers would fall, Gilchrist for 57 (48 balls) and Hayden for a relatively sedate 38 (54 balls), but any thoughts India had that the going would now get easier proved to unfounded.

In an innings that left behind the World Cup final feats of Collis King, Clive Lloyd and Viv Richards, Australian captain Ricky Ponting put on a phenomenal show. A sizzling unbroken stand of 234 for the 3rd wicket between Ponting and Damien Martyn simply put the match beyond the reach of the Indians. Ponting's hitting was so magnificent that many of his sixes were still rising as they crashed into the stands. It was batting that showed nothing but disdain for the bowling. Martyn batted with what turned out to be a broken finger, playing second fiddle to his captain and yet still scoring 88 off 84 balls himself.

Australia's score of 359-2 was the highest made by any team in a World Cup final. Ponting's sublime 140 not out came off only 121 balls and was studded with 4 fours and 8 towering sixes. Javagal Srinath proved to be the most expensive bowler, going for a whopping 87 runs in his 10 overs.

As is his wont, Glenn McGrath picked up the prized wicket of India's best player Sachin Tendulkar cheaply and in the first over of the Indian innings. If there was any glimmer of hope that India might be able to take the attack to the Australians, it was cruelly snuffed out before the first over was even done. Virender Sehwag was run out for 82 off 81, but it was never going to matter. Australia romped home by 125 runs, successfully defending their title.

Australia's Ricky Ponting and Damien Martyn discuss their destruction of India in the World Cup Final, Johannesburg, March 23, 2003. Ponting (140*) and Martyn (88*) put on a colossal, unbroken stand of 234 for the 3rd wicket, with Australia ultimately beating India by a mammoth 125 runs to win the World Cup for the third time.

It was a remarkable tournament for Australia. Undefeated through a gruelling schedule, Ricky Ponting's men never lost their edge even though many matches appeared pointless. The difference that had existed between Australia and the rest in the 1999 World Cup had grown to look an unbridgeable chasm at the conclusion of the 2003 World Cup.

The 2003 World Cup Final
Australia v India

New Wanderers Stadium, Johannesburg • 23 March 2003 (50 overs per innings)
Toss: India
Umpires: SA Bucknor (WI) and DR Shepherd (Eng) • TV Umpire: RE Koertzen
Match Referee: RS Madugalle (SL)

Australia innings (50 overs maximum)			R	M	B	4	6
+AC Gilchrist	c Sehwag	b Harbhajan Singh	57	66	48	8	1
ML Hayden	c Dravid	b Harbhajan Singh	37	93	54	5	0
*RT Ponting	not out		140	138	121	4	8
DR Martyn	not out		88	112	84	7	1
Extras	(b 2, lb 12, w 16, nb 7)		37				
Total	(2 wickets, 50 overs, 205 mins)		359				

DNB: DS Lehmann, MG Bevan, A Symonds, GB Hogg, AJ Bichel, B Lee, GD McGrath.

FoW: 1-105 (Gilchrist, 13.6 ov), 2-125 (Hayden, 19.5 ov).

Bowling	O	M	R	W	
Khan	7	0	67	0	(2nb, 6w)
Srinath	10	0	87	0	(3nb, 2w)
Nehra	10	0	57	0	(3w)
Harbhajan Singh	8	0	49	2	
Sehwag	3	0	14	0	
Tendulkar	3	0	20	0	(1w)
Mongia	7	0	39	0	(2nb)
Yuvraj Singh	2	0	12	0	

India innings (target: 360 runs from 50 overs)			R	M	B	4	6
SR Tendulkar	c & b McGrath		4	2	5	1	0
V Sehwag	run out (Lehmann)		82	107	81	10	3
*SC Ganguly	c Lehmann	b Lee	24	44	25	3	1
M Kaif	c Gilchrist	b McGrath	0	4	3	0	0
+R Dravid		b Bichel	47	87	57	2	0
Yuvraj Singh	c Lee	b Hogg	24	48	34	1	0
D Mongia	c Martyn	b Symonds	12	18	11	2	0
Harbhajan Singh	c McGrath	b Symonds	7	12	8	0	0
Z Khan	c Lehmann	b McGrath	4	20	8	0	0
J Srinath		b Lee	1	6	4	0	0
A Nehra	not out		8	7	4	2	0
Extras	(b 4, lb 4, w 9, nb 4)		21				
Total	(all out, 39.2 overs, 180 mins)		234				

FoW: 1-4 (Tendulkar, 0.5 ov), 2-58 (Ganguly, 9.5 ov), 3-59 (Kaif, 10.3 ov), 4-147 (Sehwag, 23.5 ov), 5-187 (Dravid, 31.5 ov), 6-208 (Yuvraj Singh, 34.5 ov), 7-209 (Mongia, 35.2 ov), 8-223 (Harbhajan Singh, 37.1 ov), 9-226 (Srinath, 38.2 ov), 10-234 (Khan, 39.2 ov).

Bowling	O	M	R	W	
McGrath	8.2	0	52	3	
Lee	7	1	31	2	(4nb, 2w)
Hogg	10	0	61	1	(2w)
Lehmann	2	0	18	0	
Bichel	10	0	57	1	(4w)
Symonds	2	0	7	2	(1w)

Man of the Match: RT Ponting

Result: Australia won the 2003 World Cup Final by 125 runs

The ball from Shoaib Akhtar that finally dismissed Sachin Tendulkar: India versus Pakistan, March 1, 2003, Centurion, South Africa. (See page 106.)

Allan Donald helps remove Sultan Zarawani's headgear, Rawalpindi, February 16, 1996.

The 25 Most Intriguing Moments in World Cup History,

1975 – 2003

25

Sultan Zarawani gets hit by Allan Donald • 1996

It's almost tragic when enthusiastic amateur cricket players who have strived so hard just to qualify for the World Cup finally get their chance on the big stage and then embarrass themselves in front of millions of people. However, in the case of Sultan Zarawani, the consensus is that any mirth is wholly justified. The UAE captain, reportedly a Lamborghini-driving multi-millionaire who picked up cricket while at university in Pakistan, only played seven ODIs for his country but did enough in his brief career to be remembered forever.

On February 16, 1996 in Rawalpindi, the UAE played their first match of the World Cup against a strong South African side who were legitimate contenders for the cup. Batting first, South Africa rattled up a mammoth score of 321 for the loss of only 2 wickets, with Gary Kirsten smashing a World Cup record score of 188 not out.

The UAE were never in the match, and by the time their captain came in to bat the score was 68-6. With South Africa on the rampage, and one of the world's best bowlers – the exceptionally quick Allan Donald – with the ball in his hand, most other inexperienced lower-order batsmen would have walked out to the crease with some trepidation. If Zarawani felt anything of the sort, it was obscured by the fact that he wore a sunhat instead of a helmet. Whether it was naiveté or bravado, the South Africans found Zarawani's sunhat antics to be provocative. Not pulling any punches, Donald unleashed a bouncer that Zarawani was not technically equipped to deal with. It struck the UAE captain flush on the head, knocking off the offensive headgear. Zarawani staggered around for a moment, then – to the surprise of everyone – calmly resumed his innings. Mystifyingly, the blow to the head failed to drum the sense into him to call for a helmet. Thankfully the captain avoided further injury, only lasting another six balls before being dismissed without scoring off the bowling of Brian McMillan. The UAE eventually crashed to a 169-run defeat.

24

Feiko Kloppenburg's all-round exploits • 2003

Although the minnows have on occasion upset the established teams in World Cup clashes, more often they are found to be woefully out of their depth during the course of the tournament. It is then that minnow against minnow takes on such crucial importance, for it is the one realistic chance of getting a win. The bowlers look forward to getting a crack at batsmen who may have some faults in technique and the batsmen look to make merry at the expense of bowlers who may lack the pace and/or variation of bowlers who play for Test teams. If anyone has ever made the most of a minnow versus minnow match, it's the Netherlands' Feiko Kloppenburg when his team took on Namibia at Bloemfontein.

In what was the last match of the 2003 World Cup for both teams, the Netherlands won the toss and elected to bat. Kloppenburg opened the batting with Edgar Schiferli, who fell in the 6th over after making 10 runs. This brought in Klaas-Jan van Noortwijk, and with Kloppenburg he put on 228 runs for the 2nd wicket. The pair batted through their partnership at virtually a run a ball.

Kloppenburg became the first Dutch player to score a century in ODI cricket (with van Noortwijk becoming the second, a few balls later). He was out in the 44th over, having scored 121 off 142 balls with 6 fours and 4 sixes.

However, a mammoth partnership and historic century were simply not enough. When he took the ball in his hand to bowl his medium-pacers, Kloppenburg made the first breakthrough of the Namibian innings, dismissing a well-set J.B. Burger (41 off 42 balls). The all-rounder went on to record the best bowling figures in the match, sending down a full quota of ten overs and taking 4-42. The Netherlands won the match by 64 runs, capping off an incomparable day's cricket for the Dutchman.

23

Allan Lamb steals victory from the West Indies • 1987

With Pakistan, England and the West Indies all there, Pool B contained three of the four accepted contenders for the 1987 World Cup (India being the fourth, comfortably nestled in Pool A). Of course, only two teams could progress to the semi-final stage from each pool, and it meant that a pitched battle was on the cards any time any of Pakistan, England and West Indies crossed paths. It was almost disappointing, then, to see England on the ropes, in pursuit of 244 set by the West Indies at Gujranwala in what was the first match for both teams in the 1987 World Cup.

With the top order back in the pavilion, Allan Lamb and John Emburey put on 31 runs for the seventh wicket before the latter was bowled by Patrick Patterson. It meant that England were 162-7, 82 runs adrift of their target with only 9 overs left. The next man in, Philip DeFreitas, did well to score 23 off 21 balls before Patterson bowled him too. DeFreitas and Lamb had put on 47 runs in decent time, but the fall of the 8th wicket left England the still daunting task of getting 35 runs from 3 overs at a required rate approaching 12 runs per over.

Earlier in the year, in a match against Australia at Sydney, Lamb had been in a similar position. On that occasion, he had pottered around for 97 balls and scored 58 runs without any boundaries. He then faced the last over of the match with England needing 18 runs, and promptly smashed a six, two fours, and a couple of

doubles to take England home with a ball to spare. And so the feeling was that if anyone could pull off victory in this game, it was indeed Allan Lamb. Standing in his way however, was Courtney Walsh who had been at his parsimonious best, conceding a mere 11 runs from his first 5 overs.

The 48th over of the innings, bowled by Walsh, went for 16 runs with Lamb swinging at everything and sending one ball sailing over the leg side boundary for six. With 19 now needed off 2 overs, Patterson put on the brakes allowing only six runs off the 49th over. With 13 runs needed off the last six balls, Sydney must surely have been in Lamb's thoughts. He took a double off the first ball and hit the next one for four. The equation was now a more man-ageable seven runs off four balls, which then changed to two runs off four balls after Walsh bowled one that went for four wides and then bowled a no-ball. The next legitimate delivery went for another boundary, and England were home with three balls to spare; Courtney Walsh's figures ruined with a final return of 9.3-0-65-1 and Allan Lamb finishing not out on 67 off 68 balls.

22

Asif Karim bowls maidens at Australia • 2003

In a match where Brett Lee bowled with searing pace and accuracy to snare a hat-trick, it was Kenya's Asif Karim who put in a bowling performance for the ages. With the Kenyans setting the mighty Australians a mere 175 runs to get in 50 overs, one could be forgiven for thinking that a massacre for Kenya's bowlers was on the cards. Indeed, when Australia's first wicket fell at 50, the innings was barely 6 overs old. The Australians batted at good pace, comfortably scoring over seven runs per over, when Kenya's veteran left-arm spinner Asif Karim – who had come out of retirement to play in the World Cup – was brought on to bowl.

Australian captain Ricky Ponting was dropped off Karim's second ball in the slips, but the bowler didn't have to wait long for the scalp, getting Ponting LBW with the fifth ball of what was eventually a maiden over. Karim's next over proved to be even more successful, a double-wicket maiden in which he dismissed Darren Lehmann (caught behind) and Brad Hogg (caught and bowled). However, the double strike meant that two of Australia's quickest scorers, Andrew Symonds and Ian

Kenya's Asif Karim accepts the applause after his stunning bowling perform-ance against Australia in the 2003 World Cup.

Harvey, were now at the crease. Anyone expecting fireworks from the batsmen must have been stunned to see Asif Karim bowling maiden after maiden, with the Australians unable to get the bowler away.

The target was never going to be stiff enough to trouble the Australians and by the time Karim bowled his 8th over (another maiden at Symonds), Australia's score was 171-5 with only four runs left for victory. The bowler's figure stood at a scarcely believable 8-6-2-3. The next over from Peter Ongondo only yielded two runs, and so Karim – who had already received a standing ovation from an appreciative Durban crowd – had to bowl another over. Symonds took a single off the first ball and Harvey hit the next for a boundary to seal the match in favour of the Australians in the 32nd over. Even with five runs scored off his last two balls, Asif Karim finished the day with an analysis of 8.2-6-7-3. It earned the 39-year-old spinner the man of the match award and, in a larger context, brought deserved respect to Kenya, who eventually finished the tournament as semi-finalists.

21

Sachin Tendulkar versus Shoaib Akhtar • 2003

World Cup draws have always kept Pakistan and India apart at the group stage, with the 2003 World Cup proving to be an exception. The prospect of the traditional rivals meeting so early in the tournament was thus, a rare treat. In any India/Pakistan match there are always side stories of individual battles and in this one, it was the meeting of Sachin Tendulkar and Shoaib Akhtar that had cricket enthusiasts salivating. The two already had something of a history, with Shoaib famously having bowled Tendulkar for a golden duck at Kolkata four years earlier. The World Cup clash in Centurion, billed as the match where the world's best batsman would face the world's fastest bowler, did not disappoint.

With a defendable 273 on the board, Pakistan must have felt that they were in a position to attack India's batsmen and after Wasim Akram bowled the first over of the innings, Shoaib Akhtar came out all guns blazing; his first ball was a wide sent down at a scorching 92 miles per hour. His next three balls proved to be uneventful, save for the consistency of the pace: 93.2, 94.3 and 93.8

mph. Another wide ball brought Tendulkar back on strike and then the drama well and truly began.

Shoaib sent down another quick one (93.8 mph) slightly short and wide of off-stump, and Tendulkar slashed it away for six on the offside. Centurion Park was abuzz, not only because of Tendulkar's fantastic shot but also in anticipation of what Shoaib's response would be. Shoaib steamed in to bowl again, unleashing another thunderbolt at 94.4 mph, which Tendulkar neatly clipped to the legside for four runs. Hitting Shoaib with nonchalant ease to both sides of the ground is the cricket equivalent of chucking rocks at a hornet's nest, and when Shoaib sent down his final delivery of the over, it was clocked at nearly 96 mph. Tendulkar proved equal to it. Using the pace of the ball, a gentle straight push ensured another boundary. Pakistan's strike bowler went for 18 runs in his first over, with the psychological edge ceded to Tendulkar and no doubt made worse by the Pakistan captain Waqar Younis' decision to immediately take Shoaib out of the attack.

Shoaib returned to bowl the 11th and 13th overs, with Tendulkar facing only two deliveries, one of which was dispatched for another boundary. In the 28th over however, Shoaib would get his revenge. Tendulkar, in some discomfort now after flaying the bowling to all parts of the ground, called for a runner. Shoaib, ever the hunter, was not about to show any mercy to the injured batsman and sent down a rip-snorter of a bouncer at 91.5 mph that Tendulkar could merely fend away to the point fielder. The champion batsman was out for 98 off only 75 balls, with 12 fours and that mighty six off Shoaib.

In the end, both men could gain some satisfaction. Tendulkar's came from playing a match winning innings and carting Shoaib to all parts of the ground with disdain, while Shoaib would have the satisfaction of having the final say by dismissing the batsman and depriving him of a hundred that was there for the taking.

No one who saw the clash would ever forget it.

20

Sourav Ganguly and Rahul Dravid thrash Sri Lanka • 1999

Rarely has a side fielded such an attractive array of batsmen as India did in the 1999 World Cup. Ajay Jadeja, plus the world class pair of Sachin Tendulkar and Mohammad Azharuddin aside, it was the emergence of Sourav

Ganguly and Rahul Dravid that really gave India the right to boast of having the tournament's best batting line-up.

Against a full strength but oddly sub-par Sri Lankan side at a relatively small ground at Taunton, Ganguly and Dravid took the opportunity to showcase their immense talents. Inserted by Arjuna Ranatunga, India lost their first wicket (Sadagoppan Ramesh) to the fifth ball of the match. If the Sri Lankans thought that this justified their decision to bowl first, they were sadly mistaken. The dismissal simply brought in Rahul Dravid, and while he played one elegant shot after another, Sourav Ganguly carved the bowling to all parts of the ground and beyond.

The partnership was an ideal exhibition of placement, timing, style and power hitting. Sri Lanka's stalwart bowlers Chaminda Vaas (10-0-84-1) and Muttiah Muralitharan (10-0-60-0) were unable to make any impression as the runs piled on. Dravid made 145 off 129 balls, with 17 fours and a six, while Ganguly made 183 off 158 balls, with 17 fours of his own, plus 7 massive sixes. When the pair were separated in the 46th over by Dravid being run-out, they had put on 318 runs. It was not just the highest partnership for the 2nd wicket, but for any wicket in the history of ODI cricket. India eventually made 373 runs in their 50 overs and won the match by 157 runs. It is a testament to India's batting strength at the time that this record was eclipsed later in the year, when Dravid, this time partnered by Sachin Tendulkar, put on 331 against New Zealand for the 2nd wicket at Hyderabad, Deccan.

19

Shane Warne is banned for failing a drug test • 2003

Australia arrived in South Africa for the 2003 World Cup as both defending champions and firm favourites. The mood in the Australian camp was buoyant even though key batsman Darren

Lehmann was going to be sitting out their first match while finishing up a five-match ban brought about by a racist comment against Sri Lanka several weeks prior, during the VB series in Australia.

The mercurial leg-spinner Shane Warne had announced during that series that the forthcoming World Cup would mark the end of his ODI career. He said that he wanted to help Australia retain the trophy and then focus on Test cricket for the rest of his career. It seemed ideal, as Australia were not expected to encounter any trouble during the tournament and Warne would be able to bask in World Cup glory one more time before saying goodbye to the rigours of the shortened version of the game.

Shane Warne arrives back in Australia from the World Cup in South Africa on February 12, 2003, after testing positive for a banned substance.

There was much surprise then to learn on February 11, 2003, just as Australia were getting ready to take on Pakistan in their first World Cup match, that Shane Warne was on his way back to Australia, having tested positive for a banned substance.

Warne never denied taking the tablet in question, which had the properties of being a masking agent. He maintained that it was to help him lose weight and was not in any way related to enhancing his performance, or aiding with a shoulder injury that he had been carrying.

It emerged that results of tests done in Sydney on a sample provided by Warne to the Australian Sports Drug Agency (ASDA) on January 22, 2003 revealed the presence of diuretics, hydrochlorothiazide and amiloride. Even though at a subsequent hearing there was evidence from the Australian Cricket Board's (ACB) Anti-Doping Medical Adviser that the diuretics would not give a player any advantage, the ACB ended up banning Shane Warne from cricket for one year, effective February 10, 2003.

In a statement after the committee's findings, Warne said in part, "I have made a simple and innocent error of judgement. I take full responsibility for my own actions and yes, I should have checked with someone, I should have

known better," and "I have decided to accept the decision of the committee on the chin and try to move on and deal with it the best way I can. I want to repeat again that I have never taken performance enhancing drugs and never will. It was proved by expert evidence in the hearing that fluid tablets do not enhance performance. They would not have aided recovery from the type of shoulder injury I had and would not mask any other substances."

Australia went on to win the World Cup without the champion leg-spinner, going through the tournament undefeated. Shane Warne would later admit that the year off did him good, allowing injuries to settle and refreshing him for Test cricket. All's well that ends well.

18

Sanath Jayasuriya and the birth of the pinch hitter • 1996

By their approach to the first 15 overs of the game, Sri Lanka are said to have changed the way ODI cricket was played during the 1996 World Cup. The Sri Lankans opened with Sanath Jayasuriya and wicket-keeper Romesh Kaluwitharana, both of whom attacked the bowling from ball one, looking to make the most of the fielding restrictions of the first 15 overs. In the end, their success in this regard may be more myth than reality. Kaluwitharana, for instance, managed a mere 73 runs in the entire tournament at an average of 12.17, but at a strike rate of 140.38. Jayasuriya's strike rate was high too (131.54), but he averaged 36.83 from his six innings in the World Cup, which is not bad unless compared with the rest of Sri Lanka's batting order: Aravinda de Silva (89.60), Asanka Gurusinha (51.16), Hashan Tillekaratne (64.00) and the captain Arjuna Ranatunga (120.50). And while de Silva and Ranatunga both had strike rates in excess of 100, it was Jayasuriya who set the tone with his power hitting. It wasn't his job to get a big score – that was for the powerful middle order to do. Jayasuriya had license to hit and miss and that is exactly what he did over the course of the tournament. His sequence of scores was: 6, 79, 44, 82, 1 and 9.

The best of Jayasuriya's innings was his 82 in the win against England in the quarter-final at Rawalpindi. It was a quick, brutal, yet beautiful innings. But what makes it resonate to this day is that it came against England, a team that symbolized the old order of cricket, its tradition and conservatism. And here a brash,

innovative Sri Lankan was showing the world how cricket would now be played. His 82 runs came from only 44 balls and contained 13 fours and 3 sixes, making a mockery of an entire England innings that saw only 18 fours and 2 sixes. For all that it represented, Sanath Jayasuriya's 82 surely ranks among the most influential ODI innings of all time.

17

Ian Botham's final fling with greatness • *1992*

Unlike his rivals Imran Khan of Pakistan and Kapil Dev of India, England's star all-rounder Ian Botham was never much of a force in World Cup tournaments. His last World Cup in 1992 was his best showing, with the match against Australia at the Sydney Cricket Ground indisputably his finest hour as an all-rounder, not only in the World Cup but in his entire ODI career.

In his final encounter with Australia, Ian Botham put in a splendid all-round display, having the kind of day that brought back memories of his superlative performances against the same opponents during the 1981 Ashes series.

Australia, fighting to stay alive in the tournament and dealing

Vintage Beefy: England's Ian Botham during his 4-31 versus Australia in the 1992 World Cup.

with the pressure of defending the title, won the toss and elected to bat at the SCG. After some initial discomfort, Australia found themselves at a critical juncture, being 145-4 with captain Allan Border looking like he was settled in, having made his way to 16 off 21 deliveries. And then Ian Botham came on to bowl the 38th over of the match and began to take the game away from Australia.

Botham troubled Steve Waugh a bit, and then from nowhere got one through Allan Border, hitting off-stump as the Australian captain went for a flourishing drive. The balance having only just tilted towards England, swung decisively their way when Botham came on for his next over, the 40th of the match. Wicket-keeper Ian Healy hit Botham into the hands of Neil Fairbrother posted at mid-wicket, and although new man in Peter Taylor survived the first ball he faced, he was out LBW to the next. A couple of deliveries later, Botham dismissed Craig McDermott, who chipped a catch to Philip DeFreitas. All three batsmen to fall in that over did so with the score stuck on 155. Botham finished the innings with a final bowling analysis of 10-1-31-4, the best of his ODI career.

With Australia eventually bowled out for 171, England set about the target without undue worry. Botham opened the batting with England captain Graham Gooch and by the time Botham was out in the 24th over, the pair had put on 107 for the 1st wicket, effectively sealing the match. Ian Botham's innings of 53 came off 77 balls and included six typically resounding thumps to the boundary. It was his highest score in a World Cup match and would be his last half-century in either ODI or Test cricket – indeed his 4-31 was also the last time he managed to take four wickets in an international match. This then, was Ian Botham's swansong; a virtuoso all-round performance in his last year of international cricket and fittingly it came against the old enemy.

16

Jonty Rhodes becomes the world's greatest fielder. Ever. • *1992*

The very first time that South Africa and Pakistan squared off in ODI cricket, two young cricketers were involved in a sequence of play that would set the tone for their entire careers. Inzamam-ul-Haq and Jonty Rhodes were playing only their twelfth and fifth matches respectively for their countries when Pakistan and South Africa met at Brisbane for their World Cup clash.

Apartheid had kept South Africa out of international cricket for over 20 years, so most of the cricket world was unaware of their prowess. What was rumoured about them was that the standard of their fielding was second to none. And sharpest among the South Africans was said to be Jonty Rhodes.

South Africa had set Pakistan a score of 212 in 50 overs, which after a rain delay in the 22nd over became a revised target of 194 from 36 overs. More importantly, at the time that the rain came down the required run rate had been 4.84 per over, which mutated into 8.24 runs per over upon resumption.

With the score on 135 in the 31st over, acceleration was on the mind of a young Inzamam-ul-Haq. The batsman had already scored 48 off 44 balls when he attempted a leg-bye off a ball that went to Rhodes at point. The batsman was not even halfway down the pitch when he was sent back by captain Imran Khan at the non-striker's end. Meanwhile, rather than taking a shy at the stumps, Rhodes sprinted towards the striker's end with astonishing speed and then launched himself at the stumps, taking down all three in the process and catching Inzamam short of his ground. The image of Jonty Rhodes flying through the air became iconic and his reputation as the best fielder in the world was sealed.

Rhodes' legend has grown to the point where few have any qualms about calling him the best fielder cricket has ever seen. Inzamam on the other hand, has gone on to become notorious as cricket's run out king. Statistics may have shown this notion to be false, but the legend persists and this is where it all started.

15

Chetan Sharma and Sunil Gavaskar redeem themselves • 1987

To varying degrees, India's clash with New Zealand at Nagpur during the 1987 World Cup, provided redemption to two Indian cricketers. Chetan Sharma, who had a decent Test career as Kapil Dev's new ball partner, was by this time something of a villain in India. A year earlier, during the Austral-Asia Cup final in Sharjah, with Pakistan nine wickets down and needing four runs for victory off the last ball of the match, it was Sharma who bowled the full-toss that Javed Miandad dispatched for a six over mid-wicket. It was a defeat that left Indian cricket scarred and generated ill feelings towards Sharma within India. But Nagpur provided the bowler with the chance to be a hero again.

In a patchy display of bowling where he was alternatively tight (2 maidens among his nine overs) and expensive (going for 51 runs in his other 7 overs), Chetan Sharma bowled himself into the record books with the first hat-trick in World Cup history. All three of Ken Rutherford, Ian Smith and Ewan Chatfield were bowled by straight balls, and New Zealand, who at one stage had been a comfortable 181-4, slumped to 182-8 (Ravi Shastri dismissing Dipak Patel with the score on 181 and Sharma then starting the rout with the score at 182-5). New Zealand eventually made 221 runs in their 50 overs and in the context of the tournament, Chetan Sharma's feat took on greater significance.

This was the last match of the World Cup's group stage and India were in second place in Pool A, needing a win to draw level with leaders Australia. But because Australia had a higher run rate, simply winning would not be enough for India to avoid a trip to Lahore to play the semifinal against Pakistan, Pool B's top side. India needed to beat New Zealand heavily, and in double-quick time, to boost their run rate past Australia's and become the leader in Pool A. Chetan Sharma's bowling ensured that New Zealand didn't get too many on the board and it is perhaps ironic that in his moment of glory, Sharma's bowling figures were the same (3-51) as they were in that unforgettable match at Sharjah.

India set about chasing down the target with a flourish. Openers Sunil Gavaskar and Krishnamachari Srikanth hammered New Zealand's pedestrian bowling attack. Srikanth had a reputation for big shots, but it was unusual to see Gavaskar in such a punishing mood. In the end, India surpassed New Zealand's score in the 33rd over, with Srikanth (75 off 58 balls, 9 fours and 3 sixes) the only casualty. India's win at breakneck speed meant that their tournament run rate (5.39) went past the Australians' (5.19) by a whisker.

Srikanth's innings aside, it was Sunil Gavaskar who was the real hero of India's batting that day. The legendary batsman smashed 103 not out off only 88 balls, with 10 fours and 3 sixes. It would be Gavaskar's only ODI century in what turned out to be the penultimate match of his career. With his infamous snail-paced 36 in the first World Cup a part of cricketing folklore, this sparkling innings at Nagpur went a long way to dispel the notion that Gavaskar was incapable of making quick runs. Fittingly, both Gavaskar and Chetan Sharma were declared joint men of the match.

14

Duncan Fletcher's dream debut • 1983

Few international, let alone World Cup debuts are as stellar as this – leading your country in their first ODI, rescuing the team with the bat with an unbeaten half-century and then bowling the side to victory. That Fletcher accomplished this against an Australian squad that included the likes of Allan Border, Dennis Lillee, Jeff Thomson and Rod Marsh, makes it all the more remarkable.

On June 9 1983, Zimbabwe made their ODI debut against Australia at Trent Bridge, Nottingham, in the World Cup. Led by Duncan Fletcher, now better known for being England's revolutionary coach, Zimbabwe were a team that compensated for their lack of experience with a disciplined approach to the game and top class fielding.

Inserted to bat, Zimbabwe managed to post a very creditable 55 runs for the first wicket, but then slumped to 86-4, which brought Fletcher to the crease. Only eight more runs were added when Andy Pycroft, arguably the team's best batsman at the time, was bowled by the part-time left-arm spin of Allan Border. At 94-5 there was reason for panic to set in, but Fletcher and all-rounder Kevin Curran settled down and put together a partnership of 70 runs in 15 overs before Curran was dismissed by Australia's fastest bowler on the day, Rodney Hogg. Joined by Iain Butchart now, Fletcher upped the scoring rate without taking too may liberties. Lillee and Thomson, who were now past their sell-by date, were trading mostly on reputation, and

Fletcher's calm approach in the early going meant that he had sized them up and would not be intimidated. Butchart (34 off 38 balls) and Fletcher (69 off 84 balls) shared an unbroken partnership of 75 runs for the 7th wicket at a rate of 5.76 runs per over, allowing Zimbabwe to finish with 239-6 in their 60 overs.

With the ball, the Zimbabweans bowled a tight line and fielded sharply, cutting off easy runs. Australia did not lose early wickets, but because of Zimbabwe's commitment in the field, the required run rate steadily climbed.

Graeme Wood was the first to go, caught behind off the bowling of Fletcher for 31 off 60 balls. The new man in was Australian captain Kim Hughes and Fletcher perceived his counterpart to be a key wicket, not so much for his batting ability but for the fact that he was oddly enough, the only right-hander amongst Australia's top order batsmen – and that included wicket-keeper Rod Marsh. Bowling only to left-handed batsmen would allow Fletcher's bowlers the luxury of sticking to the same line and not being forced to adjust too much for new players to the crease. And luckily for Zimbabwe, Hughes lasted a mere four balls, getting out without scoring after hitting Fletcher to a diving Ali Shah and leaving Australia at 63-2.

David Hookes and Kepler

Wessels (a batsman familiar to many in the Zimbabwe camp who had played against him in domestic South African cricket) took the score to 114 before Hookes was also dismissed by Fletcher. Thereafter, wickets continued to tumble at regular intervals. Veteran off-spinner John Traicos, who had played Test matches for South Africa before the country was banned from international cricket, benefited from the abundance of left-handers in the Australian batting line-up and bowled a miserly spell which continued to push the required run rate upwards. Traicos would end up wicketless, but his 12 overs went for a mere 27 runs.

Even with a late flourish from Rod Marsh (50 off 42 balls, 3 fours and 2 sixes), Australia fell too far behind the required run rate and finished their 60 overs with a score of 226-7. Zimbabwe's canny captain took the heart out of Australia's batting line up with his accurate medium-pace deliveries. Wessels was run out, but everyone else in the top five fell to Fletcher, whose final bowling analysis read 11-1-42-4.

Duncan Fletcher led Zimbabwe from the front with a clear plan and inspired his team with his feats with both bat and ball. In the process he scored Zimbabwe's maiden ODI half-century and captured its first 4-wicket haul. Zimbabwe's historic 13-run victory clearly owes much to Duncan Fletcher's dream performance.

13

Courtney Walsh's sporting gesture • 1987

Already reeling from a defeat against England in their first match, the West Indies knew that a win against Pakistan at Lahore was essential if they wanted to keep their hopes of a semi-final berth alive. Things did not go well with the bat and the West Indies were bowled out for 216, but were in turn able to reduce Pakistan to 110-5 with all the top order batsmen dismissed. A valiant fight back from captain Imran Khan and wicket-keeper Saleem Yousuf yielded 73 runs and with the score on 183, it was time for the pendulum to swing again. Courtney Walsh, who was seen by many as being culpable in the previous week's loss to England, dismissed Imran and then with Pakistan within striking distance of the total at 202, got rid of the danger-man Yousuf who had hit 56 off only 49 balls.

The ghosts of Gujranwala were all but exorcised when Walsh came on to bowl the final over with Pakistan needing 14 runs to win, the last pair in and neither of them a recognized batsman. With

10 needed off the last three balls, Abdul Qadir, leaving all three stumps exposed, hit a huge six. Qadir scored another two runs off the next ball and then came yet another dramatic moment in what was already an eventful over. Walsh, running in to bowl the final delivery, noticed that non-striker Saleem Jaffer had backed up too far and was out of his crease. Walsh could have run out Jaffer and with that, the West Indies would have won the match. In an unforgettable display of sportsmanship, Walsh instead chose to warn the batsman. Jaffer got back in his crease, and Abdul Qadir duly scored another double off the last ball of the match to win the game for Pakistan. It was all enough for the West Indies captain Viv Richards to collapse in a heap on the ground.

Courtney Walsh's teammates may have been of two minds about his sporting gesture, but the act went down well in Pakistan. Among the gifts that Walsh received was a gold medal from the Dawn Group of Publications and a shield from a local Karachi cricket club with the inscription, "Presented to cricketer Courtney Walsh of Kingston, Jamaica, for his generous and honourable act of sportsmanship made whilst playing with the West Indies team in the Reliance World Cup match against Pakistan at the Qaddafi Stadium, Lahore, on October 16,

by the cricketers and gentlemen sportsmen of the Karachi Parsi Gymkhana, the oldest cricket club of Karachi, with their good wishes and their gratitude that such sporting gestures do still exist in the playing of the great game of cricket." Whew.

12

John Davison scores the fastest century in World Cup history • 2003

John Davison's stunning hundred against the West Indies during the 2003 World Cup in South Africa was one of the highlights of the tournament and remains a moment loaded with significance.

Canadian-born John Davison grew up in Australia and played state cricket Down Under for Victoria and then South Australia. As an off-spinner who could also bat at number nine or come in as a stubborn night-watchman in the most testing first class cricket structure in the world, it was felt that Davison would be able to command a position high in Canada's batting order and be a key man with the ball as well.

Leading up to the World Cup, hopes continued to be high for Davison's bowling. A few months before the tournament began, in

John Davison sends another one crashing to the boundary, February 23, 2003:
The Canadian all-rounder in a match against the West Indies at Centurion,
hit a hundred off only 67 balls – the fastest in World Cup history.
Davison's record-breaking innings was studded with
8 fours and 6 sixes.

an impressive match for South Australia against a powerful New South Wales batting line-up that included Steve Waugh, Mark Waugh, Michael Bevan, Michael Slater and Simon Katich, Davison came away with 7 wickets in the match, including figures of 5-81 in the first innings. Nothing in his past, however, gave any indication of what he was about to do with the bat at the World Cup.

Opening the batting for Canada, Davison had scored 8, 31 and 0 in the first three matches. Indeed, Davison began his knock against the West Indies rather sedately,

scoring 4 runs from his first nine balls. And then things changed dramatically.

Off the third ball of the 4th over, Davison top edged Pedro Collins for four and then smashed the next ball, a short one – high over the covers for six. A single off the last ball of the over brought Davison face to face with the spearhead of the West Indies bowling attack, Merv Dillon. After pushing back the first ball of the over, Davison proceeded to smash Dillon for three consecutive fours. Fellow opener Ishwar Maraj saw off the next over from Collins, which then set up a rematch between Davison and Dillon with the batsman again winning, pulling Dillon for four and then launching a six over point.

Merv Dillon was hit out of the West Indies attack and his replacement Vasbert Drakes fared no better, conceding 13 runs in his first over, which included a four and a six by Davison. Things got worse for Drakes in his next over (16 runs conceded), when Davison dispatched him for another four and six.

Canada's first wicket fell in the 12th over with the score on 96 when Maraj was out for 16 off 34 balls faced. Canada's run rate was a dizzying eight runs per over, with John Davison still standing at 72 not out off a mere 43 balls.

John Davison continued his assault on the West Indies and when he brought up his century in the 19th over, it was fittingly with another six off Merv Dillon. Davison's hundred came off only 67 balls and shattered the World Cup record for fastest hundred held by India's Kapil Dev.

When Davison eventually fell for 111, it was while attempting another six and it took a spectacular catch by Vasbert Drakes, held one-handed while falling back after the ball had gone past him. Davison's dismissal reduced

Canada to 156-3 and the team eventually collapsed to 202 all out in the 43rd over.

That the West Indies chased down the target nonchalantly, with some powerful hitting of their own, cannot obscure John Davison's achievement. The first century to be made by a Canadian in ODI cricket, Davison's 111 was scored off only 76 balls with 8 fours and 6 sixes. For too long in World Cups had the Test teams feasted on the bowling of the so-called minnows. Davison's shining innings was only the second occasion of a player from a team without Test status scoring a hundred off a Test team in a World Cup match (Zimbabwe's Dave Houghton scored 141 against New Zealand in 1987). But more than just the century itself, it was the manner in which Davison scored his runs that was so impressive. He treated the West Indies as if they, and not Canada, were the rookies, smashing their bowling with utter disdain. The West Indies may have won the match, but they will always consider the episode to be an embarrassment and an example of how far their cricket had fallen. At the same time, Canada and John Davison can always feel pride in what truly was one of the greatest batting performances in World Cup history.

11

Aamer Sohail versus Venkatesh Prasad (as well as the universe) • 1996

This incident took place in a match where the Pakistan side was under unimaginable pressure. The World Cup holders found themselves facing their archrivals in the quarter-final match, in the vociferously partial cauldron of Bangalore, India. The teams had not played each other on Indian soil in seven years and the tournament's format had meant that at one stage the Pakistanis had the option of losing a game and ensuring that they played their quarter-final clash at home. Pakistan dismissed any suggestion of taking their matches lightly and confidently announced that they would have no trouble facing India in Bangalore.

Moments before the captains were to come out to the pitch for the toss, the Pakistan team management came to the grim realization that captain and strike bowler Wasim Akram was unfit to play. Akram had picked up an injury during a first-round match against New Zealand, but had been confident that he would be able to play in the crucial quarter-final match. Wasim Akram pulling out of the match and the circumstances surrounding the event are the subject of some controversy, but what is not in dispute is that Aamer Sohail learned that he would be leading the side in this match mere minutes before the captains were to take the field for the toss.

Reportedly there were heated arguments within the Pakistan dressing room upon learning that Wasim Akram would not be playing. The team composition became an issue, as did the very notion of who would skipper the side. There were some within the team who thought a player with more experience than Sohail should take over the reigns in a match of such paramount importance. In the end, team management opted to have vice captain Sohail lead the side. One can only imagine what would have been going through the player's head among the chaos of the big occasion.

India, no doubt relieved not to be facing Wasim Akram, and buoyed by the 55,000 strong home crowd, not to mention the rattled look of their opposition, made merry and rang up a formidable total of 287 in 50 overs. Pakistan's other bowling stalwart, Waqar Younis, conceded 40 runs in his last two overs to further demoralize the side. Pakistan were slow in their over rate too and when they came out to bat they were docked one over by the match referee.

The tension thick in the air and the weight of the world on his shoulders, Aamer Sohail came out to bat with fellow opener Saeed Anwar under newly installed floodlights to chase 288 in 49 overs, at a required run rate of 5.88.

Sohail, well known as a fiery and combative individual, decided not to let the occasion get to him and set about the task at hand with astonishing aggression. The required run rate, the squabbling of his teammates, the absence of his captain, the tension of an India-Pakistan match, the pressure of a do-or-die clash while defending the World Championship and – last but not least – the burden of unexpected leadership all seemed to go out the window or perhaps even focussed Sohail into playing what could have been the innings of his life. He and Saeed Anwar launched into India's bowling with such gusto that the capacity crowd was stunned into silence. The duo put on 84 runs in a mere 10 overs, with Anwar falling for 48 off a mere 32 balls. Pakistan were cruising at a scoring rate of over 8 runs an over and even with the loss of his opening partner, Sohail kept blazing away. And then his aggression got the better of him.

Venkatesh Prasad, a bowler of gentle medium pace, had been getting some stick from Pakistan's openers. In the 15th over, such was Sohail's brashness that he stepped out of his crease to smash Prasad to the boundary and then had a few words with the bowler, pointing to where he hit the ball and indicating that he would do it again. It was a gesture that said to the crowd and the tens of millions watching the match on television that he was untroubled by the bowling and was going to win this match against the odds, on his own, and in incredible style. It was courageous, arrogant, calculated and ultimately foolish. Prasad, somewhat chastened, came back to bowl the next delivery and pitched it in line with off-stump. Sohail had another violent swing and completely missed the ball, which crashed into the stumps. The stadium erupted and Sohail walked back to the pavilion not bothering to look at the destruction behind him. In the end he made a whirlwind, fighting 55 off only 46 balls, with 9 fours and a six. Pakistan never recovered from Sohail's loss and went down to India by 39 runs, their World Cup defence over.

10

Wasim Akram's two-wicket burst in the World Cup final • 1992.

Perhaps the most memorable moment of Pakistan's victory over England in the final of the 1992 World Cup was the moment when Wasim Akram came on to bowl the 35th over of the England innings. The match was delicately poised with England in pursuit of 250, on 141-4 and Allan Lamb, one of the world's best ODI batsmen and a cool head under pressure, batting on a composed 31. Charging in to bowl from around the wicket, Akram dismissed Lamb with what Tony Cozier described on the day as "an absolutely magnificent delivery, as near as to unplayable as you can possibly get." The ball swung in to Lamb at high speed and once it pitched, moved away from him to crash into off-stump, leaving the batsman utterly bewildered. Rarely has a cricketer looked as delighted with a wicket as Wasim Akram did with that one. But he wasn't done yet. The next man in was Chris Lewis and this time Akram pitched the ball well outside of off-stump and it swung in sharply, hitting the top of off and middle-stump. England were now 141-6 and the writing was on the wall.

In an illustrious career where Wasim Akram became the record holder for the most wickets in ODI history, it is saying something about the quality and magnitude of what he did that day that he still regards those two scalps as his favourites.

9

Sunil Gavaskar's 36 not out • 1975

Few if any innings are as vilified as Sunil Gavaskar's 36 not out in the very first match ever played in the World Cup on June 7, 1975. In later years, Gavaskar himself described the innings as the worst of his career. Indeed, one would be hard pressed to find a worse batting display anywhere in the history of ODI cricket.

After England had rattled up a score of 334-4 in 60 overs on the back of Dennis Amiss' fine 137 off 147 balls with 18 fours, India replied as if they were utterly uninterested in the outcome of the match. Sunil Gavaskar and his opening partner Eknath Solkar plodded along,without troubling the scorers too much. Solkar departed for 8 off 34 balls, but the loss didn't have too much of an impact on the run rate.

When the Indian innings drew to a close, they had lost the match by the embarrassing margin of 202 runs, managing a meagre 132-3 off 60 overs at a run rate of 2.2. Worse was that Sunil Gavaskar, who had faced the first ball of the innings, returned to the pavilion not out, scoring 36 runs with one boundary off a whopping 174 balls faced – a dreadful strike rate of 20.68. Comparatively, Gavaskar's teammate Gundappa Vishwanath, no hare with the bat himself, had faced only 59 balls for his 37.

There have been many explanations for what went wrong with Gavaskar that day. Some have suggested that he was unhappy about team selection or the choice of captain and chose to make his displeasure known this way. Others have said he was not equipped to play ODI cricket, particularly when it was this new and others too were finding their feet. Bizarrely, and one hopes facetiously, there is the suggestion that Gavaskar really didn't understand ODI cricket and was playing for a draw. Whatever the reason, it was an absolutely irritating, even infuriating innings for those who watched it. Even Indian supporters at the ground felt ashamed and voiced their displeasure to Gavaskar when he made his way back the pavilion. On the plus side, it was good to get the worst innings out of the way in the very first match of the competition's history. Things could only get better.

8

Kapil Dev's 175 not out • 1983

Leaving aside the fact that Zimbabwe were minnows of the game at the time (*la plus ça change?*), Kapil Dev's blistering, unbeaten 175 is one of the most remarkable innings in World Cup history. It is also among the finest examples of a captain's innings in the annals of ODI cricket. It came against the odds, blended caution with aggression and ultimately left the team with no choice but to be humbled about their own efforts and to feel pride at the achievement of their captain.

The tale of Kapil Dev's epic innings begins in the unlikely setting of the tiny Nevill Ground at Tunbridge Wells, on June 18, 1983 during India's second meeting of the tournament with Zimbabwe. India won the toss and decided to bat on a pitch that was closest to the edge of the boundary, resulting in one boundary square of the wicket being ominously short. The pitch had some dampness, but India did not expect to be troubled too much by Zimbabwe's bowlers – an underestimation of their opponents that proved to be costly.

Sunil Gavaskar was LBW to the second ball of the match courtesy of Peter Rawson, and the normally aggressive Krishnamachari Srikanth was also out without scoring, having dawdled for 13 deliveries. Both openers falling for ducks was bad enough, but the wickets kept tumbling such that when the captain Kapil Dev came out to bat the score-line was a dismal 9-4. The captain's presence failed to calm nerves and soon batting partner Yashpal Sharma also edged the rampant Rawson to the wicket-keeper Dave Houghton, leaving India 5 down now, for only 17 runs.

Zimbabwe captain Duncan Fletcher took Rawson and his other opening bowler, Kevin Curran, out of the attack and things began to settle down. Without further loss, Kapil Dev in the company of fellow all-rounder Roger Binny, brought the score up to 77, but just as it looked that an Indian recovery was underway, both Binny and Ravi Shastri fell in quick succession, leaving the score-line again looking perilous at 78-7.

Madan Lal (17 off 39 balls) and later Syed Kirmani (24 off 56 balls) lent good support to Kapil Dev who took advantage of the short boundary and launched into the Zimbabwean bowling in a manner that was still uncommon in ODI cricket. Kapil's swashbuckling innings contained 16 fours and 6 sixes, with the century being reached off only 72 balls. He eventually finished not out on 175 off only 138 balls, taking India's total to 266. It proved to be too much for Zimbabwe, who eventually fell short by 31 runs.

Kapil Dev's innings was a landmark for a number of reasons. Its immediate significance from India's perspective was that it was the first century scored by an Indian player in ODI cricket. The game as a whole was also impacted by the Indian captain's wondrous knock. At the time, Kapil Dev's 175 not out was the highest score by a batsman not only in World Cup history, but in all of ODI cricket. The mere 72 balls it took Kapil to reach three figures equalled the then world record for fastest ODI century (held by Pakistan's Zaheer Abbas) and the unbroken 126-run partnership between Kapil Dev and Syed Kirmani, remains an ODI record for the ninth wicket.

Kapil Dev would never score another century in his ODI career, but his heroics in this match are an integral part of the chronicle of India's successful 1983 World Cup campaign.

7

Andy Flower and Henry Olonga protest against the government of Zimbabwe

• *2003*

Zimbabwe opened their account in the 2003 World Cup with a comfortable win against Namibia in Harare. Batting first, Zimbabwe made their highest team score in history at 340-2 with Craig Wishart also recording the highest individual score by a Zimbabwean with an undefeated 172. However, the real news story of Zimbabwe's first match was that two of its most prominent cricketers chose the moment to go public with a protest against their government.

On the morning of the match, Andy Flower, the best player to ever represent Zimbabwe, and Henry Olonga, the national team's first black player, issued a joint statement that was essentially an expression of acute distress felt by the two about not only the human rights situation in their country but also of the related issues of starvation, poverty and AIDS. The pair mentioned in the statement that they would be wearing black armbands when on the field, going on to explain that, "In doing so we are mourning the death of democracy in our beloved Zimbabwe. In doing so we are making a silent plea to those responsible to stop the abuse of human rights in Zimbabwe. In doing so we pray that our small action may help to restore sanity and dignity to our Nation."

The statement also made it clear that neither Flower nor Olonga had any expectation that the rest of the team would join in the protest. Indeed, it came to pass that during the World Cup, no other Zimbabwean player donned the black armband. It was however reported that the stance by Flower and Olonga had widespread support in the

Zimbabwe's Andy Flower and Henry Olonga in contemplative mood, during the 2003 World Cup.

Zimbabwean dressing room and that the courage of the two players was widely admired by their teammates.

With Zimbabwe's President Robert Mugabe also being the patron of the Zimbabwe Cricket Union, both Flower and Olonga knew that going public with their criticism and protest meant that their careers would be over. Olonga even feared for his life and did not return to Zimbabwe after the World Cup, remaining first in South Africa and then going to the UK. Andy Flower had been rumoured to be mulling retirement from international cricket after the World Cup anyway in order to play county cricket in England, and that is what he ended up doing.

In what was indicative of the Zimbabwean cricket establishment's feeling on the issue, Givemore Makoni, the chairman of the Zimbabwean club that Henry Olonga played for, characterized Olonga and Flower's behaviour as "disgraceful" and said that by taking political issues onto the field, the pair had brought the game into disrepute. Andy Flower and Henry Olonga predictably never played for Zimbabwe again, but maintain that they have no regrets over their statement or protest.

6

Herschelle Gibbs drops Steve Waugh (and possibly the World Cup) • *1999*

Losses to New Zealand and Pakistan in the first round of the 1999 World Cup meant that Australia entered the Super Six stage of the tournament without any lives. A single loss would have been enough to prevent

Herschelle Gibbs, World Cup 1999: Quite possibly Steve Waugh's favourite South African player.

them from reaching the semi-finals and so when South Africa rattled up an imposing 271 in the last Super Six match of the tournament, and then reduced Australia to 48-3 in the 12th over, Aussie captain Steve Waugh had reason to be worried. The South Africans bowled tightly in the first half of the innings and at the end of the 21st over Australia only had 63 runs on the board and a required run rate that had needled over 7 runs per over. While Ricky Ponting was uncharacteristically bogged down (eventually falling for a dogged 69 off 110 balls), Waugh kept the scoreboard ticking along, looking steely and purposeful as he made an urgent half-century. And shortly after he reached the landmark came the moment that would define the match.

Wickets could tumble at the other end, but it was becoming clear to South Africa that as long as Steve Waugh was sticking around, victory could not be taken for granted. Hearts skipped a beat then when Waugh, who had made 56 off 52 balls at that point, chipped Lance Klusener on the last ball of 31st over, straight to Herschelle Gibbs at mid-wicket. Gibbs, regarded as not just one of South Africa's best fielders but one of the world's best, appeared to take the catch easily enough, but before he had complete control of the ball, it slipped out of his hand as he attempted to toss it away in celebration. The story goes that Waugh rubbed salt into the wounds by taunting Gibbs with, "You just dropped the World Cup, mate." Australia were 152-3 at the time and in a tight match, eventually reaching their target with two balls and 5 wickets to spare. Steve Waugh made his highest ODI score, finishing not out on 120 off 110 balls. Australia's victory in this match set up what would become an even more memorable clash with South Africa in the semi-final.

In Herschelle Gibbs' defence, there has been some suggestion that his hand had been sprayed and may still have been numb after being hit while batting earlier in the day. If so, he would not have properly felt whether he had the ball or not. Others suggest that there is the likelihood that the catch would have been considered clean if Gibbs' reaction had not been of dismay when the ball went down.

Steve Waugh's quip, meanwhile, has become legendary. Gibbs has said the first he heard of it was at the press conference after the match, and even Waugh has distanced himself from the remark. The accuracy of the barb aside, Herschelle Gibbs' spill and Steve Waugh's "You just dropped the World Cup, mate" will forever be a part of World Cup folklore.

5

Inzamam-ul-Haq spoils New Zealand's party •
1992

Simply the greatest knock ever played in a World Cup semi-final, Inzamam-ul-Haq's whirlwind 60 was the brightest contribution in Pakistan's historic win.

New Zealand were the form side of the tournament and playing their semi-final at home, were buoyed by a stadiumful of support. Chasing an imposing New Zealand total of 262 at Eden Park, Auckland, Pakistan were bogged down by some tight Kiwi bowling. When Inzamam came out to bat, joining Javed Miandad, Pakistan were 140-4 with only 15 overs left and no other recognized batsmen to come. With 123 runs still needed, the required run rate was over 8 runs per over. The 22-year-old Inzamam's response to the pressure was to step out of his crease and swing mightily at the ball.

He soon had the New Zealanders running around the park trying to stop his full-blooded swats to the fence. In between the boundaries, Javed Miandad, legendary for pinching tight singles, had Inzamam sprinting any time there was even the remote possibility of a run. By the time Inzamam was out in the 45th over, he had made 60 runs off

A star is born: Pakistan's Inzamam-ul-Haq during his match-winning innings of 60 off 37 balls in the 1992 World Cup Semi-Final against New Zealand.

only 37 balls with 7 fours and a six, whittling down a near impossible target to a more manageable 36 runs off 32 balls. Javed Miandad (57* off 69 balls), Rameez Raja (44 off 59 balls) and Imran Khan (44 off 93 balls) all played well in difficult batting conditions, but it is Inzamam's cool-headed blitz that was the major factor in the win. Adding to the folklore of the innings is the fact that the young Inzamam's innings was terminated by what would become a customary form of dismissal: He was run out.

4

Rain knocks South Africa out of the World Cup. Again. • *2003*

South Africa have had their share of heartbreak in the World Cup. In the 1992 semi-final against England, an adjustment after a rain delay meant that South Africa needed an impossible 22 runs off 1 ball, whereas before the rain came down the target was 22 runs off 13 balls. And then there was the 1999 World Cup semi-final against Australia, where a powerful South African misse going through to the final by only one run. South Africa's elimination in the 2003 World Cup was a cruel

combination of both of those painful incidents.

Not quite as strong as the 1999 team led by Hansie Cronje, hosts South Africa were still one of the favourites to reach the final of the 2003 World Cup. Losing matches to the West Indies and New Zealand however, meant that South Africa needed to win their final match of the group stage in order to progress to the next round. With rain forecast for later in the day, and Durban a notoriously tricky place to bat under floodlights, the Sri Lankans had no hesitation in winning the toss and deciding to bat first.

A 152-run partnership between Marvan Atapattu (124) and Aravinda de Silva (73) formed the cornerstone of Sri Lanka's imposing 268-9. In reply, South Africa got off to a bright start with Graeme Smith and Herschelle Gibbs putting on 65 for the first wicket in 11 overs. Wickets then began to fall at regular intervals and at 149-5, with all the specialist batsmen gone, things looked bleak for South Africa. The threat of rain also meant that South Africa had to keep one eye on the evolving Duckworth-Lewis equation.

Mark Boucher and captain Shaun Pollock kept the dream alive with a 63-run partnership, but when Pollock was run out in the 43rd over, the rain came down almost on cue. The score was 212 and the new man in was the hero of the 1999 World Cup, the big hitting Lance Klusener, fatefully the man who was also at the crease in the 1999 semi-final when South Africa crashed out.)

With Boucher and Klusener batting in tandem, South Africa did have the firepower to reach their target but the rain and lights, coupled with Klusener's waning powers, meant that he struggled with his timing and ultimately scored only 1 run from the eight balls that he faced.

With the rain getting heavier, South Africa had their calculators going, knowing that they would soon have to come off the field and the Duckworth-Lewis formula would be employed. At the end of 45 overs, the par score would be 229 and when Boucher smashed the penultimate ball of the 44th over for a huge six, he

Heartbroken again: Captain Shaun Pollock watches the rain wash away South Africa's World Cup dreams, Durban, March 3, 2003

punched the air in delight as it brought the score up to 229. He patted the last ball of the over to a fielder and the players came off the field in the pouring rain. Unbeknownst to the batsmen, a par score meant exactly that – a tie. South Africa had needed to score at least one more run to win the match, which they likely would have done had they not misinterpreted the rule. South Africa's only hope was for the rain to stop and as captain Shaun Pollock looked out from the dressing room in utter despair, the rain just got heavier. The match ended in a tie and the hosts crashed out of the tournament in the first round, the blunder ultimately costing Pollock the captaincy.

3
Mike Gatting's reverse sweep • 1987

Brimming with confidence after defeating hosts and defending champion India in the semi-final, England were considered a good bet to lift the1987 World Cup. Considered a better team, England did not expect too much trouble from an Australian side that they had just recently defeated in the Ashes as well as in a couple of ODI tournaments. If anything, Australia had done England a favour by knocking out

Mike Gatting , 1987 World Cup Final: "What's the harm, I'll just play a fancy reverse-sweep around the corner here and … oh."

hot favourites Pakistan, who had troubled England in the group stages.

Chasing a decent Australian total of 254, England were going along nicely at 135-2 from 31 overs with Bill Athey and captain Mike Gatting well set. Gatting was one of England's in form men, having hit three half-centuries in the previous seven matches. He was set for his fourth fifty of the tournament when he played what can only be described as the most injudicious shot ever played in a World Cup final.

Having used five bowlers and not denting England's top order to the degree he would have liked, Australian captain Allan Border decided to bring himself on. A part-time left-arm spinner, Border would never have predict-

ed what happened next. His first delivery was pitched on leg stump and Gatting, perhaps over-confident about his own abilities and somewhat disdainful of his opposite number's bowling credentials, played a reverse sweep shot. After taking the top-edge of the bat, the ball hit Gatting's shoulder and then lodged comfortably in the gloves of wicket-keeper Greg Dyer. A shot of such extravagance was ill-advised and unnecessary at that juncture of the match. The England captain who had looked so good and in control prior to that shot, departed for 41 off 45 balls. It was a gift of a wicket and Gatting would later go on to admit that he should have at least had more of a look at Border's bowling before having a go at him. England went on to lose the final by a mere seven runs

2

Lance Klusener runs out Allan Donald in the semi-final • 1999

With nine runs needed off the last over of the World Cup semi-final and the last pair batting, most teams would feel exorbitant pressure. But in the 1999 World Cup, such was the form and confidence of Lance Klusener that nothing seemed impossible for him. Throughout the tournament he performed wonders for South Africa, bludgeoning the bowlers to all parts of the ground and ultimately finishing the tournament with 281 runs at a scarcely believable average of 140.50. More significantly, Klusener's strike rate of 122.17 is testament to how quickly he scored his runs and as his average indicates, he proved to be a difficult batsmen to dismiss too, getting out only twice in eight innings. In short, Lance Klusener was exactly the man South Africa wanted to be on strike when the last over began.

Things could not have started off better. Damien Fleming's first ball of that fateful over was just outside of off-stump and Klusener smashed it through the offside, all

The final act of one of the greatest cricket matches ever played: Allan Donald goes for a suicidal run; South Africa versus Australia World Cup Semi-Final, Birmingham, June 17, 1999.

along the ground and straight to the boundary for four. Klusener swaggered around the pitch and with the equation now changed to five runs off five balls, Fleming's next ball, pitched right on off-stump this time, disappeared to a similar, thundering shot for four more. The scores were now tied and with only one run needed for a win and four balls left, inexplicably the nerves finally showed. Fleming's next ball was hit to a fielder and Allan Donald at the non-striker's end attempted a run that wasn't there and barely missed being run out. This appears to have panicked Klusener and it seems he made up his mind not to wait around and take the required run off the very next ball. Fleming's fourth ball of the over was hit straight back past the bowler. Without waiting to see if a fielder picked it up, Klusener bolted for an ill-advised run. At the other end, Donald had kept his eye on the fielder and had not noticed Klusener bounding down the pitch. By the time Donald set off for the single, it was too late. The Australians had run him out, taking the last South African wicket and booking their place in the final, not to mention capping off the most dramatic moment of arguably the most dramatic match in World Cup history.

1

Imran Khan wins the World Cup • 1992.

A fairytale ending if there ever was one, Imran Khan's triumph in the 1992 World Cup final could not have been scripted better. In what would be the last game of his career, the inspirational captain led from the front, made the highest score in the match and then took the final wicket to seal the win. But to understand the real gravitas of what Imran Khan accomplished, one has to go back not just to the start of the tournament where Pakistan appeared to be done and dusted in the preliminary round but earlier still to the 1987 World Cup.

Pakistan had entered the 1987 World Cup as favourites and their captain Imran Khan, then very much in prime form as an all-rounder, had announced his intention to retire after the tournament. A shocking semi-final loss to the unfancied Australians saw Imran's career end on a sad note. The Pakistan cricket team, while still a powerful force in the world game, went into depression at the inability to win the World Cup, but more so at the loss of their charismatic captain, who at the time was still the team's best fast bowler. An impending tour of the

West Indies and a direct request from the President of Pakistan is what it took for Imran to reconsider his retirement and he returned to the side as captain in 1988.

Although 1987 had been a watershed year for Imran and Pakistan, with series wins away from home in India and England, there was a noticeable change in Imran's approach to the game after his return from retirement. There seemed to be a greater sense of urgency in wanting to achieve the lofty goal of establishing Pakistan as cricket's best team and solidifying that status with a win in the next World Cup.

The 1988 series in the West Indies saw Imran bowling as well as ever, but having crossed the age of 35, Imran knew that his days as a bowling spearhead were coming to an end. The role was ceded to the exceptionally talented Wasim Akram and when Waqar Younis, another young man of phenomenal bowling talent, emerged in late 1989, Imran demoted himself to a mere support bowler, occasionally choosing not to bowl at all in matches. Worth his place in the side as captain alone, Imran chose to focus on his batting and in doing so over the next few seasons came to be regarded as his team's most reliable batsman – a remarkable feat during his last years as a player. But more than cricket,

Imran was now focussed on the noble goal of establishing Pakistan's first cancer hospital, in honour of his mother who had succumbed to the disease. Imran has admitted to the cancer hospital being an obsession for him. Knowing that initial fundraising efforts depended on his remaining a visible and successful cricketer, Imran continued to work extremely hard at his game and played cricket to the best of his abilities.

Pakistan approached the 1992 World Cup with high hopes that were immediately dealt a body blow when the lightning quick Waqar Younis, who was to have been Pakistan's chief weapon, was ruled out of the tournament due to injury. The Pakistan side for the tournament was filled with rookies, some of whom, such as Inzamam-ul-Haq and Moin Khan, would go on to notable international careers while others, like Wasim Haider and Iqbal Sikandar, would fade into obscurity. There was a clutch of players who were sufficiently experienced at this point, chief among them Wasim Akram, Rameez Raja and Saleem Malik, but all eyes rested on the two battle-hardened veterans; the two poles of Pakistani cricket, the country's greatest bowler and greatest batsman, the urbane Oxford graduate and the excitable so-called street fighter, the captain and vice-captain – Imran Khan and Javed Miandad, the only two players on the planet who had played in every World Cup. But by this time Imran was 39 years old and hampered by a shoulder injury that he carried throughout the tournament and which restricted his ability to bowl in the World Cup. Javed Miandad himself was 35 years old and was also suffering from two ailments, a bad back that had kept him out of cricket leading up to the tournament, and an adverse reaction to medication that resulted in severely painful stomach inflammation. Pakistan were looking decidedly ragged and were down and out at the halfway stage of the World Cup, with only one win in five games. Pakistan languished at number eight out of the nine teams in the tournament and there appeared little hope that they could qualify for the semi-finals.

With morale sinking in the team, Imran Khan delivered his famous speech where he told his team to play like cornered tigers. Imran's belief in Pakistan's ability to win the World Cup never wavered and certainly had an impact on his young team. Wasim Akram, Mushtaq Ahmed, Inzamam and even the likes of the suave Rameez Raja have admitted to Imran's passion having a profound motivational affect.

The stars aligned, and not only did Pakistan start winning themselves, but all the results they needed from other teams battling each other also came to pass. From being dead in the water, Pakistan managed an incredible recovery to finish among the top four teams at the end of the round-robin stage.

After seeing off New Zealand, the tournament's most in form team, in a thrilling semi-final, Imran Khan's Pakistan side also made short work of England in the final at Melbourne. And for this to be such a great story, it had to be England – Imran's second home; the country where he truly learned his cricket; the country where he felt Pakistan had never been given the respect they deserved as a cricketing nation in spite of their success. And that it was England meant that the larger cricketing world was behind Pakistan too, vicariously enjoying the prospect of giving one to the old colonial master.

Playing through his shoulder pain, Imran led from the front in that World Cup final, coming in to bat at number three. He paced his innings perfectly, using all of his experience in not panicking when the run rate slowed to a crawl and then unleashing some power hitting when it was really needed. His 72 was the top score of the match and as a captain he used his resources marvellously well, shuffling the batting order, which allowed the explosive pairing of Wasim Akram and Inzamam-ul-

Haq to have a go at England's bowling in the last few overs, ahead of the more recognized batsmen Saleem Malik and Ijaz Ahmed.

In the field too, Imran made canny bowling changes, having the leg-spinner Mushtaq Ahmed attack Graeme Hick and then the masterstroke of bringing his trump card on for a spell earlier than anyone expected. It was Wasim Akram's removal of Allan Lamb and Chris Lewis in the 35th over of the England innings which decisively swung the match Pakistan's way. Imran himself went on to take the final wicket.

There could be no better way for Imran Khan to cap off a wonderful career than by leading Pakistan to victory in the World Cup. His victory as captain justified his decision to return to cricket and meant that the preceding four years had purpose. The respect and glory that Imran had sought to bring to Pakistan was achieved, but more than that Imran knew that the World Cup win would go a long way in boosting fundraising efforts and helping to bring his dream of the cancer hospital to reality. Indeed, it would prove to be so. Imran would go on to dedicate all proceeds from Pakistan's World Cup win to the hospital, which would formally open two years later in December 1994.

From a cricketing perspective, who could ask for more – a half-century with the bat, a wicket with your final delivery in international cricket and then lifting the World Cup as not only the captain of a proud team, but also as the crowning achievement of a glorious career. Imran Khan's win of 1992 is the greatest story in World Cup history.

Now that's the way to cap off a career: The legendary Imran Khan with the 1992 World Cup

World Champions Australia, 2003

World Cup Statistics,

Batting and Bowling by Country, 1975 – 2003

ENGLAND
Winners: Never
Runner's Up: 1979, 1987, 1992
Semi-Final Finish: 1975, 1983
Participants: All World Cups

Always the bridesmaid, England were in the thick of things in all World Cups until 1992. Never quite the favourites in any edition of the tournament, England's best chance of lifting the trophy was against Ashes rivals Australia in 1987. The only team that had troubled England in the tournament that year was Pakistan, and when they fell in the semi-final to Australia, Mike Gatting's men must have had visions of a victory parade in Trafalgar Square. It was not to be, and after another finals appearance in 1992, England have been innocuous in subsequent World Cups. In 1996, England were unable to beat any quality opposition and looked like a team that was archaic in its approach and completely out of step with the evolution of ODI cricket. Worse was to come.

Best World Cup: 1979. England sailed into the final undefeated.

Worst World Cup: 1999. England showed that they hadn't learned any lessons from the previous tournament and selected a team of what the British media described as "pie-throwers." England, the hosts of the tournament, humiliatingly crashed out in the first round. In their last match, a do-or-die clash with India, the home team found that there was more Indian support in the ground than English – quite possibly the lowest ebb of modern English cricket.

ENGLAND RESULTS

		M	Won	Lost	Tied	NR
v	Australia	5	2	3	0	0
v	Canada	1	1	0	0	0
v	East Africa	1	1	0	0	0
v	India	6	3	3	0	0
v	Kenya	1	1	0	0	0
v	Namibia	1	1	0	0	0
v	Netherlands	2	2	0	0	0
v	New Zealand	6	3	3	0	0
v	Pakistan	9	4	4	0	1
v	South Africa	4	2	2	0	0
v	Sri Lanka	7	6	1	0	0
v	United Arab Emirates	1	1	0	0	0
v	West Indies	4	3	1	0	0
v	Zimbabwe	2	1	1	0	0
	Total	50	31	18	0	1

Success Percentage: 63.26%

ENGLAND BATTING RECORDS

Name	Mat	I	NO	Runs	HS	Ave	SR	100	50	Ct	St
PJW Allott	7	3	1	8	8	4.00	53.33	-	-	1	-
DL Amiss	4	4	0	243	137	60.75	84.37	1	1	1	-
JM Anderson	5	2	1	2	2	2.00	25.00	-	-	-	-
GG Arnold	3	1	1	18	18*	-	60.00	-	-	1	-
MA Atherton	6	6	0	119	66	19.83	68.00	-	1	-	-
CWJ Athey	6	6	2	211	86	52.75	64.92	-	2	4	-
ID Austin	2	0	-	-	-	-	-	-	-	-	-
ID Blackwell	2	2	1	38	22*	38.00	26.66	-	-	-	-
IT Botham	22	18	2	297	53	18.56	62.39	-	1	10	-
G Boycott	5	5	1	92	57	23.00	42.99	-	1	-	-
JM Brearley	5	5	0	161	64	32.20	39.85	-	2	4	-
BC Broad	3	3	0	67	36	22.33	44.66	-	-	1	-
AR Caddick	5	4	3	25	13*	25.00	43.85	-	-	-	-
PD Collingwood	5	5	2	137	66*	45.66	74.45	-	1	4	-
DG Cork	5	3	0	36	19	12.00	78.26	-	-	2	-
NG Cowans	1	0	-	-	-	-	-	-	-	1	-
RDB Croft	2	1	0	12	12	12.00	48.00	-	-	-	-
PAJ DeFreitas	22	13	3	184	67	18.40	98.92	-	1	5	-
MH Denness	4	4	2	113	37*	56.50	75.83	-	-	-	-
GR Dilley	6	4	2	90	31*	45.00	120.00	-	-	1	-
PR Downton	8	5	1	19	9	4.75	59.37	-	-	8	1
MA Ealham	5	2	0	5	5	2.50	25.00	-	-	1	-
PH Edmonds	3	2	1	7	5*	7.00	22.58	-	-	-	-
JE Emburey	8	7	2	96	30*	19.20	109.09	-	-	3	-
NH Fairbrother	19	15	5	430	75*	43.00	63.60	-	3	8	-
KWR Fletcher	4	3	0	207	131	69.00	69.23	1	1	1	-
A Flintoff	10	7	0	171	64	24.42	69.23	-	1	3	-
NA Foster	7	4	3	42	20*	42.00	113.51	-	-	1	-
G Fowler	7	7	2	360	81*	72.00	62.82	-	4	-	-
ARC Fraser	3	2	1	18	15*	18.00	51.42	-	-	3	-
MW Gatting	15	13	2	437	60	39.72	87.05	-	3	3	-
AF Giles	2	2	0	19	17	9.50	63.33	-	-	4	-
GA Gooch	21	21	1	897	115	44.85	63.21	1	8	3	-
D Gough	11	6	2	95	26*	23.75	73.64	-	-	2	-
IJ Gould	7	4	1	66	35	22.00	64.70	-	-	11	1
DI Gower	12	11	3	434	130	54.25	82.35	1	1	2	-
AW Greig	4	4	0	29	9	7.25	42.02	-	-	-	-
FC Hayes	3	3	0	90	52	30.00	66.17	-	1	-	-

Another tough day at the office: England captain Alec Stewart, during the 1999 World Cup

Name	Mat	I	NO	Runs	HS	Ave	SR	100	50	Ct	St
EE Hemmings	6	1	1	4	4*	-	133.33	-	-	2	-
M Hendrick	5	2	1	1	1*	1.00	16.66	-	-	3	-
GA Hick	20	19	4	635	104*	42.33	74.00	1	6	12	-
AJ Hollioake	3	1	0	6	6	6.00	46.15	-	-	-	-
N Hussain	9	8	2	218	88*	36.33	58.60	-	2	4	-
RK Illingworth	10	5	3	31	14	15.50	81.57	-	-	3	-
RC Irani	2	2	0	12	12	6.00	133.33	-	-	-	-
JA Jameson	2	2	0	32	21	16.00	43.83	-	-	-	-
NV Knight	5	5	0	103	51	20.60	76.86	-	1	3	-
APE Knott	4	2	1	18	18*	18.00	75.00	-	-	1	-
AJ Lamb	19	17	4	656	102	50.46	84.10	1	3	9	-
W Larkins	2	2	0	7	7	3.50	18.42	-	-	-	-
P Lever	4	1	0	5	5	5.00	38.46	-	-	1	-
CC Lewis	9	6	2	81	33	20.25	142.10	-	-	4	-
VJ Marks	7	3	0	18	8	6.00	47.36	-	-	2	-
PJ Martin	5	4	2	6	3	3.00	40.00	-	-	-	-
G Miller	1	0	-	-	-	-	-	-	-	-	-
AD Mullally	5	2	1	1	1*	1.00	12.50	-	-	-	-
CM Old	9	7	2	91	51*	18.20	119.73	-	1	2	-
DR Pringle	11	7	2	50	18*	10.00	66.66	-	-	2	-
DW Randall	5	5	1	64	42*	16.00	70.32	-	-	1	-
DA Reeve	11	7	3	117	35	29.25	86.66	-	-	5	-
RT Robinson	7	7	0	142	55	20.28	55.90	-	1	1	-
RC Russell	6	4	0	27	12	6.75	41.53	-	-	7	1
GC Small	13	4	1	8	5	2.66	34.78	-	-	-	-

Name	Mat	I	NO	Runs	HS	Ave	SR	100	50	Ct	St
NMK Smith	3	3	1	69	31	34.50	78.40	-	-	1	-
RA Smith	10	10	2	293	91	36.62	62.87	-	2	4	-
JA Snow	3	1	0	2	2	2.00	14.28	-	-	-	-
AJ Stewart	25	22	1	606	88	28.85	61.52	-	4	21	2
CJ Tavare	7	7	0	212	58	30.28	49.07	-	1	2	-
RW Taylor	5	3	1	32	20*	16.00	37.64	-	-	4	-
GP Thorpe	11	10	3	379	89	54.14	73.73	-	3	11	-
ME Trescothick	5	5	0	116	58	23.20	77.33	-	1	2	-
PCR Tufnell	4	2	2	3	3*	-	60.00	-	-	-	-
DL Underwood	2	0	-	-	-	-	-	-	-	2	-
MP Vaughan	5	5	0	139	52	27.80	76.79	-	2	2	-
C White	7	5	1	92	35	23.00	98.92	-	-	1	-
RGD Willis	11	4	1	25	24	8.33	56.81	-	-	4	-
B Wood	3	2	0	83	77	41.50	52.86	-	1	-	-

ENGLAND BOWLING RECORDS

Name	Mat	O	M	R	W	Ave	Best	4w	5w	SR	Econ
PJW Allott	7	80.3	10	335	8	41.87	3-41	-	-	60.3	4.16
DL Amiss	4	-	-	-	-	-	-	-	-	-	-
JM Anderson	5	47	3	225	10	22.50	4-25	2	-	28.2	4.78
GG Arnold	3	29.4	7	70	3	23.33	1-15	-	-	59.3	2.35
MA Atherton	6	-	-	-	-	-	-	-	-	-	-
CWJ Athey	6	1	0	10	0	-	-	-	-	-	10.00
ID Austin	2	18.4	1	66	3	22.00	2-25	-	-	37.3	3.53
ID Blackwell	2	10	0	37	2	18.50	2-37	-	-	30.0	3.70
IT Botham	22	222	33	762	30	25.40	4-31	1	-	44.4	3.43
G Boycott	5	27	1	94	5	18.80	2-14	-	-	32.4	3.48
JM Brearley	5	-	-	-	-	-	-	-	-	-	-
BC Broad	3	1	0	6	0	-	-	-	-	-	6.00
AR Caddick	5	44	8	178	8	22.25	4-35	1	-	33.0	4.04
PD Collingwood	5	4	0	15	1	15.00	1-15	-	-	24.0	3.75
DG Cork	5	48	2	216	8	27.00	2-33	-	-	36.0	4.50
NG Cowans	1	12	3	31	2	15.50	2-31	-	-	36.0	2.58
RDB Croft	2	12	1	45	1	45.00	1-32	-	-	72.0	3.75
PAJ DeFreitas	22	187.5	30	742	29	25.58	3-28	-	-	38.8	3.95
MH Denness	4	-	-	-	-	-	-	-	-	-	-
GR Dilley	6	66	4	243	7	34.71	4-45	1	-	56.5	3.68
PR Downton	8	-	-	-	-	-	-	-	-	-	-
MA Ealham	5	50	5	191	10	19.10	2-28	-	-	30.0	3.82
PH Edmonds	3	26	3	73	3	24.33	2-40	-	-	52.0	2.80
JE Emburey	8	79	4	295	6	49.16	2-26	-	-	79.0	3.73
NH Fairbrother	19	-	-	-	-	-	-	-	-	-	-
KWR Fletcher	4	-	-	-	-	-	-	-	-	-	-
A Flintoff	10	66.4	9	236	9	26.22	2-15	-	-	44.4	3.54
NA Foster	7	70	1	313	9	34.77	3-47	-	-	46.6	4.47
G Fowler	7	-	-	-	-	-	-	-	-	-	-
ARC Fraser	3	30	2	111	1	111.00	1-27	-	-	180.0	3.70
MW Gatting	15	12	3	48	1	48.00	1-35	-	-	72.0	4.00
AF Giles	2	10	0	42	2	21.00	2-42	-	-	30.0	4.20
GA Gooch	21	23	2	115	1	115.00	1-42	-	-	138.0	5.00
D Gough	11	99.4	8	430	15	28.66	4-34	1	-	39.8	4.31
IJ Gould	7	-	-	-	-	-	-	-	-	-	-
DI Gower	12	-	-	-	-	-	-	-	-	-	-
AW Greig	4	31	2	89	6	14.83	4-45	1	-	31.0	2.87
FC Hayes	3	-	-	-	-	-	-	-	-	-	-
EE Hemmings	6	59.3	4	274	13	21.07	4-52	1	-	27.4	4.60

Name	Mat	O	M	R	W	Ave	Best	4w	5w	SR	Econ
M Hendrick	5	56	14	149	10	14.90	4-15	1	-	33.6	2.66
GA Hick	20	37.2	0	208	5	41.60	2-44	-	-	44.8	5.57
AJ Hollioake	3	18	0	90	1	90.00	1-21	-	-	108.0	5.00
N Hussain	9	-	-	-	-	-	-	-	-	-	-
RK Illingworth	10	98.1	6	424	12	35.33	3-33	-	-	49.0	4.31
RC Irani	2	14	0	58	3	19.33	3-30	-	-	28.0	4.14
JA Jameson	2	2	1	3	0	-	-	-	-	-	1.50
NV Knight	5	-	-	-	-	-	-	-	-	-	-
APE Knott	4	-	-	-	-	-	-	-	-	-	-
AJ Lamb	19	1	0	3	0	-	-	-	-	-	3.00
W Larkins	2	2	0	21	0	-	-	-	-	-	10.50
P Lever	4	36	3	92	5	18.40	3-32	-	-	43.2	2.55
CC Lewis	9	50.4	5	214	7	30.57	4-30	1	-	43.4	4.22
VJ Marks	7	78	9	246	13	18.92	5-39	-	1	36.0	3.15
PJ Martin	5	44	2	198	6	33.00	3-33	-	-	44.0	4.50
G Miller	1	2	1	1	0	-	-	-	-	-	0.50
AD Mullally	5	50	6	176	10	17.60	4-37	1	-	30.0	3.52
CM Old	9	90.3	18	243	16	15.18	4-8	1	-	33.9	2.68
DR Pringle	11	90.4	15	366	8	45.75	3-8	-	-	68.0	4.03
DW Randall	5	-	-	-	-	-	-	-	-	-	-
DA Reeve	11	45.2	5	177	9	19.66	3-38	-	-	30.2	3.90
RT Robinson	7	-	-	-	-	-	-	-	-	-	-
RC Russell	6	-	-	-	-	-	-	-	-	-	-
GC Small	13	103	5	458	11	41.63	2-29	-	-	56.1	4.44
NMK Smith	3	25.3	2	96	4	24.00	3-29	-	-	38.2	3.76
RA Smith	10	-	-	-	-	-	-	-	-	-	-
JA Snow	3	36	8	65	6	10.83	4-11	1	-	36.0	1.80
AJ Stewart	25	-	-	-	-	-	-	-	-	-	-
CJ Tavare	7	-	-	-	-	-	-	-	-	-	-
RW Taylor	5	-	-	-	-	-	-	-	-	-	-
GP Thorpe	11	8	0	45	0	-	-	-	-	-	5.62
ME Trescothick	5	-	-	-	-	-	-	-	-	-	-
PCR Tufnell	4	28	2	133	3	44.33	2-36	-	-	56.0	4.75
DL Underwood	2	22	7	41	2	20.50	2-30	-	-	66.0	1.86
MP Vaughan	5	8	0	41	0	-	-	-	-	-	5.12
C White	7	51.3	6	202	9	22.44	3-33	-	-	34.3	3.92
RGD Willis	11	118.1	27	315	18	17.50	4-11	2	-	39.3	2.66
B Wood	3	12	5	14	0	-	-	-	-	-	1.16

AUSTRALIA
Winners: 1987, 1999, 2003
Runner's Up: 1975, 1996
Semi-Final Finish: None
Participants: All World Cups

Three-time winners Australia are the most successful team in the history of the World Cup. The defending champions have made a record five appearances in the final and their success percentage of 68.96 is higher than any other country.

Australia have only been out and out favourites in two editions of the tournament, at home defending the title in 1992 and then again as defending champions in South Africa in 2003. The weight of expectations proved to be too much in 1992 with the team crashing out of the tournament before the semi-final stage, but 2003 proved to be just the opposite. Australia emphatically justified their top billing and went undefeated through the course of the tournament. Never was the gulf between Australia and the rest of the cricket world felt more acutely than when Ricky Ponting held the trophy aloft in Johannesburg on March 23, 2003.

Best World Cup: 1999. Steve Waugh's 1999 win must rank as Australia's best World Cup win. In arguably the strongest edition of the tournament, the Australians found themselves in a heap of trouble, losing two of their first three matches, after which every single game became do or die. Steve Waugh's tough as nails team responded to the challenge and went undefeated for seven successive matches in order to lift the trophy. Along the way they also took part in what many regard as the greatest ever ODI match, the legendary semi-final against South Africa.

Worst World Cup: 1992. Defending the title in 1992, Allan Border's side got beat up by all and sundry at home, and in a tournament that they were supposed to win without any fuss.

AUSTRALIA RESULTS

		M	Won	Lost	Tied	NR
v	Bangladesh	1	1	0	0	0
v	Canada	1	1	0	0	0
v	England	5	3	2	0	0
v	India	9	7	2	0	0
v	Kenya	2	2	0	0	0
v	Namibia	1	1	0	0	0
v	Netherlands	1	1	0	0	0
v	New Zealand	6	4	2	0	0
v	Pakistan	7	4	3	0	0
v	South Africa	3	1	1	1	0
v	Scotland	1	1	0	0	0
v	Sri Lanka	5	4	1	0	0
v	West Indies	8	3	5	0	0
v	Zimbabwe	8	7	1	0	0
	Total	58	40	17	1	0

Success percentage: 68.96

AUSTRALIA BATTING RECORDS

Name	Mat	I	NO	Runs	HS	Ave	SR	100	50	Ct	St
MG Bevan	26	18	6	537	74*	44.75	64.38	-	5	6	-
AJ Bichel	8	3	2	117	64	117.00	83.57	-	1	2	-
DC Boon	16	16	1	815	100	54.33	73.75	2	5	2	-
AR Border	25	24	0	452	67	18.83	70.40	-	1	10	-
GS Chappell	5	5	0	129	50	25.80	75.43	-	1	3	-
IM Chappell	5	5	0	121	62	24.20	57.07	-	1	-	-
TM Chappell	4	4	0	139	110	34.75	77.65	1	-	1	-
GJ Cosier	3	2	0	6	6	3.00	28.57	-	-	1	-
AC Dale	2	1	1	3	3*	-	60.00	-	-	2	-
WM Darling	3	3	0	51	25	17.00	50.00	-	-	-	-
GC Dyer	8	4	0	50	27	12.50	116.27	-	-	9	2
G Dymock	3	2	1	14	10	14.00	46.66	-	-	-	-
R Edwards	5	4	1	166	80*	55.33	79.80	-	2	-	-
DW Fleming	16	4	2	12	8*	6.00	70.58	-	-	5	-
AC Gilchrist	20	20	0	632	99	31.60	94.18	-	6	33	2
JN Gillespie	4	1	1	6	6*	-	150.00	-	-	-	-
GJ Gilmour	2	2	1	42	28*	42.00	107.69	-	-	1	-
IJ Harvey	6	5	2	66	28*	22.00	76.74	-	-	-	-
ML Hayden	11	11	1	328	88	32.80	80.00	-	1	-	-
IA Healy	14	11	2	110	31	12.22	88.70	-	-	18	3
AMJ Hilditch	3	3	0	143	72	47.66	53.55	-	1	1	-
TG Hogan	4	4	2	24	11	12.00	80.00	-	-	2	-
GB Hogg	10	6	1	42	19*	8.40	67.74	-	-	4	-
RM Hogg	8	5	4	29	19*	29.00	67.44	-	-	1	-
DW Hookes	6	6	0	133	56	22.16	68.55	-	1	3	-
KJ Hughes	8	8	1	218	69	31.14	57.51	-	2	3	-
MG Hughes	1	1	1	0	0*	-	0.00	-	-	-	-
AG Hurst	3	2	2	6	3*	-	50.00	-	-	-	-
DM Jones	16	16	2	590	90	42.14	72.74	-	5	6	-
BP Julian	2	1	0	9	9	9.00	150.00	-	-	-	-
TJ Laughlin	1	1	0	8	8	8.00	36.36	-	-	-	-
SG Law	7	6	2	204	72	51.00	85.71	-	1	-	-
GF Lawson	4	4	0	24	16	6.00	68.57	-	-	-	-
B Lee	10	3	1	23	15*	11.50	65.71	-	-	8	-
S Lee	4	2	0	11	9	5.50	61.11	-	-	1	-
DS Lehmann	19	16	5	360	76	32.72	81.08	-	3	2	-

Name	Mat	I	NO	Runs	HS	Ave	SR	100	50	Ct	St
DK Lillee	9	3	1	19	16*	9.50	57.57	-	-	-	-
RB McCosker	5	5	0	120	73	24.00	45.45	-	1	-	-
CJ McDermott	17	11	0	43	14	3.90	74.13	-	-	4	-
GD McGrath	28	4	3	3	3*	3.00	60.00	-	-	4	-
KH MacLeay	4	4	0	19	9	4.75	67.85	-	-	1	-
JP Maher	2	2	0	35	26	17.50	58.33	-	-	3	-
AA Mallett	3	1	0	0	0	0.00	0.00	-	-	1	-
GR Marsh	13	13	1	579	126*	48.25	58.66	2	2	2	-
RW Marsh	11	11	4	220	52*	31.42	85.93	-	2	17	1
DR Martyn	12	10	3	352	88*	50.28	80.00	-	4	5	-
TBA May	6	3	1	16	15	8.00	123.07	-	-	1	-
TM Moody	18	16	5	329	57	29.90	73.27	-	3	5	-
JK Moss	1	1	0	7	7	7.00	43.75	-	-	2	-
SP O'Donnell	7	4	0	15	7	3.75	45.45	-	-	4	-
RT Ponting	28	27	3	998	140*	41.58	74.98	3	2	18	-
GD Porter	2	1	0	3	3	3.00	33.33	-	-	1	-
BA Reid	14	5	2	10	5*	3.33	24.39	-	-	4	-
PR Reiffel	11	6	3	28	13*	9.33	66.66	-	-	4	-
A Symonds	9	5	3	326	143*	163.00	90.55	1	2	4	-
MA Taylor	9	9	0	206	74	22.88	62.80	-	2	1	-
PL Taylor	9	7	3	34	17*	8.50	100.00	-	-	1	-
JR Thomson	8	5	2	51	21	17.00	102.00	-	-	1	-
A Turner	5	5	0	201	101	40.20	77.60	1	-	3	-
MRJ Veletta	4	4	1	136	48	45.33	112.39	-	-	-	-
MHN Walker	5	3	0	33	18	11.00	55.93	-	-	1	-
KD Walters	5	5	1	123	59	30.75	64.39	-	1	-	-
SK Warne	17	9	3	66	24	11.00	91.66	-	-	2	-
ME Waugh	22	22	3	1004	130	52.84	83.04	4	4	11	-
SR Waugh	33	30	10	978	120*	48.90	81.02	1	6	14	-
KC Wessels	12	12	2	405	85	40.50	53.78	-	4	8	-
MR Whitney	7	3	2	22	9*	22.00	43.13	-	-	-	-
GM Wood	5	5	1	144	73	36.00	56.25	-	1	1	-
KJ Wright	3	2	0	29	23	14.50	55.76	-	-	5	-
GN Yallop	9	9	3	247	66*	41.16	67.48	-	2	-	-
AK Zesers	2	2	2	10	8*	-	71.42	-	-	1	-

AUSTRALIA BOWLING RECORDS

Name	Mat	O	M	R	W	Ave	Best	4w	5w	SR	Econ
MG Bevan	26	50	2	237	4	59.25	2-35	-	-	75.0	4.74
AJ Bichel	8	57	7	197	16	12.31	7-20	-	1	21.3	3.45
DC Boon	16	1	0	17	0	-	-	-	-	-	17.00
AR Border	25	73	1	342	9	38.00	2-27	-	-	48.6	4.68
GS Chappell	5	18	0	88	0	-	-	-	-	-	4.88
IM Chappell	5	7	1	23	2	11.50	2-14	-	-	21.0	3.28
TM Chappell	4	19.4	0	98	4	24.50	3-47	-	-	29.5	4.98
GJ Cosier	3	27.2	4	95	5	19.00	3-54	-	-	32.8	3.47
AC Dale	2	15	3	53	1	53.00	1-18	-	-	90.0	3.53
WM Darling	3	-	-	-	-	-	-	-	-	-	-
GC Dyer	8	-	-	-	-	-	-	-	-	-	-
G Dymock	3	31	7	64	2	32.00	1-17	-	-	93.0	2.06
R Edwards	5	-	-	-	-	-	-	-	-	-	-
DW Fleming	16	133.2	12	583	26	22.42	5-36	-	1	30.7	4.37
AC Gilchrist	20	-	-	-	-	-	-	-	-	-	-
JN Gillespie	4	30	4	98	8	12.25	3-13	-	-	22.5	3.26
GJ Gilmour	2	24	8	62	11	5.63	6-14	-	2	13.0	2.58
IJ Harvey	6	36	3	157	8	19.62	4-58	1	-	27.0	4.36

Name	Mat	O	M	R	W	Ave	Best	4w	5w	SR	Econ
ML Hayden	11	-	-	-	-	-	-	-	-	-	-
IA Healy	14	-	-	-	-	-	-	-	-	-	-
AMJ Hilditch	3	-	-	-	-	-	-	-	-	-	-
TG Hogan	4	47	2	172	6	28.66	2-33	-	-	47.0	3.65
GB Hogg	10	75.4	4	322	13	24.76	3-46	-	-	34.9	4.25
RM Hogg	8	78	9	271	10	27.10	3-40	-	-	46.8	3.47
DW Hookes	6	-	-	-	-	-	-	-	-	-	-
KJ Hughes	8	-	-	-	-	-	-	-	-	-	-
MG Hughes	1	9	1	49	1	49.00	1-49	-	-	54.0	5.44
AG Hurst	3	32	6	119	7	17.00	5-21	-	1	27.4	3.71
DM Jones	16	1	0	5	0	-	-	-	-	-	5.00
BP Julian	2	17	2	80	0	-	-	-	-	-	4.70
TJ Laughlin	1	9.1	0	38	2	19.00	2-38	-	-	27.5	4.14
SG Law	7	5	0	23	0	-	-	-	-	-	4.60
GF Lawson	4	38	7	127	5	25.40	3-29	-	-	45.6	3.34
B Lee	10	83.1	9	394	22	17.90	5-42	-	1	22.6	4.73
S Lee	4	19	3	80	1	80.00	1-25	-	-	114.0	4.21
DS Lehmann	19	38	0	155	6	25.83	2-22	-	-	38.0	4.07
DK Lillee	9	98	8	400	12	33.33	5-34	-	1	49.0	4.08
RB McCosker	5	-	-	-	-	-	-	-	-	-	-
CJ McDermott	17	149	8	599	27	22.18	5-44	1	1	33.1	4.02
GD McGrath	28	245	37	935	45	20.77	7-15	-	2	32.6	3.81
KH MacLeay	4	44.5	6	163	8	20.37	6-39	-	1	33.6	3.63
JP Maher	2	-	-	-	-	-	-	-	-	-	-
AA Mallett	3	35	3	156	3	52.00	1-35	-	-	70.0	4.45
GR Marsh	13	-	-	-	-	-	-	-	-	-	-
RW Marsh	11	-	-	-	-	-	-	-	-	-	-
DR Martyn	12	6	0	46	0	-	-	-	-	-	7.66
TBA May	6	44	1	213	4	53.25	2-29	-	-	66.0	4.84
TM Moody	18	102	7	460	14	32.85	3-25	-	-	43.7	4.50
JK Moss	1	-	-	-	-	-	-	-	-	-	-
SP O'Donnell	7	60.4	6	261	9	29.00	4-39	1	-	40.4	4.30
RT Ponting	28	-	-	-	-	-	-	-	-	-	-
GD Porter	2	18	5	33	3	11.00	2-13	-	-	36.0	1.83
BA Reid	14	122.4	10	512	9	56.88	2-38	-	-	81.7	4.17
PR Reiffel	11	93	6	401	12	33.41	3-55	-	-	46.5	4.31
A Symonds	9	27	1	123	2	61.50	2-7	-	-	81.0	4.55
MA Taylor	9	-	-	-	-	-	-	-	-	-	-
PL Taylor	9	47.4	1	218	6	36.33	2-14	-	-	47.6	4.57
JR Thomson	8	76.5	10	290	7	41.42	3-51	-	-	65.8	3.77
A Turner	5	-	-	-	-	-	-	-	-	-	-
MRJ Veletta	4	-	-	-	-	-	-	-	-	-	-
MHN Walker	5	57.2	10	210	6	35.00	3-22	-	-	57.3	3.66
KD Walters	5	17	1	85	1	85.00	1-29	-	-	102.0	5.00
SK Warne	17	162.5	16	624	32	19.50	4-29	4	-	30.5	3.83
ME Waugh	22	62	1	313	5	62.60	3-38	-	-	74.4	5.04
SR Waugh	33	173.1	7	814	27	30.14	3-36	-	-	38.4	4.70
KC Wessels	12	-	-	-	-	-	-	-	-	-	-
MR Whitney	7	66	12	215	9	23.88	4-34	1	-	44.0	3.25
GM Wood	5	-	-	-	-	-	-	-	-	-	-
KJ Wright	3	-	-	-	-	-	-	-	-	-	-
GN Yallop	9	22	0	110	3	36.66	2-28	-	-	44.0	5.00
AK Zesers	2	15	1	74	1	74.00	1-37	-	-	90.0	4.93

SOUTH AFRICA
Winners: Never
Runner's Up: Never
Semi-Final Finish: 1992, 1999
Participants: 1992 and onwards

South Africa were banned from playing any international cricket through the 1970s and 1980s due to apartheid. As a result of the country's sporting isolation, their maiden World Cup appearance wasn't until the 1992 tournament, which would mark the first time that most cricket teams – not to mention an entire generation of fans – would see the Proteas in action. The world was stunned to find a team that walked into international cricket from the cold and immediately established itself as a bonafide contender to be the best in the world. The South Africans lost a controversial semi-final to England that year and then choked in the 1996 quarter-final against the West Indies, when they had been favourites for the trophy in the eyes of many. More heartbreak followed with South Africa's inability to overcome Australia in the 1999 semi-final, in the tournament that Hansie Cronje's men were widely expected to win. And then there was the entirely self-inflicted wound four years later on home soil, where South Africa's miscalculation of the Duckworth-Lewis formula prevented them from progressing to the next round. Any insinuation of South Africa being chokers is however denied by the team quite strenuously and, it must be said, with a straight face.

Best World Cup: 1999. In a tight World Cup where Australia and Pakistan were also considered viable contenders, South Africa were seen as being a nose in front. They played wonderful cricket in the tournament, with Cronje as captain and Bob Woolmer as coach forming a potent duo. All-rounder Lance Klusener set the tournament alight with his ferocious hitting and it was the stuff of Greek tragedy that blade in hand, it was Klusener alone who was left standing, as the Australians denied South Africa.

Worst World Cup: 2003. A strong South Africa failed to make it out of the first round of the tournament; an utter humiliation considering that they were the host nation. The captain Shaun Pollock was scapegoated and subsequently lost the captaincy.

SOUTH AFRICA RESULTS		M	Won	Lost	Tied	NR
v	Australia	3	1	1	1	0
v	Bangladesh	1	1	0	0	0
v	Canada	1	1	0	0	0
v	England	4	2	2	0	0
v	India	2	2	0	0	0
v	Kenya	2	2	0	0	0
v	Netherlands	1	1	0	0	0
v	New Zealand	4	2	2	0	0
v	Pakistan	3	3	0	0	0
v	Sri Lanka	3	1	1	1	0
v	United Arab Emirates	1	1	0	0	0
v	West Indies	3	1	2	0	0
v	Zimbabwe	2	1	1	0	0
	Total	30	19	9	2	0

Success Percentage: 63.33

SOUTH AFRICA BATTING RECORDS

Name	Mat	I	NO	Runs	HS	Ave	SR	100	50	Ct	St
PR Adams	2	1	0	10	10	10.00	71.42	-	-	-	-
N Boje	5	2	1	54	29	54.00	87.09	-	-	2	-
T Bosch	1	0	-	-	-	-	-	-	-	-	-
MV Boucher	15	12	4	204	49	25.50	73.91	-	-	22	-
WJ Cronje	23	20	4	476	78	29.75	80.67	-	2	10	-
DJ Cullinan	15	15	3	471	69	39.25	67.67	-	3	11	-
PS de Villiers	1	1	0	12	12	12.00	109.09	-	-	-	-
HH Dippenaar	6	3	0	108	80	36.00	68.35	-	1	3	-
AA Donald	25	5	2	13	7	4.33	32.50	-	-	3	-
S Elworthy	8	3	0	25	23	8.33	53.19	-	-	-	-
HH Gibbs	15	15	2	725	143	55.76	85.49	2	4	3	-
AJ Hall	3	1	1	22	22*	-	200.00	-	-	-	-
O Henry	1	1	0	11	11	11.00	84.61	-	-	-	-
AC Hudson	12	12	0	571	161	47.58	76.95	1	4	2	-
JH Kallis	19	16	4	438	96	36.50	66.76	-	4	4	-
G Kirsten	21	21	4	806	188*	47.41	75.46	1	5	9	-
PN Kirsten	8	8	2	410	90	68.33	66.55	-	4	2	-
L Klusener	14	11	8	372	57	124.00	121.17	-	3	2	-
AP Kuiper	9	8	1	113	36	16.14	71.51	-	-	3	-
CK Langeveldt	1	0	-	-	-	-	-	-	-	-	-
BM McMillan	15	9	4	145	33*	29.00	74.74	-	-	8	-
CR Matthews	6	2	2	17	9*	-	68.00	-	-	1	-
M Ntini	6	2	0	14	14	7.00	175.00	-	-	-	-
SJ Palframan	6	3	0	45	28	15.00	70.31	-	-	8	-
RJ Peterson	1	0	-	-	-	-	-	-	-	1	-
SM Pollock	21	13	1	216	52	18.00	78.26	-	1	10	-
MW Pringle	7	1	1	5	5*	-	83.33	-	-	1	-
JN Rhodes	24	20	3	354	43	20.82	88.05	-	-	7	-
DJ Richardson	9	5	2	66	28	22.00	66.66	-	-	14	1
MW Rushmere	3	3	0	49	35	16.33	47.57	-	-	1	-
GC Smith	3	3	0	121	63	40.33	85.81	-	1	2	-

Name	Mat	I	NO	Runs	HS	Ave	SR	100	50	Ct	St
RP Snell	9	4	2	24	11*	12.00	120.00	-	-	1	-
PL Symcox	4	2	0	25	24	12.50	104.16	-	-	-	-
KC Wessels	12	12	2	405	85	40.50	53.78	-	4	8	-
M Zondeki	3	1	1	1	1*	-	100.00	-	-	2	-

SOUTH AFTRICA BOWLING RECORDS

Name	Mat	O	M	R	W	Ave	Best	4w	5w	SR	Econ
PR Adams	2	18	0	87	3	29.00	2-45	-	-	36.0	4.83
N Boje	5	22	1	144	1	144.00	1-44	-	-	132.0	6.54
T Bosch	1	2.3	0	19	0	-	-	-	-	-	7.60
MV Boucher	15	-	-	-	-	-	-	-	-	-	-
WJ Cronje	23	74	2	329	8	41.12	2-17	-	-	55.5	4.44
DJ Cullinan	15	2	0	7	0	-	-	-	-	-	3.50
PS de Villiers	1	7	1	27	2	13.50	2-27	-	-	21.0	3.85
HH Dippenaar	6	-	-	-	-	-	-	-	-	-	-
AA Donald	25	218.5	14	913	38	24.02	4-17	2	-	34.5	4.17
S Elworthy	8	72	9	262	10	26.20	2-20	-	-	43.2	3.63
HH Gibbs	15	-	-	-	-	-	-	-	-	-	-
AJ Hall	3	23	3	103	5	20.60	2-15	-	-	27.6	4.47
O Henry	1	10	0	31	1	31.00	1-31	-	-	60.0	3.10
AC Hudson	12	-	-	-	-	-	-	-	-	-	-
JH Kallis	19	120	9	510	11	46.36	3-26	-	-	65.4	4.25
G Kirsten	21	3	1	9	0	-	-	-	-	-	3.00
PN Kirsten	8	18	1	87	5	17.40	3-31	-	-	21.6	4.83
L Klusener	14	100.5	7	487	22	22.13	5-21	1	1	27.5	4.82
AP Kuiper	9	41	0	235	9	26.11	3-40	-	-	27.3	5.73
CK Langeveldt	1	5	0	24	0	-	-	-	-	-	4.80
BM McMillan	15	116	12	433	17	25.47	3-11	-	-	40.9	3.73
CR Matthews	6	59.3	2	226	7	32.28	2-30	-	-	51.0	3.79
M Ntini	6	52.1	6	176	10	17.60	4-24	1	-	31.3	3.37
SJ Palframan	6	-	-	-	-	-	-	-	-	-	-
RJ Peterson	1	6	0	21	0	-	-	-	-	-	3.50
SM Pollock	21	185	27	674	23	29.30	5-36	-	1	48.2	3.64
MW Pringle	7	57	6	236	8	29.50	4-11	1	-	42.7	4.14
JN Rhodes	24	-	-	-	-	-	-	-	-	-	-
DJ Richardson	9	-	-	-	-	-	-	-	-	-	-
MW Rushmere	3	-	-	-	-	-	-	-	-	-	-
GC Smith	3	1	0	10	0	-	-	-	-	-	10.00
RP Snell	9	72.5	10	310	8	38.75	3-42	-	-	54.6	4.25
PL Symcox	4	40	2	149	6	24.83	2-22	-	-	40.0	3.72
KC Wessels	12	-	-	-	-	-	-	-	-	-	-
M Zondeki	3	20	2	76	2	38.00	1-17	-	-	60.0	3.80

Graeme Smith hangs on to Makhaya Ntini: The Proteas stars will be keen to dispel the notion that South Africa have a habit of choking in the World Cup.

WEST INDIES
Winners: 1975, 1979
Runner's Up: 1983
Semi-Final Finish: 1996
Participants: All World Cups

Cricket's first World Champions, the West Indies won consecutive tournaments in 1975 and 1979. Going into the 1983 edition, they were considered the heavy favourites to win the tournament and were also among the legitimate contenders for the 1987 World Cup. Their fall from grace began in 1992, when the team embarked for the World Cup, having shed some stalwarts of old, including the legendary Viv Richards. Although the West Indies made it to the semi-final in 1996, this was considered a surprise and their failure in the match was predictable. In spite of their largely non-threatening presence in the past four World Cups, the West Indies still own a win percentage that is second only to Australia courtesy of their form in the first three editions of the tournament.

Best World Cup: 1975. Going undefeated through the inaugural tournament, the West Indies showed the world that they were the kings of cricket. In the final against a tough Australian team, Clive Lloyd played a captain's innings, a scorching 102 off only 85 deliveries that would typify how the West Indies would play the game through the 1970s and 1980s. Fittingly it was Lloyd who held that first World Cup trophy aloft at the end of the day's play.

Worst World Cup: 2003. This was supposed to be the tournament where the West Indies turned things around, with Brian Lara returning to the fold and bowler Vasbert Drakes, with his extensive experience in South African conditions, expected to make a significant contribution. Aside from a win against the hosts, the West Indies were not able to challenge the other big fish in their pool. What's more, Canada's John Davison embarrassed the West Indies bowling attack, caning them for a belligerent century.

WEST INDIES RESULTS

		M	Won	Lost	Tied	NR
v	Australia	8	5	3	0	0
v	Bangladesh	2	1	0	0	1
v	Canada	1	1	0	0	0
v	England	4	1	3	0	0
v	India	6	3	3	0	0
v	Kenya	2	1	1	0	0
v	New Zealand	5	3	2	0	0
v	Pakistan	7	5	2	0	0
v	South Africa	3	2	1	0	0
v	Scotland	1	1	0	0	0
v	Sri Lanka	5	4	1	0	0
v	Zimbabwe	4	4	0	0	0
	Total	48	31	16	0	1

Success Percentage: 65.95

WEST INDIES BATTING RECORDS

Name	Mat	I	NO	Runs	HS	Ave	SR	100	50	Ct	St
JC Adams	9	8	3	120	53*	24.00	49.18	-	1	7	1
CEL Ambrose	17	10	2	48	15*	6.00	53.93	-	-	1	-
KLT Arthurton	14	13	1	241	58*	20.08	62.43	-	2	2	-
SFAF Bacchus	8	5	1	157	80*	39.25	62.54	-	1	-	-
EAE Baptiste	1	1	0	14	14	14.00	70.00	-	-	1	-
WKM Benjamin	13	10	5	69	24*	13.80	85.18	-	-	4	-
CA Best	2	2	0	23	18	11.50	51.11	-	-	1	-
IR Bishop	6	4	1	35	17	11.66	36.84	-	-	1	-
KD Boyce	5	2	0	41	34	20.50	95.34	-	-	-	-
CO Browne	5	4	0	64	26	16.00	64.64	-	-	3	2
HR Bryan	2	0	-	-	-	-	-	-	-	1	-
SL Campbell	9	8	0	112	47	14.00	44.97	-	-	2	-
S Chanderpaul	17	15	2	541	80	41.61	66.05	-	5	5	-
PT Collins	3	1	1	1	1*	-	100.00	-	-	-	-
CD Collymore	1	1	1	0	0*	-	-	-	-	-	-
CEH Croft	4	1	1	0	0*	-	0.00	-	-	-	-
CE Cuffy	1	1	0	1	1	1.00	12.50	-	-	1	-
AC Cummins	6	2	1	11	6	11.00	32.35	-	-	-	-
WW Daniel	3	1	1	16	16*	-	133.33	-	-	-	-
WW Davis	5	1	1	0	0*	-	0.00	-	-	-	-
M Dillon	10	5	0	28	10	5.60	54.90	-	-	4	-
VC Drakes	6	4	2	42	25	21.00	60.00	-	-	1	-
PJL Dujon	14	9	1	112	46	14.00	46.86	-	-	19	1
RC Fredericks	5	5	0	116	58	23.20	64.08	-	1	2	-
J Garner	8	5	3	52	37	26.00	65.82	-	-	4	-
CH Gayle	6	6	0	206	119	34.33	69.83	1	1	3	-
LR Gibbs	1	0	-	-	-	-	-	-	-	-	-
OD Gibson	3	2	0	7	6	3.50	100.00	-	-	1	-
HA Gomes	8	7	3	258	78	64.50	55.96	-	3	3	-
CG Greenidge	15	15	2	591	106*	45.46	59.15	2	4	1	-
RA Harper	14	13	2	118	24	10.72	76.12	-	-	6	-
DL Haynes	25	25	2	854	105	37.13	57.50	1	3	12	-
WW Hinds	6	6	0	108	64	18.00	80.59	-	1	-	-
RIC Holder	2	2	0	5	5	2.50	41.66	-	-	-	-
VA Holder	5	2	1	22	16	22.00	73.33	-	-	2	-
MA Holding	11	5	0	36	20	7.20	61.01	-	-	5	-
CL Hooper	20	18	4	261	63	18.64	70.73	-	1	13	-
RD Jacobs	11	8	4	270	80*	67.50	54.00	-	3	21	1
BD Julien	5	3	2	48	26*	48.00	58.53	-	-	-	-

Brian Lara: 956 World Cup runs at an average of 43.45 and a strike rate of 87.70

Name	Mat	I	NO	Runs	HS	Ave	SR	100	50	Ct	St
AI Kallicharran	9	8	1	251	78	35.85	70.90	-	2	6	-
RB Kanhai	5	4	2	109	55	54.50	55.05	-	1	3	-
CL King	4	3	0	132	86	44.00	121.10	-	1	2	-
RD King	4	1	0	1	1	1.00	3.33	-	-	-	-
BC Lara	25	25	3	956	116	43.45	87.70	2	6	11	-
JJC Lawson	1	0	-	-	-	-	-	-	-	-	-
CH Lloyd	17	11	2	393	102	43.66	84.88	1	2	12	-
AL Logie	15	13	2	282	65*	25.63	91.85	-	2	4	-
NAM McLean	1	1	0	5	5	5.00	71.42	-	-	-	-
MD Marshall	11	7	0	40	18	5.71	38.09	-	-	-	-
DL Murray	9	5	2	122	61*	40.66	73.49	-	1	16	-
BP Patterson	7	2	2	4	4*	-	33.33	-	-	2	-
RL Powell	7	6	1	117	50	23.40	130.00	-	1	4	-
IVA Richards	23	21	5	1013	181	63.31	85.05	3	5	9	-
RB Richardson	20	20	3	639	110	37.58	62.89	1	4	6	-
AME Roberts	16	8	3	85	37*	17.00	54.14	-	-	-	-
MN Samuels	1	1	0	14	14	14.00	82.35	-	-	-	-
RR Sarwan	5	5	3	209	75	104.50	95.87	-	1	1	-
PV Simmons	13	11	0	336	110	30.54	74.66	1	2	3	-
CA Walsh	17	8	3	37	9*	7.40	75.51	-	-	3	-
D Williams	8	6	2	52	32*	13.00	74.28	-	-	11	3
SC Williams	4	3	1	17	14*	8.50	48.57	-	-	5	-

WEST INDIES BOWLING RECORDS

Name	Mat	O	M	R	W	Ave	Best	4w	5w	SR	Econ
JC Adams	9	30	0	167	3	55.66	3-53	-	-	60.0	5.56
CEL Ambrose	17	164.3	20	499	24	20.79	3-28	-	-	41.1	3.03
KLT Arthurton	14	36	0	186	3	62.00	2-40	-	-	72.0	5.16
SFAF Bacchus	8	-	-	-	-	-	-	-	-	-	-
EAE Baptiste	1	8	1	33	0	-	-	-	-	-	4.12

Name	Mat	O	M	R	W	Ave	Best	4w	5w	SR	Econ
WKM Benjamin	13	123	10	515	14	36.78	3-27	-	-	52.7	4.18
CA Best	2	-	-	-	-	-	-	-	-	-	-
IR Bishop	6	49	6	194	3	64.66	2-35	-	-	98.0	3.95
KD Boyce	5	52	3	185	10	18.50	4-50	1	-	31.2	3.55
CO Browne	5	-	-	-	-	-	-	-	-	-	-
HR Bryan	2	15.2	0	59	3	19.66	2-29	-	-	30.6	3.84
SL Campbell	9	-	-	-	-	-	-	-	-	-	-
S Chanderpaul	17	2	0	6	0	-	-	-	-	-	3.00
PT Collins	3	26	1	151	2	75.50	1-35	-	-	78.0	5.80
CD Collymore	1	-	-	-	-	-	-	-	-	-	-
CEH Croft	4	43	3	140	8	17.50	3-29	-	-	32.2	3.25
CE Cuffy	1	8	0	31	1	31.00	1-31	-	-	48.0	3.87
AC Cummins	6	59	1	246	12	20.50	4-33	1	-	29.5	4.16
WW Daniel	3	24	6	84	3	28.00	3-28	-	-	48.0	3.50
WW Davis	5	54.3	6	206	8	25.75	7-51	-	1	40.8	3.77
M Dillon	10	86	4	332	13	25.53	4-46	1	-	39.6	3.86
VC Drakes	6	51.5	7	208	16	13.00	5-33	-	2	19.4	4.01
PJL Dujon	14	-	-	-	-	-	-	-	-	-	-
RC Fredericks	5	-	-	-	-	-	-	-	-	-	-
J Garner	8	90	12	289	13	22.23	5-38	-	1	41.5	3.21
CH Gayle	6	34	2	168	4	42.00	2-60	-	-	51.0	4.94
LR Gibbs	1	4	0	17	0	-	-	-	-	-	4.25
OD Gibson	3	19.4	1	90	1	90.00	1-27	-	-	118.0	4.57
HA Gomes	8	74	4	304	9	33.77	2-46	-	-	49.3	4.10
CG Greenidge	15	-	-	-	-	-	-	-	-	-	-
RA Harper	14	132	10	488	18	27.11	4-47	1	-	44.0	3.69
DL Haynes	25	-	-	-	-	-	-	-	-	-	-
WW Hinds	6	19.5	0	88	7	12.57	3-35	-	-	17.0	4.43
RIC Holder	2	-	-	-	-	-	-	-	-	-	-
VA Holder	5	43.2	4	184	5	36.80	3-30	-	-	52.0	4.24
MA Holding	11	115.5	16	341	20	17.05	4-33	1	-	34.7	2.94
CL Hooper	20	154	3	659	18	36.61	3-42	-	-	51.3	4.27
RD Jacobs	11	-	-	-	-	-	-	-	-	-	-
BD Julien	5	60	11	177	10	17.70	4-20	2	-	36.0	2.95
AI Kallicharran	9	-	-	-	-	-	-	-	-	-	-
RB Kanhai	5	-	-	-	-	-	-	-	-	-	-
CL King	4	32	2	128	2	64.00	1-36	-	-	96.0	4.00
RD King	4	31.3	4	95	8	11.87	3-30	-	-	23.6	3.01
BC Lara	25	-	-	-	-	-	-	-	-	-	-
JJC Lawson	1	8	0	16	2	8.00	2-16	-	-	24.0	2.00
CH Lloyd	17	36	4	125	3	41.66	1-31	-	-	72.0	3.47
AL Logie	15	-	-	-	-	-	-	-	-	-	-
NAM McLean	1	6	0	38	0	-	-	-	-	-	6.33
MD Marshall	11	113	13	349	14	24.92	3-28	-	-	48.4	3.08
DL Murray	9	-	-	-	-	-	-	-	-	-	-
BP Patterson	7	66	2	278	15	18.53	3-31	-	-	26.4	4.21
RL Powell	7	7	2	38	1	38.00	1-8	-	-	42.0	5.42
IVA Richards	23	83	2	345	10	34.50	3-41	-	-	49.8	4.15
RB Richardson	20	4	0	24	0	-	-	-	-	-	6.00
AME Roberts	16	170.1	29	552	26	21.23	3-32	-	-	39.2	3.24
MN Samuels	1	-	-	-	-	-	-	-	-	-	-
RR Sarwan	5	-	-	-	-	-	-	-	-	-	-
PV Simmons	13	59	6	227	8	28.37	2-33	-	-	44.2	3.84
CA Walsh	17	158	23	547	27	20.25	4-25	2	-	35.1	3.46
D Williams	8	-	-	-	-	-	-	-	-	-	-
SC Williams	4	-	-	-	-	-	-	-	-	-	-

NEW ZEALAND
Winners: Never
Runner's Up: Never
Semi-Final Finish: 1975, 1979, 1992, 1999
Participants: All World Cups

Despite never making it to a World Cup final, New Zealand have a healthy showing when it comes to reaching the semi-final stage of the tournament. They have a losing record only to Australia, West Indies and Pakistan – teams which ultimately account for six of the eight World Championships. Although New Zealand's performances have generally been quite good, the impression has been of a team punching above its weight class. New Zealand have never entered a World Cup tournament as favourites and other than in 1992, were not expected to win any of their semi-final clashes.

Best World Cup: 1992. Martin Crowe threw opposition captains for a loop when he decided to open the bowling with spinner Dipak Patel. Crowe's own form with the bat was excellent, and New Zealand beat team after team until the Pakistanis somehow managed to get the better of them. That set up a semi-final clash between the two teams and based on the overall form of both sides in the tournament, New Zealand were expected to win the game. Even though the Kiwis lost the match and exited the tournament, World Cup 1992 is still remembered for Crowe's brilliance and his team's golden run.

Worst World Cup: 1987. New Zealand only managed to win their matches against Zimbabwe – and even those wins came with difficulty. Without Richard Hadlee, the bowling looked toothless, as evidenced by Zimbabwe's Dave Houghton, who struck a memorable 142 off the Kiwi attack, and perhaps more notably by India's Sunil Gavaskar. The man who played the most infamous knock in World Cup history (36 not out in 60 overs in 1975), struck his only ODI hundred, a blazing, unbeaten 103 off only 88 balls in a match against New Zealand.

NEW ZEALAND RESULTS

		M	Won	Lost	Tied	NR
v	Australia	6	2	4	0	0
v	Bangladesh	2	2	0	0	0
v	Canada	1	1	0	0	0
v	East Africa	1	1	0	0	0
v	England	6	3	3	0	0
v	India	7	4	3	0	0
v	Netherlands	1	1	0	0	0
v	Pakistan	7	1	6	0	0
v	South Africa	4	2	2	0	0
v	Scotland	1	1	0	0	0
v	Sri Lanka	5	3	2	0	0
v	United Arab Emirates	1	1	0	0	0
v	West Indies	5	2	3	0	0
v	Zimbabwe	5	4	0	0	1
	Total	52	28	23	0	1

Success Percentage: 54.90

NEW ZEALAND BATTING RECORDS

Name	Mat	I	NO	Runs	HS	Ave	SR	100	50	Ct	St
AR Adams	7	5	1	90	36	22.50	118.42	-	-	1	-
GI Allott	9	1	1	0	0*	-	0.00	-	-	1	-
NJ Astle	22	22	2	403	102*	20.15	70.45	2	1	9	-
SE Bond	8	3	2	5	3	5.00	23.80	-	-	3	-
SL Boock	4	3	2	19	12	19.00	118.75	-	-	2	-
JG Bracewell	7	7	2	80	34	16.00	84.21	-	-	1	-
CE Bulfin	1	0	-	-	-	-	-	-	-	-	-
MG Burgess	4	2	0	45	35	22.50	72.58	-	-	2	-
BL Cairns	11	9	0	43	14	4.77	84.31	-	-	4	-
CL Cairns	28	24	7	565	60	33.23	82.60	-	3	16	-
EJ Chatfield	13	8	7	45	19*	45.00	44.11	-	-	2	-
RO Collinge	4	2	0	8	6	4.00	80.00	-	-	1	-
JV Coney	10	8	2	244	66*	40.66	54.83	-	2	4	-
JJ Crowe	8	8	1	220	88*	31.42	77.19	-	1	4	-
MD Crowe	21	21	5	880	100*	55.00	83.49	1	8	8	-
BA Edgar	8	8	1	194	84*	27.71	43.49	-	1	5	-
SP Fleming	23	23	2	722	134*	34.38	73.00	1	2	10	-
LK Germon	6	6	3	191	89	63.66	84.88	-	1	2	1
MJ Greatbatch	7	7	0	313	73	44.71	87.92	-	3	4	-
BG Hadlee	1	1	0	19	19	19.00	24.67	-	-	-	-
DR Hadlee	4	3	1	28	20	14.00	47.45	-	-	-	-
RJ Hadlee	13	10	1	149	42	16.55	61.06	-	-	3	-
CZ Harris	28	20	5	431	130	28.73	68.84	1	-	7	-
MN Hart	1	1	0	0	0	0.00	0.00	-	-	-	-
BF Hastings	4	4	1	76	34	25.33	54.67	-	-	3	-
MJ Horne	8	8	0	199	74	24.87	56.21	-	1	1	-
PA Horne	1	1	0	18	18	18.00	51.42	-	-	-	-
GP Howarth	11	11	1	374	76	37.40	65.72	-	4	2	-
HJ Howarth	4	2	1	1	1*	1.00	12.50	-	-	2	-
AH Jones	13	13	2	416	78	37.81	61.81	-	4	3	-
RJ Kennedy	3	1	0	2	2	2.00	66.66	-	-	1	-
GR Larsen	19	6	3	76	37	25.33	59.37	-	-	7	-
RT Latham	7	7	0	136	60	19.42	62.38	-	1	3	-
WK Lees	8	6	1	88	26	17.60	80.00	-	-	10	-
BB McCullum	7	3	1	41	36*	20.50	53.94	-	-	9	-
BJ McKechnie	8	4	2	45	27	22.50	40.17	-	-	2	-
CD McMillan	15	15	0	278	75	18.53	60.69	-	1	4	-

Name	Mat	I	NO	Runs	HS	Ave	SR	100	50	Ct	St
KD Mills	1	0	-	-	-	-	-	-	-	-	-
DK Morrison	11	4	3	27	12	27.00	50.94	-	-	2	-
JFM Morrison	6	5	0	102	55	20.40	45.73	-	1	3	-
DJ Nash	13	6	3	50	21*	16.66	51.02	-	-	3	-
JDP Oram	8	3	0	35	23	11.66	46.66	-	-	3	-
JM Parker	4	4	0	71	66	17.75	75.53	-	1	-	-
AC Parore	14	11	2	206	55	22.88	85.12	-	1	7	-
DN Patel	17	11	2	97	40	10.77	74.61	-	-	3	-
KR Rutherford	14	12	2	416	75	41.60	70.86	-	4	5	-
MS Sinclair	1	0	-	-	-	-	-	-	-	-	-
IDS Smith	17	13	3	138	29	13.80	132.69	-	-	9	-
MC Snedden	9	8	0	218	64	27.25	63.00	-	1	2	-
CM Spearman	6	6	0	191	78	31.83	100.00	-	2	1	-
LW Stott	1	0	-	-	-	-	-	-	-	1	-
SB Styris	8	7	2	268	141	53.60	101.90	1	1	5	-
SA Thomson	5	5	2	101	31*	33.66	68.70	-	-	3	-
GB Troup	3	1	1	3	3*	-	100.00	-	-	-	-
DR Tuffey	2	2	0	15	11	7.50	93.75	-	-	-	-
GM Turner	14	14	4	612	171*	61.20	64.01	2	2	2	-
RG Twose	15	15	5	493	92	49.30	74.35	-	4	5	-
DL Vettori	7	3	0	36	13	12.00	48.64	-	-	-	-
L Vincent	4	3	0	17	9	5.66	48.57	-	-	2	-
KJ Wadsworth	4	4	0	68	25	17.00	75.55	-	-	3	1
W Watson	14	5	4	29	12*	29.00	55.76	-	-	2	-
JG Wright	18	18	0	493	69	27.38	57.19	-	3	4	-

NEW ZEALAND BOWLING RECORDS

Name	Mat	O	M	R	W	Ave	Best	4w	5w	SR	Econ
AR Adams	7	57.4	3	347	10	34.70	4-44	1	-	34.6	6.01
GI Allott	9	87.4	7	325	20	16.25	4-37	2	-	26.3	3.70
NJ Astle	22	87.3	2	418	11	38.00	3-34	-	-	47.7	4.77
SE Bond	8	78	12	305	17	17.94	6-23	-	1	27.5	3.91
SL Boock	4	32.4	2	156	4	39.00	2-42	-	-	49.0	4.77
JG Bracewell	7	59	2	310	1	310.00	1-66	-	-	354.0	5.25
CE Bulfin	1	6	0	31	0	-	-	-	-	-	5.16
MG Burgess	4	-	-	-	-	-	-	-	-	-	-
BL Cairns	11	115.2	16	436	14	31.14	3-36	-	-	49.4	3.78
CL Cairns	28	146.4	9	755	18	41.94	3-19	-	-	48.8	5.14
EJ Chatfield	13	131.3	16	524	14	37.42	2-24	-	-	56.3	3.98
RO Collinge	4	48	13	137	6	22.83	3-28	-	-	48.0	2.85
JV Coney	10	89	7	303	12	25.25	3-28	-	-	44.5	3.40
JJ Crowe	8	-	-	-	-	-	-	-	-	-	-
MD Crowe	21	18	2	116	1	116.00	1-15	-	-	108.0	6.44
BA Edgar	8	-	-	-	-	-	-	-	-	-	-
SP Fleming	23	2	0	8	1	8.00	1-8	-	-	12.0	4.00
LK Germon	6	-	-	-	-	-	-	-	-	-	-
MJ Greatbatch	7	1	0	5	0	-	-	-	-	-	5.00
BG Hadlee	1	-	-	-	-	-	-	-	-	-	-
DR Hadlee	4	46	5	162	8	20.25	3-21	-	-	34.5	3.52
RJ Hadlee	13	146.1	38	421	22	19.13	5-25	-	1	39.8	2.88
CZ Harris	28	194.2	10	861	32	26.90	4-7	1	-	36.4	4.43
MN Hart	1	-	-	-	-	-	-	-	-	-	-
BF Hastings	4	-	-	-	-	-	-	-	-	-	-
MJ Horne	8	-	-	-	-	-	-	-	-	-	-
PA Horne	1	-	-	-	-	-	-	-	-	-	-
GP Howarth	11	-	-	-	-	-	-	-	-	-	-

Chris Cairns (left) and Chris Harris: The all-rounders share the record for the most appearances for New Zealand in the World Cup, with 28 caps each.

Name	Mat	O	M	R	W	Ave	Best	4w	5w	SR	Econ
HJ Howarth	4	40	5	148	5	29.60	3-29	-	-	48.0	3.70
AH Jones	13	12	0	52	2	26.00	2-42	-	-	36.0	4.33
RJ Kennedy	3	21	2	88	4	22.00	2-36	-	-	31.5	4.19
GR Larsen	19	170	12	599	18	33.27	3-16	-	-	56.6	3.52
RT Latham	7	23	0	136	1	136.00	1-35	-	-	138.0	5.91
WK Lees	8	-	-	-	-	-	-	-	-	-	-
BB McCullum	7	-	-	-	-	-	-	-	-	-	-
BJ McKechnie	8	89.5	9	304	13	23.38	3-24	-	-	41.4	3.38
CD McMillan	15	4	1	23	0	-	-	-	-	-	5.75
KD Mills	1	6	0	32	0	-	-	-	-	-	5.33
DK Morrison	11	79	2	396	8	49.50	3-42	-	-	59.2	5.01
JFM Morrison	6	8	0	31	0	-	-	-	-	-	3.87
DJ Nash	13	116	15	473	9	52.55	3-26	-	-	77.3	4.07
JDP Oram	8	70	8	295	14	21.07	4-52	1	-	30.0	4.21
JM Parker	4	-	-	-	-	-	-	-	-	-	-
AC Parore	14	-	-	-	-	-	-	-	-	-	-
DN Patel	17	140	9	556	13	42.76	3-36	-	-	64.6	3.97
KR Rutherford	14	1.4	0	11	0	-	-	-	-	-	6.60
MS Sinclair	1	-	-	-	-	-	-	-	-	-	-
IDS Smith	17	-	-	-	-	-	-	-	-	-	-
MC Snedden	9	81.5	6	455	10	45.50	2-36	-	-	49.1	5.56
CM Spearman	6	-	-	-	-	-	-	-	-	-	-
LW Stott	1	12	1	48	3	16.00	3-48	-	-	24.0	4.00
SB Styris	8	34.4	0	183	4	45.75	2-23	-	-	52.0	5.27
SA Thomson	5	42.3	2	197	5	39.40	3-20	-	-	51.0	4.63
GB Troup	3	32	3	104	4	26.00	2-36	-	-	48.0	3.25
DR Tuffey	2	15	1	77	1	77.00	1-41	-	-	90.0	5.13
GM Turner	14	-	-	-	-	-	-	-	-	-	-
RG Twose	15	13	0	77	0	-	-	-	-	-	5.92
DL Vettori	7	65	1	259	2	129.50	1-38	-	-	195.0	3.98
L Vincent	4	-	-	-	-	-	-	-	-	-	-
KJ Wadsworth	4	-	-	-	-	-	-	-	-	-	-
W Watson	14	132	14	571	19	30.05	3-37	-	-	41.6	4.32
JG Wright	18	-	-	-	-	-	-	-	-	-	-

INDIA
Winners: 1983
Runner's Up: 2003
Semi- Final Finish: 1987, 1996
Participants: All World Cups

Apart from the first two events when they were still finding their way in ODI cricket, India have always been a presence in World Cup tournaments. Even in 1992, when they failed to qualify for the semi-final, the win over Pakistan made their rivals' road to glory all the more difficult. In 1999, in spite of again not making the final four, the Indians boasted arguably the best batting line-up in the tournament. India's passionate fans have made headlines too for their extreme behaviour – a fan is known to have committed suicide when India lost their opening match in the 1987 World Cup to Australia. Despair can also quickly turn to anger, as the team found out when a slow start to what was ultimately a very good 2003 campaign, saw effigies of the players burned on the streets. Most notorious of all is undoubtedly the rioting in the 1996 semi-final match in Nagpur, when the hosts had to forfeit the match to Sri Lanka amid bonfires in the stands. At their best however, India's fans have given their team unparalleled support in the World Cup, often by virtue of their sheer numbers at the grounds.

Best World Cup: 1983. India's win in 1983 was the biggest upset in the history of the World Cup. Although the Indians had played well throughout the tournament, no one expected them to win the final against the mighty West Indies, who were the two time defending champions. India won the low-scoring match in style and planted the seeds that would a few short years later, make India the centre of the cricket universe.

Worst World Cup: 1979. India were unable to win a single match during the tournament. Most humiliating of all was the loss to Sri Lanka, who were still a few years away from gaining Test status.

INDIA RESULTS

		M	Won	Lost	Tied	NR
v	Australia	9	2	7	0	0
v	East Africa	1	1	0	0	0
v	England	6	3	3	0	0
v	Kenya	4	4	0	0	0
v	Namibia	1	1	0	0	0
v	Netherlands	1	1	0	0	0
v	New Zealand	7	3	4	0	0
v	Pakistan	4	4	0	0	0
v	South Africa	2	0	2	0	0
v	Sri Lanka	6	2	3	0	1
v	West Indies	6	3	3	0	0
v	Zimbabwe	8	7	1	0	0
	Total	55	31	23	0	1

Success Percentage: 57.40

INDIA BATTING RECORDS

Name	Mat	I	NO	Runs	HS	Ave	SR	100	50	Ct	St
S Abid Ali	3	1	0	70	70	70.00	71.42	-	1	-	-
AB Agarkar	3	1	0	1	1	1.00	20.00	-	-	1	-
M Amarnath	14	12	0	254	80	21.16	46.60	-	1	2	-
PK Amre	4	3	1	27	22	13.50	67.50	-	-	-	-
SA Ankola	1	0	-	-	-	-	-	-	-	-	-
KBJ Azad	3	2	0	15	15	7.50	71.42	-	-	-	-
M Azharuddin	30	25	4	826	93	39.33	77.19	-	8	11	-
ST Banerjee	2	2	1	36	25*	36.00	144.00	-	-	2	-
BS Bedi	5	4	1	25	13	8.33	47.16	-	-	-	-
RMH Binny	9	7	0	73	27	10.42	52.51	-	-	2	-
N Chopra	1	0	-	-	-	-	-	-	-	-	-
R Dravid	19	18	6	779	145	64.91	75.26	2	5	17	1
FM Engineer	3	2	1	78	54*	78.00	60.46	-	1	2	-
AD Gaekwad	6	5	0	113	37	22.60	53.80	-	-	2	-
SC Ganguly	18	18	3	844	183	56.26	81.78	4	1	1	-
SM Gavaskar	19	19	3	561	103*	35.06	57.36	1	4	4	-
KD Ghavri	4	3	0	35	20	11.66	62.50	-	-	-	-
Harbhajan Singh	10	6	2	58	28	14.50	98.30	-	-	2	-
A Jadeja	21	18	3	522	100*	34.80	71.40	1	2	5	-
M Kaif	11	10	1	182	68*	20.22	57.59	-	1	5	-
VG Kambli	12	11	3	205	106	25.62	71.92	1	-	1	-
N Kapil Dev	26	24	6	669	175*	37.16	115.14	1	1	12	-
AR Kapoor	2	1	0	0	0	0.00	0.00	-	-	-	-
Z Khan	11	5	1	18	13*	4.50	66.66	-	-	6	-
SC Khanna	3	3	0	17	10	5.66	37.77	-	-	1	-
SMH Kirmani	8	6	1	61	24*	12.20	41.78	-	-	12	2
A Kumble	17	8	4	62	17	15.50	70.45	-	-	14	-
S Madan Lal	11	7	3	122	27	30.50	60.69	-	-	1	-
Maninder Singh	7	2	1	4	4	4.00	80.00	-	-	1	-
SV Manjrekar	11	11	0	295	62	26.81	66.89	-	1	5	-
DS Mohanty	6	1	0	0	0	0.00	0.00	-	-	1	-
D Mongia	11	6	0	120	42	20.00	57.41	-	-	8	-
NR Mongia	14	12	6	115	28	19.16	80.98	-	-	12	4
KS More	14	10	5	100	42*	20.00	116.27	-	-	12	6
A Nehra	9	1	1	8	8*	-	200.00	-	-	-	-
CS Pandit	2	1	0	24	24	24.00	80.00	-	-	1	-
BP Patel	6	5	1	88	38	22.00	45.12	-	-	-	-
SM Patil	8	8	1	216	51*	30.85	90.00	-	2	2	-
M Prabhakar	19	11	2	45	11*	5.00	34.09	-	-	4	-

Name	Mat	I	NO	Runs	HS	Ave	SR	100	50	Ct	St
BKV Prasad	14	5	2	4	2*	1.33	26.66	-	-	2	-
SLV Raju	11	3	1	4	3*	2.00	80.00	-	-	2	-
S Ramesh	5	5	0	144	55	28.80	65.75	-	1	1	-
BS Sandhu	8	4	2	28	11*	14.00	45.16	-	-	2	-
V Sehwag	11	11	0	299	82	27.18	86.66	-	2	8	-
C Sharma	4	1	0	0	0	0.00	0.00	-	-	-	-
RJ Shastri	14	11	1	185	57	18.50	54.09	-	1	6	-
NS Sidhu	12	10	0	454	93	45.40	78.81	-	6	3	-
RR Singh	6	6	1	157	75	31.40	80.51	-	1	2	-
L Sivaramakrishnan	2	0	-	-	-	-	-	-	-	1	-
ED Solkar	3	2	0	21	13	10.50	47.72	-	-	1	-
K Srikkanth	23	23	1	521	75	23.68	68.28	-	2	9	-
J Srinath	34	18	9	85	18	9.44	106.25	-	-	4	-
SR Tendulkar	33	32	3	1732	152	59.72	87.56	4	12	10	-
DB Vengsarkar	11	10	3	252	63	36.00	75.90	-	1	3	-
S Venkataraghavan	6	4	3	49	26*	49.00	49.49	-	-	1	-
GR Viswanath	6	5	0	145	75	29.00	52.91	-	1	-	-
Yashpal Sharma	8	8	1	240	89	34.28	64.00	-	2	2	-
Yuvraj Singh	11	10	3	240	58*	34.28	85.40	-	2	1	-

As formidable as they come: (left to right) Sachin Tendulkar (ave. 59.72), Rahul Dravid (ave. 64.91) and Sourav Ganguly (ave. 56.26) have stellar records in the World Cup.

INDIA BOWLING RECORDS

Name	Mat	O	M	R	W	Ave	Best	4w	5w	SR	Econ
S Abid Ali	3	36	7	115	6	19.16	2-22	-	-	36.0	3.19
AB Agarkar	3	28	0	162	3	54.00	1-35	-	-	56.0	5.78
M Amarnath	14	110.3	9	431	16	26.93	3-12	-	-	41.4	3.90
PK Amre	4	-	-	-	-	-	-	-	-	-	-
SA Ankola	1	5	0	28	0	-	-	-	-	-	5.60
KBJ Azad	3	17	1	42	1	42.00	1-28	-	-	102.0	2.47
M Azharuddin	30	23.5	0	109	5	21.80	3-19	-	-	28.6	4.57
ST Banerjee	2	13	1	85	1	85.00	1-45	-	-	78.0	6.53
BS Bedi	5	60	17	148	2	74.00	1-6	-	-	180.0	2.46
RMH Binny	9	95	9	382	19	20.10	4-29	1	-	30.0	4.02
N Chopra	1	10	2	33	1	33.00	1-33	-	-	60.0	3.30
R Dravid	19	-	-	-	-	-	-	-	-	-	-
FM Engineer	3	-	-	-	-	-	-	-	-	-	-
AD Gaekwad	6	-	-	-	-	-	-	-	-	-	-
SC Ganguly	18	58	1	283	9	31.44	3-22	-	-	38.6	4.87
SM Gavaskar	19	-	-	-	-	-	-	-	-	-	-
KD Ghavri	4	43	4	195	0	-	-	-	-	-	4.53
Harbhajan Singh	10	85.2	5	335	11	30.45	2-28	-	-	46.5	3.92
A Jadeja	21	28.2	0	143	3	47.66	2-32	-	-	56.6	5.04
M Kaif	11	-	-	-	-	-	-	-	-	-	-
VG Kambli	12	-	-	-	-	-	-	-	-	-	-
N Kapil Dev	26	237	27	892	28	31.85	5-43	-	1	50.7	3.76
AR Kapoor	2	20	2	81	1	81.00	1-41	-	-	120.0	4.05
Z Khan	11	88.2	5	374	18	20.77	4-42	1	-	29.4	4.23
SC Khanna	3	-	-	-	-	-	-	-	-	-	-
SMH Kirmani	8	-	-	-	-	-	-	-	-	-	-
A Kumble	17	164	5	670	28	23.92	4-32	1	-	35.1	4.08
S Madan Lal	11	116.2	12	426	22	19.36	4-20	1	-	31.7	3.66
Maninder Singh	7	70	1	280	14	20.00	3-21	-	-	30.0	4.00
SV Manjrekar	11	-	-	-	-	-	-	-	-	-	-
DS Mohanty	6	52	2	260	10	26.00	4-56	1	-	31.2	5.00
D Mongia	11	32.1	1	135	5	27.00	2-24	-	-	38.6	4.19
NR Mongia	14	-	-	-	-	-	-	-	-	-	-
KS More	14	-	-	-	-	-	-	-	-	-	-
A Nehra	9	69.1	9	289	15	19.26	6-23	1	1	27.6	4.17
CS Pandit	2	-	-	-	-	-	-	-	-	-	-
BP Patel	6	-	-	-	-	-	-	-	-	-	-
SM Patil	8	9	0	61	0	-	-	-	-	-	6.77
M Prabhakar	19	145.1	10	640	24	26.66	4-19	1	-	36.2	4.40
BKV Prasad	14	129.5	5	578	17	34.00	5-27	-	1	45.8	4.45
SLV Raju	11	88.1	7	366	13	28.15	3-30	-	-	40.6	4.15
S Ramesh	5	-	-	-	-	-	-	-	-	-	-
BS Sandhu	8	83	10	297	8	37.12	2-26	-	-	62.2	3.57
V Sehwag	11	22	2	88	2	44.00	1-3	-	-	66.0	4.00
C Sharma	4	36.1	2	170	6	28.33	3-51	-	-	36.1	4.70
RJ Shastri	14	92.3	2	389	12	32.41	3-26	-	-	46.2	4.20
NS Sidhu	12	-	-	-	-	-	-	-	-	-	-
RR Singh	6	32.3	1	153	8	19.12	5-31	-	1	24.3	4.70
L Sivaramakrishnan	2	17	0	70	1	70.00	1-36	-	-	102.0	4.11
ED Solkar	3	4	0	28	0	-	-	-	-	-	7.00
K Srikkanth	23	2.1	0	15	0	-	-	-	-	-	6.92
J Srinath	34	283.2	21	1224	44	27.81	4-30	2	-	38.6	4.32
SR Tendulkar	33	104	1	469	6	78.16	2-28	-	-	104.0	4.50
DB Vengsarkar	11	-	-	-	-	-	-	-	-	-	-
S Venkataraghavan	6	72	7	217	0	-	-	-	-	-	3.01
GR Viswanath	6	-	-	-	-	-	-	-	-	-	-
Yashpal Sharma	8	-	-	-	-	-	-	-	-	-	-
Yuvraj Singh	11	14.3	2	70	5	14.00	4-6	1	-	17.4	4.82

PAKISTAN
Winners: 1992
Runner's Up: 1999
Semi-Final Finish: 1979, 1983, 1987
Participants: All World Cups

Predictably unpredictable, Pakistan have a history of being an interesting commodity at the World Cup. Since the inaugural competition when they went toe to toe with the mighty West Indies, Pakistan's performances have one way or another been eyebrow raising. Hot favourites to lift the trophy in 1987, Pakistan crashed out in the semi-final. But led by the inspirational Imran Khan for the third successive World Cup, the team went on to lift the trophy in the next edition of the tournament in 1992 after languishing near the bottom of the standings at the halfway point of the competition. When on song, Pakistan have played breathtaking cricket in the World Cup, but when they've been bad, they've been very, very bad.

Best World Cup: 1992. After reaching the semi-final stage in the previous three World Cups, Pakistan went the extra step and won the tournament in 1992; a fairytale triumph if ever there was one.

Worst World Cup: 2003. The watershed World Cup of 2003, a campaign so disastrous that Pakistan realized it was time to bid farewell to their stalwarts: the legendary Wasim Akram, the mercurial Waqar Younis and the elegant Saeed Anwar. The rain-ruined match against Zimbabwe was the last time the trio ever played for Pakistan.

PAKISTAN RESULTS

		M	Won	Lost	Tied	NR
v	Australia	7	3	4	0	0
v	Bangladesh	1	0	1	0	0
v	Canada	1	1	0	0	0
v	England	9	4	4	0	1
v	India	4	0	4	0	0
v	Namibia	1	1	0	0	0
v	Netherlands	2	2	0	0	0
v	New Zealand	7	6	1	0	0
v	South Africa	3	0	3	0	0
v	Scotland	1	1	0	0	0
v	Sri Lanka	6	6	0	0	0
v	United Arab Emirates	1	1	0	0	0
v	West Indies	7	2	5	0	0
v	Zimbabwe	3	2	0	0	1
	Total	53	29	22	0	2

Success percentage: 56.86

PAKISTAN BATTING RECORDS

Name	Mat	I	NO	Runs	HS	Ave	SR	100	50	Ct	St
Aamer Sohail	16	16	0	598	114	37.37	69.29	2	4	4	-
Aaqib Javed	15	3	3	8	6*	-	18.60	-	-	2	-
Abdul Qadir	13	9	7	118	41*	59.00	79.72	-	-	3	-
Abdul Razzaq	14	13	0	269	60	20.69	49.81	-	1	3	-
Asif Iqbal	5	4	0	182	61	45.50	65.94	-	3	5	-
Asif Masood	3	1	0	6	6	6.00	85.71	-	-	-	-
Ata-ur-Rehman	1	1	0	0	0	0.00	0.00	-	-	-	-
Azhar Mahmood	11	8	1	116	37	16.57	67.44	-	-	1	-
Haroon Rashid	4	4	1	69	37*	23.00	51.11	-	-	-	-
Ijaz Ahmed	29	26	4	516	70	23.45	71.96	-	4	11	-
Ijaz Faqih	6	5	1	61	42*	15.25	54.46	-	-	1	-
Imran Khan	28	24	5	666	102*	35.05	65.61	1	4	6	-
Inzamam-ul-Haq	32	30	3	643	81	23.81	74.76	-	4	12	-
Iqbal Sikander	4	1	1	1	1*	-	33.33	-	-	-	-
Javed Miandad	33	30	5	1083	103	43.32	67.89	1	8	10	1
Majid Khan	7	7	0	359	84	51.28	68.51	-	5	1	-
Mansoor Akhtar	8	8	0	108	33	13.50	43.72	-	-	2	-
Manzoor Elahi	1	1	1	4	4*	-	66.66	-	-	-	-
Mohammad Sami	1	0	-	-	-	-	-	-	-	-	-
Mohsin Khan	7	7	0	223	82	31.85	44.15	-	2	3	-
Moin Khan	20	14	4	286	63	28.60	106.31	-	1	23	7
Mudassar Nazar	12	10	1	149	40	16.55	41.27	-	-	6	-
Mushtaq Ahmed	15	5	1	27	17	6.75	47.36	-	-	5	-
Mushtaq Mohammad	3	3	0	89	55	29.66	54.26	-	1	1	-
Naseer Malik	3	1	1	0	0*	-	0.00	-	-	-	-
Pervez Mir	2	2	1	8	4*	8.00	50.00	-	-	1	-
Rameez Raja	16	16	3	700	119*	53.84	64.22	3	2	4	-
Rashid Khan	7	1	0	9	9	9.00	42.85	-	-	1	-
Rashid Latif	12	7	1	148	36	24.66	111.27	-	-	14	3
Sadiq Mohammad	7	7	1	189	74	31.50	53.69	-	2	3	-
Saeed Anwar	21	21	4	915	113*	53.82	79.08	3	3	3	-
Saleem Elahi	4	4	0	102	63	25.50	68.00	-	1	-	-
Saleem Jaffar	5	3	2	9	8*	9.00	42.85	-	-	-	-
Saleem Malik	27	23	5	591	100	32.83	82.65	1	4	6	-
Saleem Yousuf	7	6	3	112	56	37.33	123.07	-	1	9	-
Saqlain Mushtaq	14	10	6	56	21	14.00	46.28	-	-	4	-
Sarfraz Nawaz	11	8	1	65	17	9.28	73.86	-	-	2	-

Name	Mat	I	NO	Runs	HS	Ave	SR	100	50	Ct	St
Shahid Afridi	11	10	0	109	37	10.90	87.20	-	-	5	-
Shahid Mahboob	5	3	0	100	77	33.33	59.88	-	1	1	-
Shoaib Akhtar	16	8	7	76	43	76.00	115.15	-	-	2	-
Shoaib Mohammad	1	1	0	0	0	0.00	0.00	-	-	-	-
Sikander Bakht	4	2	1	3	2	3.00	13.04	-	-	1	-
Tahir Naqqash	1	1	1	0	0*	-	-	-	-	1	-
Taufeeq Umar	3	3	0	91	48	30.33	62.32	-	-	1	-
Tauseef Ahmed	6	2	0	1	1	0.50	25.00	-	-	1	-
Wajahatullah Wasti	5	5	0	151	84	30.20	56.76	-	1	-	-
Waqar Younis	13	6	1	32	11	6.40	50.00	-	-	5	-
Wasim Akram	38	30	8	426	43	19.36	100.70	-	-	8	-
Wasim Bari	14	8	4	87	34	21.75	52.40	-	-	18	4
Wasim Haider	3	2	0	26	13	13.00	36.61	-	-	-	-
Wasim Raja	8	8	0	154	58	19.25	75.86	-	1	4	-
Younis Khan	5	5	1	84	32	21.00	64.61	-	-	4	-
Yousuf Youhana	10	10	1	331	81*	36.77	75.91	-	2	2	-
Zaheer Abbas	14	14	2	597	103*	49.75	78.34	1	4	7	-
Zahid Fazal	2	2	0	13	11	6.50	23.21	-	-	1	-

PAKISTAN BOWLING RECORDS

Name	Mat	O	M	R	W	Ave	Best	4w	5w	SR	Econ
Aamer Sohail	16	86	3	384	8	48.00	2-26	-	-	64.5	4.46
Aaqib Javed	15	124.2	13	517	18	28.72	3-21	-	-	41.4	4.15
Abdul Qadir	13	135.4	8	506	24	21.08	5-44	2	1	33.9	3.72
Abdul Razzaq	14	103	5	431	14	30.78	3-25	-	-	44.1	4.18
Asif Iqbal	5	59	5	215	10	21.50	4-56	1	-	35.4	3.64
Asif Masood	3	30	3	128	2	64.00	1-50	-	-	90.0	4.26
Ata-ur-Rehman	1	10	0	40	1	40.00	1-40	-	-	60.0	4.00
Azhar Mahmood	11	84	4	349	13	26.84	3-24	-	-	38.7	4.15
Haroon Rashid	4	-	-	-	-	-	-	-	-	-	-
Ijaz Ahmed	29	40	1	170	1	170.00	1-28	-	-	240.0	4.25
Ijaz Faqih	6	37	2	125	0	-	-	-	-	-	3.37
Imran Khan	28	169.3	18	655	34	19.26	4-37	2	-	29.9	3.86
Inzamam-ul-Haq	32	-	-	-	-	-	-	-	-	-	-
Iqbal Sikander	4	35	2	147	3	49.00	1-30	-	-	70.0	4.20
Javed Miandad	33	22	2	73	4	18.25	2-22	-	-	33.0	3.31
Majid Khan	7	47	8	117	7	16.71	3-27	-	-	40.2	2.48
Mansoor Akhtar	8	17	2	75	2	37.50	1-7	-	-	51.0	4.41
Manzoor Elahi	1	9.4	0	32	1	32.00	1-32	-	-	58.0	3.31
Mohammad Sami	1	-	-	-	-	-	-	-	-	-	-
Mohsin Khan	7	1	0	3	0	-	-	-	-	-	3.00
Moin Khan	20	-	-	-	-	-	-	-	-	-	-
Mudassar Nazar	12	105	8	397	8	49.62	3-43	-	-	78.7	3.78
Mushtaq Ahmed	15	135	5	549	26	21.11	3-16	-	-	31.1	4.06
Mushtaq Mohammad	3	7	0	23	0	-	-	-	-	-	3.28
Naseer Malik	3	30	5	98	5	19.60	2-37	-	-	36.0	3.26
Pervez Mir	2	15	2	59	2	29.50	1-17	-	-	45.0	3.93
Rameez Raja	16	-	-	-	-	-	-	-	-	-	-
Rashid Khan	7	71	11	266	8	33.25	3-47	-	-	53.2	3.74
Rashid Latif	12	-	-	-	-	-	-	-	-	-	-
Sadiq Mohammad	7	6	1	20	2	10.00	2-20	-	-	18.0	3.33
Saeed Anwar	21	4	0	15	1	15.00	1-15	-	-	24.0	3.75
Saleem Elahi	4	-	-	-	-	-	-	-	-	-	-
Saleem Jaffar	5	39.4	0	210	5	42.00	3-30	-	-	47.6	5.29
Saleem Malik	27	56	2	282	4	70.50	2-41	-	-	84.0	5.03
Saleem Yousuf	7	-	-	-	-	-	-	-	-	-	-

Name	Mat	O	M	R	W	Ave	Best	4w	5w	SR	Econ
Saqlain Mushtaq	14	112.2	7	494	23	21.47	5-35	-	1	29.3	4.39
Sarfraz Nawaz	11	119	15	435	16	27.18	4-44	1	-	44.6	3.65
Shahid Afridi	11	48.3	1	259	4	64.75	2-36	-	-	72.7	5.34
Shahid Mahboob	5	52	4	228	4	57.00	1-37	-	-	78.0	4.38
Shoaib Akhtar	16	124.5	8	643	27	23.81	4-46	1	-	27.7	5.15
Shoaib Mohammad	1	-	-	-	-	-	-	-	-	-	-
Sikander Bakht	4	41	10	108	7	15.42	3-32	-	-	35.1	2.63
Tahir Naqqash	1	8	0	49	1	49.00	1-49	-	-	48.0	6.12
Taufeeq Umar	3	-	-	-	-	-	-	-	-	-	-
Tauseef Ahmed	6	60	4	230	5	46.00	1-35	-	-	72.0	3.83
Wajahatullah Wasti	5	-	-	-	-	-	-	-	-	-	-
Waqar Younis	13	93.1	8	466	22	21.18	4-26	1	-	25.4	5.00
Wasim Akram	38	324.3	17	1311	55	23.83	5-28	2	1	35.4	4.04
Wasim Bari	14	-	-	-	-	-	-	-	-	-	-
Wasim Haider	3	19	1	79	1	79.00	1-36	-	-	114.0	4.15
Wasim Raja	8	13.4	4	46	1	46.00	1-7	-	-	82.0	3.36
Younis Khan	5	6	0	36	0	-	-	-	-	-	6.00
Yousuf Youhana	10	-	-	-	-	-	-	-	-	-	-
Zaheer Abbas	14	19.4	2	74	2	37.00	1-8	-	-	59.0	3.76
Zahid Fazal	2	-	-	-	-	-	-	-	-	-	-

*The Pakistan team,
World Cup 2003.*

SRI LANKA
Winner: 1996
Runner's Up: Never
Semi-Final Finish: 2003
Participants: All World Cups

Sri Lanka have not had a particularly good time at the World Cup. Not counting matches against Zimbabwe and the minnows, Sri Lanka have managed to win a paltry nine games, spanning eight tournaments. The team's overall winning percentage of 37.7 is the worst of any country that has participated in all World Cups. But in 1996 the shackles were broken in the most decisive manner possible, when Sri Lanka ran away with the World Cup. That win established Sri Lanka as a team to be taken seriously, and a hiccup in the 1999 World Cup aside, there has been no looking back.

Best World Cup: 1996. The Sri Lankans benefited from the fact that the West Indies and Australia citing security concerns, refused to play against them in Colombo and forfeited their matches. This turn of events contributed to Sri Lanka going through the tournament undefeated. The team was a near perfect mix of youth and experience and were ably led by the battle-hardened Arjuna Ranatunga. This tournament is also where Sri Lanka revolutionized ODI cricket by having their opening batsmen attack the bowling during the initial fielding restrictions.

Worst World Cup: 1999. Unable to mount anything resembling a fight in defence of their crown, Sri Lanka went home humiliated. In spite of having a strong batting line-up, the Sri Lankans struggled to put runs on the board. Their bowlers were carted from pillar to post, with India and Kenya posting World Cup record stands of 318 and 161 for the second and sixth wicket respectively. The stunning assault by the Indian pair of Sourav Ganguly and Rahul Dravid remains the highest stand for any wicket in World Cup history

SRI LANKA RESULTS

		M	Won	Lost	Tied	NR
v	Australia	5	1	4	0	0
v	Bangladesh	1	1	0	0	0
v	Canada	1	1	0	0	0
v	England	7	1	6	0	0
v	India	6	3	2	0	1
v	Kenya	3	2	1	0	0
v	New Zealand	5	2	3	0	0
v	Pakistan	6	0	6	0	0
v	South Africa	3	1	1	1	0
v	West Indies	5	1	4	0	0
v	Zimbabwe	4	4	0	0	0
	Total	46	17	27	1	1

Success percentage: 37.77

SRI LANKA BATTING RECORDS

Name	Mat	I	NO	Runs	HS	Ave	SR	100	50	Ct	St
SD Anurasiri	11	5	2	21	11	7.00	53.84	-	-	3	-
RP Arnold	10	8	2	92	34*	15.33	54.11	-	-	2	-
MS Atapattu	15	15	3	521	124	43.41	79.29	2	3	3	-
UDU Chandana	2	2	0	9	9	4.50	39.13	-	-	-	-
RG de Alwis	6	6	3	167	59*	55.66	105.03	-	2	5	-
ALF de Mel	9	7	0	66	27	9.42	65.34	-	-	-	-
DLS de Silva	2	1	0	10	10	10.00	28.57	-	-	1	-
DS de Silva	11	10	1	148	35	16.44	49.66	-	-	2	-
GRA de Silva	2	2	1	2	2*	2.00	8.69	-	-	-	-
PA de Silva	35	32	3	1064	145	36.68	86.57	2	6	14	-
HDPK Dharmasena	6	1	0	9	9	9.00	45.00	-	-	1	-
RL Dias	10	10	1	310	80	34.44	57.72	-	3	5	-
CRD Fernando	9	4	2	30	13*	15.00	88.23	-	-	-	-
ER Fernando	3	3	0	47	22	15.66	71.21	-	-	-	-
PW Gunaratne	6	1	1	15	15*	-	100.00	-	-	1	-
FRMD Gunatilleke	1	0	-	-	-	-	-	-	-	-	-
DA Gunawardene	2	2	0	42	41	21.00	63.63	-	-	-	-
AP Gurusinha	18	17	0	488	87	28.70	61.85	-	3	3	-
UC Hathurusingha	4	3	0	26	16	8.66	41.26	-	-	1	-
PD Heyn	2	2	0	3	2	1.50	15.00	-	-	1	-
SA Jayasinghe	2	1	0	1	1	1.00	33.33	-	-	1	-
ST Jayasuriya	27	26	2	698	120	29.08	86.17	1	4	15	-
DPMD Jayawardene	13	11	0	123	45	11.18	75.00	-	-	2	-
S Jeganathan	3	3	1	24	20*	12.00	68.57	-	-	1	-
VB John	11	9	7	46	15	23.00	54.11	-	-	1	-
RS Kalpage	7	6	2	67	14	16.75	60.36	-	-	3	-
LWS Kaluperuma	3	2	2	19	13*	-	41.30	-	-	-	-
RS Kaluwitharana	11	11	1	163	57	16.30	91.57	-	1	8	4
DSBP Kuruppu	11	11	0	251	72	22.81	49.90	-	2	4	1
GF Labrooy	1	1	0	19	19	19.00	55.88	-	-	-	-
RS Madugalle	11	10	0	193	60	19.30	55.14	-	1	4	-
RS Mahanama	25	21	3	596	89	33.11	56.54	-	5	6	-
LRD Mendis	16	16	2	412	64	29.42	69.71	-	3	2	-
J Mubarak	1	1	0	0	0	0.00	0.00	-	-	-	-
M Muralitharan	21	9	3	59	16	9.83	92.18	-	-	7	-
RAP Nissanka	4	2	0	2	2	1.00	7.40	-	-	-	-
ARM Opatha	5	3	0	29	18	9.66	52.72	-	-	3	-
SP Pasqual	2	2	1	24	23*	24.00	85.71	-	-	-	-
HSM Pieris	3	3	1	19	16	9.50	32.20	-	-	-	-
KR Pushpakumara	2	0	-	-	-	-	-	-	-	-	-

Name	Mat	I	NO	Runs	HS	Ave	SR	100	50	Ct	St
CPH Ramanayake	8	6	2	25	12	6.25	38.46	-	-	4	-
AN Ranasinghe	3	3	1	23	14*	11.50	53.48	-	-	-	-
A Ranatunga	30	29	8	969	88*	46.14	80.95	-	7	7	-
RJ Ratnayake	9	8	2	81	20*	13.50	69.82	-	-	3	-
JR Ratnayeke	6	5	0	52	22	10.40	46.84	-	-	-	-
MAR Samarasekera	8	8	0	224	75	28.00	78.32	-	1	1	-
KC Sangakkara	10	9	2	176	39*	25.14	73.64	-	-	15	2
APB Tennekoon	4	4	0	137	59	34.25	66.18	-	1	3	-
HP Tillakaratne	24	19	5	386	81*	27.57	54.75	-	2	8	1
MH Tissera	3	3	0	78	52	26.00	53.06	-	1	-	-
KEA Upashantha	3	2	0	16	11	8.00	38.09	-	-	-	-
WPUJC Vaas	21	14	6	185	29*	23.12	71.98	-	-	4	-
B Warnapura	5	5	0	79	31	15.80	36.40	-	-	3	-
S Wettimuny	6	6	0	128	50	21.33	40.37	-	1	-	-
SRD Wettimuny	3	3	1	136	67	68.00	56.19	-	2	-	-
GP Wickramasinghe	17	8	6	53	21*	26.50	58.24	-	-	4	-
KIW Wijegunawardene	3	0	-	-	-	-	-	-	-	-	-

SRI LANKA BOWLING RECORDS

Name	Mat	O	M	R	W	Ave	Best	4w	5w	SR	Econ
SD Anurasiri	11	105	4	455	9	50.55	3-41	-	-	70.0	4.33
RP Arnold	10	23.3	0	132	3	44.00	3-47	-	-	47.0	5.61
MS Atapattu	15	-	-	-	-	-	-	-	-	-	-
UDU Chandana	2	8	0	39	0	-	-	-	-	-	4.87
RG de Alwis	6	-	-	-	-	-	-	-	-	-	-
ALF de Mel	9	90.2	13	449	18	24.94	5-32	-	2	30.1	4.97
DLS de Silva	2	20	2	54	2	27.00	2-36	-	-	60.0	2.70
DS de Silva	11	110	12	463	10	46.30	3-29	-	-	66.0	4.20
GRA de Silva	2	19	2	85	1	85.00	1-39	-	-	114.0	4.47
PA de Silva	35	135	2	671	16	41.93	3-42	-	-	50.6	4.97
HDPK Dharmasena	6	56	1	249	6	41.50	2-30	-	-	56.0	4.44
RL Dias	10	-	-	-	-	-	-	-	-	-	-
CRD Fernando	9	48	2	268	8	33.50	3-47	-	-	36.0	5.58
ER Fernando	3	-	-	-	-	-	-	-	-	-	-
PW Gunaratne	6	38	1	230	4	57.50	2-24	-	-	57.0	6.05
FRMD Gunatilleke	1	9	1	34	0	-	-	-	-	-	3.77
DA Gunawardene	2	-	-	-	-	-	-	-	-	-	-
AP Gurusinha	18	53	0	307	7	43.85	2-67	-	-	45.4	5.79
UC Hathurusingha	4	17	0	97	5	19.40	4-57	1	-	20.4	5.70
PD Heyn	2	-	-	-	-	-	-	-	-	-	-
SA Jayasinghe	2	-	-	-	-	-	-	-	-	-	-
ST Jayasuriya	27	151.5	4	758	20	37.90	3-12	-	-	45.5	4.99
DPMD Jayawardene	13	24	0	131	2	65.50	2-56	-	-	72.0	5.45
S Jeganathan	3	29	2	123	4	30.75	2-45	-	-	43.5	4.24
VB John	11	99.2	10	477	4	119.25	1-49	-	-	149.0	4.80
RS Kalpage	7	50	0	241	4	60.25	2-33	-	-	75.0	4.82
LWS Kaluperuma	3	27.4	2	102	1	102.00	1-50	-	-	166.0	3.68
RS Kaluwitharana	11	-	-	-	-	-	-	-	-	-	-
DSBP Kuruppu	11	-	-	-	-	-	-	-	-	-	-
GF Labrooy	1	10	1	68	1	68.00	1-68	-	-	60.0	6.80
RS Madugalle	11	-	-	-	-	-	-	-	-	-	-
RS Mahanama	25	-	-	-	-	-	-	-	-	-	-
LRD Mendis	16	-	-	-	-	-	-	-	-	-	-
J Mubarak	1	-	-	-	-	-	-	-	-	-	-
M Muralitharan	21	187.5	13	693	30	23.10	4-28	1	-	37.5	3.68
RAP Nissanka	4	25	3	112	4	28.00	4-12	1	-	37.5	4.48

Name	Mat	O	M	R	W	Ave	Best	4w	5w	SR	Econ
ARM Opatha	5	42.1	1	180	5	36.00	3-31	-	-	50.6	4.26
SP Pasqual	2	4.4	0	20	0	-	-	-	-	-	4.28
HSM Pieris	3	22	0	135	2	67.50	2-68	-	-	66.0	6.13
KR Pushpakumara	2	15	0	99	1	99.00	1-53	-	-	90.0	6.60
CPH Ramanayake	8	64.4	6	265	5	53.00	2-37	-	-	77.6	4.09
AN Ranasinghe	3	10	0	65	0	-	-	-	-	-	6.50
A Ranatunga	30	81.1	2	460	6	76.66	2-26	-	-	81.1	5.66
RJ Ratnayake	9	89	6	437	12	36.41	2-18	-	-	44.5	4.91
JR Ratnayeke	6	54	2	313	10	31.30	3-41	-	-	32.4	5.79
MAR Samarasekera	8	16.2	2	71	0	-	-	-	-	-	4.34
KC Sangakkara	10	-	-	-	-	-	-	-	-	-	-
APB Tennekoon	4	-	-	-	-	-	-	-	-	-	-
HP Tillakaratne	24	1	0	4	0	-	-	-	-	-	4.00
MH Tissera	3	-	-	-	-	-	-	-	-	-	-
KEA Upashantha	3	28	1	161	1	161.00	1-43	-	-	168.0	5.75
WPUJC Vaas	21	184	24	754	36	20.94	6-25	1	1	30.6	4.09
B Warnapura	5	36	0	159	4	39.75	3-42	-	-	54.0	4.41
S Wettimuny	6	3	0	15	0	-	-	-	-	-	5.00
SRD Wettimuny	3	-	-	-	-	-	-	-	-	-	-
GP Wickramasinghe	17	136.1	8	625	16	39.06	3-30	-	-	51.0	4.58
KIW Wijegunawardene	3	17	1	88	0	-	-	-	-	-	5.17

Aravinda de Silva: The most matches (35) and most runs (1064) for Sri Lanka in the World Cup.

ZIMBABWE
Winners: Never
Runner's Up: Never
Semi-Final Finish: Never
Participants: 1983 and onwards

Like other minnows before them, Zimbabwe made their debut as an ODI side during the World Cup. What sets the Zimbabweans apart however, is that rather than looking out of their depth, they actually won their inaugural match. That victory against Australia in 1983 set the precedent for Zimbabwe to come away with upset wins in subsequent tournaments. The losses have been many, but Zimbabwe have also shown some upward mobility, qualifying for the second round of the tournament in both 1999 and 2003.

Best World Cup: 1999. Zimbabwe fielded one of their best ever line-ups in the 1999 World Cup. This was a side that was coached by David Houghton and had the likes of Neil Johnson, Andy Flower, Alistair Campbell, Heath Streak, Henry Olonga and Pommie Mbangwa. There was no shortage of talent or brains in this team, and in arguably the strongest edition of the tournament, Zimbabwe did well to qualify for the second round, beating India and South Africa in the process.

Worst World Cup: 1992. It was a long World Cup for Zimbabwe, losing seven matches in a row before finally winning one. It was however a sweet victory, coming against an England side that included Harare-born Graeme Hick.

ZIMBABWE RESULTS

		M	Won	Lost	Tied	NR
v	Australia	8	1	7	0	0
v	England	2	1	1	0	0
v	India	8	1	7	0	0
v	Kenya	4	2	1	0	1
v	Namibia	1	1	0	0	0
v	Netherlands	1	1	0	0	0
v	New Zealand	5	0	4	0	1
v	Pakistan	3	0	2	0	1
v	South Africa	2	1	1	0	0
v	Sri Lanka	4	0	4	0	0
v	West Indies	4	0	4	0	0
	Total	42	8	31	0	3

Success Percentage: 20.51

ZIMBABWE BATTING RECORDS

Name	Mat	I	NO	Runs	HS	Ave	SR	100	50	Ct	St
KJ Arnott	9	8	1	206	60	29.42	49.51	-	3	2	-
AM Blignaut	7	6	0	123	58	20.50	138.20	-	2	1	-
EA Brandes	16	12	4	120	23	15.00	74.07	-	-	5	-
RD Brown	7	7	0	110	38	15.71	32.93	-	-	5	-
MG Burmester	4	3	1	17	12	8.50	40.47	-	-	1	-
IP Butchart	17	14	2	240	54	20.00	66.48	-	1	4	-
ADR Campbell	19	18	1	281	75	16.52	53.32	-	1	10	-
SV Carlisle	6	5	1	62	27	15.50	58.49	-	-	-	-
KM Curran	11	11	0	287	73	26.09	66.74	-	2	1	-
SG Davies	1	1	0	9	9	9.00	25.71	-	-	-	-
KG Duers	6	2	1	7	5	7.00	35.00	-	-	2	-
DD Ebrahim	7	5	0	79	32	15.80	64.22	-	-	1	-
SM Ervine	3	2	1	43	31*	43.00	130.30	-	-	-	-
CN Evans	6	5	2	92	39*	30.66	82.14	-	-	-	-
DAG Fletcher	6	6	2	191	71*	47.75	66.08	-	2	-	-
A Flower	30	29	4	815	115*	32.60	68.25	1	4	12	3
GW Flower	21	20	2	512	78*	28.44	57.20	-	1	8	-
TJ Friend	1	1	0	21	21	21.00	105.00	-	-	-	-
MW Goodwin	8	8	0	201	57	25.12	63.80	-	1	4	-
JG Heron	6	6	0	50	18	8.33	30.67	-	-	1	-
VR Hogg	2	1	1	7	7*	-	36.84	-	-	-	-
DT Hondo	8	4	2	3	2	1.50	11.53	-	-	2	-
DL Houghton	20	19	0	567	142	29.84	63.00	1	4	14	2
AG Huckle	3	2	0	0	0	0.00	0.00	-	-	1	-
WR James	4	3	0	35	17	11.66	44.30	-	-	1	-
MP Jarvis	10	5	3	37	17	18.50	55.22	-	-	1	-
NC Johnson	8	8	1	367	132*	52.42	73.99	1	3	1	-
ACI Lock	6	3	2	8	5	8.00	40.00	-	-	-	-
DA Marillier	5	4	0	41	21	10.25	73.21	-	-	1	-
S Matsikenyeri	1	1	1	1	1*	-	33.33	-	-	-	-
M Mbangwa	3	1	0	0	0	0.00	0.00	-	-	-	-
MA Meman	1	1	0	19	19	19.00	86.36	-	-	-	-
BA Murphy	5	2	0	3	2	1.50	27.27	-	-	2	-
HK Olonga	9	6	4	16	5*	8.00	26.22	-	-	1	-
AH Omarshah	16	16	1	266	60*	17.73	45.39	-	1	3	-
GA Paterson	10	10	0	123	27	12.30	37.61	-	-	2	-
SG Peall	5	2	0	9	9	4.50	50.00	-	-	1	-
GE Peckover	3	3	1	33	16*	16.50	61.11	-	-	-	-
AJ Pycroft	20	19	2	295	61	17.35	52.67	-	2	6	-
PWE Rawson	10	8	3	80	24*	16.00	65.04	-	-	4	-

All-rounder Neil Johnson was a star performer for Zimbabwe in the 1999 World Cup, scoring 367 runs at an average of 52.42 and taking 12 wickets at 19.41.

Name	Mat	I	NO	Runs	HS	Ave	SR	100	50	Ct	St
BC Strang	4	2	0	3	3	1.50	20.00	-	-	2	-
PA Strang	12	9	3	109	29	18.16	65.66	-	-	2	-
HH Streak	22	18	7	328	72*	29.81	73.37	-	1	7	-
T Taibu	8	6	2	117	53	29.25	58.50	-	1	7	-
AJ Traicos	20	12	5	70	19	10.00	51.47	-	-	2	-
MA Vermeulen	3	3	0	66	39	22.00	49.62	-	-	-	-
DP Viljoen	1	1	0	5	5	5.00	38.46	-	-	-	-
AC Waller	20	20	3	479	83*	28.17	72.13	-	2	3	-
AR Whittall	4	1	0	3	3	3.00	50.00	-	-	4	-
GJ Whittall	20	18	1	246	35	14.47	49.49	-	-	2	-
CB Wishart	8	7	1	293	172*	48.83	85.42	1	-	1	-

ZIMBABWE BOWLING RECORDS

Name	Mat	O	M	R	W	Ave	Best	4w	5w	SR	Econ
KJ Arnott	9	-	-	-	-	-	-	-	-	-	-
AM Blignaut	7	57	2	255	4	63.75	2-41	-	-	85.5	4.47
EA Brandes	16	129.1	11	641	16	40.06	4-21	1	-	48.4	4.96
RD Brown	7	-	-	-	-	-	-	-	-	-	-
MG Burmester	4	21.5	0	138	4	34.50	3-36	-	-	32.7	6.32
IP Butchart	17	117	6	640	12	53.33	3-57	-	-	58.5	5.47
ADR Campbell	19	3	0	13	0	-	-	-	-	-	4.33
SV Carlisle	6	-	-	-	-	-	-	-	-	-	-
KM Curran	11	84.2	3	398	9	44.22	3-65	-	-	56.2	4.71
SG Davies	1	-	-	-	-	-	-	-	-	-	-
KG Duers	6	50	2	256	3	85.33	1-17	-	-	100.0	5.12
DD Ebrahim	7	-	-	-	-	-	-	-	-	-	-
SM Ervine	3	12	0	87	3	29.00	1-19	-	-	24.0	7.25
CN Evans	6	-	-	-	-	-	-	-	-	-	-
DAG Fletcher	6	50.1	5	221	7	31.57	4-42	1	-	43.0	4.40
A Flower	30	-	-	-	-	-	-	-	-	-	-
GW Flower	21	64.1	2	268	4	67.00	2-14	-	-	96.2	4.17
TJ Friend	1	2	0	13	0	-	-	-	-	-	6.50
MW Goodwin	8	-	-	-	-	-	-	-	-	-	-
JG Heron	6	-	-	-	-	-	-	-	-	-	-
VR Hogg	2	15	4	49	0	-	-	-	-	-	3.26
DT Hondo	8	50.2	4	265	6	44.16	1-16	-	-	50.3	5.26
DL Houghton	20	2	0	19	1	19.00	1-19	-	-	12.0	9.50
AG Huckle	3	20	1	78	1	78.00	1-43	-	-	120.0	3.90
WR James	4	-	-	-	-	-	-	-	-	-	-
MP Jarvis	10	83.1	5	384	7	54.85	1-21	-	-	71.2	4.61
NC Johnson	8	50	4	233	12	19.41	4-42	1	-	25.0	4.66
ACI Lock	6	32	3	141	3	47.00	2-57	-	-	64.0	4.40
DA Marillier	5	30	1	133	4	33.25	2-49	-	-	45.0	4.43
S Matsikenyeri	1	2	0	13	0	-	-	-	-	-	6.50
M Mbangwa	3	23	1	93	2	46.50	2-28	-	-	69.0	4.04
MA Meman	1	6.5	0	34	0	-	-	-	-	-	4.97
BA Murphy	5	30	3	139	5	27.80	3-44	-	-	36.0	4.63
HK Olonga	9	43.2	2	259	9	28.77	3-22	-	-	28.8	5.97
AH Omarshah	16	104.3	9	456	11	41.45	2-17	-	-	57.0	4.36
GA Paterson	10	-	-	-	-	-	-	-	-	-	-
SG Peall	5	23	1	101	1	101.00	1-23	-	-	138.0	4.39
GE Peckover	3	-	-	-	-	-	-	-	-	-	-
AJ Pycroft	20	-	-	-	-	-	-	-	-	-	-
PWE Rawson	10	95.1	10	427	12	35.58	3-47	-	-	47.5	4.48
BC Strang	4	18	1	66	3	22.00	2-24	-	-	36.0	3.66
PA Strang	12	86.4	6	388	15	25.86	5-21	1	1	34.6	4.47
HH Streak	22	175	13	804	22	36.54	3-35	-	-	47.7	4.59
T Taibu	8	-	-	-	-	-	-	-	-	-	-
AJ Traicos	20	188	13	673	16	42.06	3-35	-	-	70.5	3.57
MA Vermeulen	3	-	-	-	-	-	-	-	-	-	-
DP Viljoen	1	-	-	-	-	-	-	-	-	-	-
AC Waller	20	-	-	-	-	-	-	-	-	-	-
AR Whittall	4	27	1	143	3	47.66	2-41	-	-	54.0	5.29
GJ Whittall	20	79.3	3	396	11	36.00	3-35	-	-	43.3	4.98
CB Wishart	8	-	-	-	-	-	-	-	-	-	-

BANGLADESH
Winners: Never
Runner's Up: Never
Semi-Final Finish: Never
Participants: 1999 and onwards

Bangladesh have only participated in two editions of the
World Cup. They were not expected to win any games in
1999, yet came away with two creditable victories. The win
over equally lowly Scotland was not too much of a surprise,
but the win over Pakistan proved to be the requisite upset
match of the World Cup. The act of giant killing resulted in
a national holiday in Bangladesh and somewhat ridiculously,
fast tracked the team to Test status. Many remained uncon-
vinced and rumours circulated that the match was fixed, so
much so that Pakistan had the matter judicially reviewed.
The subsequent inquiry found no evidence of match fixing,
and so the victory remains the highlight of Bangladesh's
World Cup experience.

Best World Cup: 1999. Two wins make 1999 the good World
Cup.

Worst World Cup: 2003. Unable to win any matches in 2003,
Bangladesh even lost to Canada, the only team ever to do
so in a World Cup match.

BANGLADESH RESULTS	M	Won	Lost	Tied	NR
v Australia	1	0	1	0	0
v Canada	1	0	1	0	0
v Kenya	1	0	1	0	0
v New Zealand	2	0	2	0	0
v Pakistan	1	1	0	0	0
v South Africa	1	0	1	0	0
v Scotland	1	1	0	0	0
v Sri Lanka	1	0	1	0	0
v West Indies	2	0	1	0	1
Total	11	2	8	0	1

Success Percentage: 20.00

*Khaled Mahmud: Bangladesh's leading
wicket taker in the World Cup.*

BANGLADESH BATTING RECORDS

Name	Mat	I	NO	Runs	HS	Ave	SR	100	50	Ct	St
Akram Khan	7	7	0	119	44	17.00	50.21	-	-	1	-
Alok Kapali	6	5	0	80	32	16.00	63.49	-	-	2	-
Al Sahariar	5	5	0	38	14	7.60	55.07	-	-	2	-
Aminul Islam	5	5	0	45	15	9.00	36.88	-	-	2	-
Ehsanul Haque	4	4	0	28	13	7.00	38.88	-	-	-	-
Enamul Haque	4	4	1	59	19	19.66	57.84	-	-	-	-
Faruk Ahmed	2	2	0	16	9	8.00	40.00	-	-	1	-
Habibul Bashar	2	2	0	0	0	0.00	0.00	-	-	-	-
Hannan Sarkar	3	3	0	34	25	11.33	56.66	-	-	-	-
Hasibul Hossain	4	3	0	23	16	7.66	46.93	-	-	2	-
Khaled Mahmud	9	8	0	87	27	10.87	58.00	-	-	2	-
Khaled Mashud	11	10	2	139	35*	17.37	42.12	-	-	4	2
Manjural Islam	10	7	5	13	6*	6.50	37.14	-	-	3	-
Mashrafe Mortaza	2	2	0	28	28	14.00	112.00	-	-	-	-
Mehrab Hossain	5	5	0	120	64	24.00	44.44	-	1	2	-
Minhajul Abedin	4	4	2	140	68*	70.00	56.22	-	2	-	-
Mohammad Ashraful	5	5	1	71	56	17.75	66.98	-	1	2	-
Mohammad Rafique	8	7	1	71	41*	11.83	62.83	-	-	-	-
Naimur Rahman	5	5	0	114	45	22.80	55.33	-	-	1	-
Niamur Rashid	1	1	0	1	1	1.00	50.00	-	-	-	-
Sanwar Hossain	6	6	1	63	25	12.60	73.25	-	-	4	-
Shafiuddin Ahmed	1	1	1	2	2*	-	66.66	-	-	-	-
Shahriar Hossain	3	3	0	41	39	13.66	60.29	-	-	1	-
Talha Jubair	2	1	1	4	4*	-	50.00	-	-	-	-
Tapash Baisya	4	3	1	7	5	3.50	22.58	-	-	1	-
Tushar Imran	3	2	0	57	48	28.50	54.28	-	-	-	-

BANGLADESH BOWLING RECORDS

Name	Mat	O	M	R	W	Ave	Best	4w	5w	SR	Econ
Akram Khan	7	-	-	-	-	-	-	-	-	-	-
Alok Kapali	6	23	1	96	2	48.00	1-3	-	-	69.0	4.17
Al Sahariar	5	-	-	-	-	-	-	-	-	-	-
Aminul Islam	5	-	-	-	-	-	-	-	-	-	-
Ehsanul Haque	4	10	0	34	2	17.00	2-34	-	-	30.0	3.40
Enamul Haque	4	23.2	1	115	3	38.33	2-40	-	-	46.6	4.92
Faruk Ahmed	2	-	-	-	-	-	-	-	-	-	-
Habibul Bashar	2	-	-	-	-	-	-	-	-	-	-
Hannan Sarkar	3	-	-	-	-	-	-	-	-	-	-
Hasibul Hossain	4	29	4	111	3	37.00	2-26	-	-	58.0	3.82
Khaled Mahmud	9	68.5	8	298	12	24.83	3-31	-	-	34.4	4.32
Khaled Mashud	11	-	-	-	-	-	-	-	-	-	-
Manjural Islam	10	69.1	7	301	8	37.62	3-62	-	-	51.8	4.35
Mashrafe Mortaza	2	13	0	76	2	38.00	2-38	-	-	39.0	5.84
Mehrab Hossain	5	-	-	-	-	-	-	-	-	-	-
Minhajul Abedin	4	20	2	107	4	26.75	1-12	-	-	30.0	5.35
Mohammad Ashraful	5	6.3	0	33	0	-	-	-	-	-	5.07
Mohammad Rafique	8	44.1	3	205	4	51.25	1-22	-	-	66.2	4.64
Naimur Rahman	5	30	2	126	2	63.00	1-5	-	-	90.0	4.20
Niamur Rashid	1	5	1	20	0	-	-	-	-	-	4.00
Sanwar Hossain	6	24	0	108	5	21.60	3-49	-	-	28.8	4.50
Shafiuddin Ahmed	1	8	0	26	1	26.00	1-26	-	-	48.0	3.25
Shahriar Hossain	3	-	-	-	-	-	-	-	-	-	-
Talha Jubair	2	10	0	70	0	-	-	-	-	-	7.00
Tapash Baisya	4	22	1	125	2	62.50	1-22	-	-	66.0	5.68
Tushar Imran	3	-	-	-	-	-	-	-	-	-	-

KENYA
Winners: Never
Runner's Up: Never
Semi-Final Finish: 2003
Participants: 1996 and onwards

For a team without Test status, Kenya have done remarkably well in World Cups. The so-called minnows are only expected to compete with other minnows, but from time to time Kenya have managed to spring surprises on the established teams. Their best victory remains the one in 1996, when the West Indies were bowled out for a shocking score of 93 and lost to the Kenyans by 73 runs.

Best World Cup: 2003. New Zealand's refusal to play in Kenya due to security concerns and their subsequent forfeiture of the match, in conjunction with a famous win over Sri Lanka, meant that Kenya were on their way to the World Cup semi-final. No non-Test playing nation had ever come this far.

Worst World Cup: 1999. Battered and bruised, Kenya lost every match in the 1999 World Cup. Sachin Tendulkar was a notable assailant, giving a batting clinic while taking 140 runs (101 balls, 16 fours and 3 sixes) off the Kenyan bowling attack.

KENYA RESULTS		M	Won	Lost	Tied	NR
v	Australia	2	0	2	0	0
v	Bangladesh	1	1	0	0	0
v	Canada	1	1	0	0	0
v	England	1	0	1	0	0
v	India	4	0	4	0	0
v	South Africa	2	0	2	0	0
v	Sri Lanka	3	1	2	0	0
v	West Indies	2	1	1	0	0
v	Zimbabwe	4	1	2	0	1
	Total	20	5	14	0	1

Success Percentage: 26.31

Steve Tikolo: Kenya's most successful batsman, with 569 runs in the World Cup.

KENYA BATTING RECORDS

Name	Mat	I	NO	Runs	HS	Ave	SR	100	50	Ct	St
RW Ali	6	2	2	6	6*	-	31.57	-	-	1	-
JO Angara	4	2	1	6	6	6.00	85.71	-	-	1	-
DN Chudasama	7	6	0	106	34	17.66	59.55	-	-	2	-
SK Gupta	2	2	0	1	1	0.50	12.50	-	-	-	-
IT Iqbal	3	2	0	17	16	8.50	32.69	-	-	2	-
JK Kamande	2	0	-	-	-	-	-	-	-	-	-
AY Karim	15	10	4	79	22	13.16	53.37	-	-	2	-
HS Modi	18	14	1	195	41	15.00	40.20	-	-	5	-
CO Obuya	9	7	1	88	29	14.66	64.23	-	-	4	-
DO Obuya	4	4	1	11	4*	3.66	31.42	-	-	8	-
TM Odoyo	17	16	4	315	43*	26.25	68.62	-	-	1	-
EO Odumbe	6	5	1	54	20	13.50	41.53	-	-	3	-
MO Odumbe	19	18	3	452	82	30.13	73.13	-	3	3	-
PJ Ongondo	9	8	1	84	24	12.00	77.06	-	-	-	-
LN Onyango	1	1	0	23	23	23.00	127.77	-	-	1	-
KO Otieno	20	19	0	427	85	22.47	52.20	-	4	11	4
BJ Patel	6	5	0	56	32	11.20	48.27	-	-	2	-
RD Shah	14	14	0	419	61	29.92	60.37	-	3	5	-
M Sheikh	2	2	0	15	8	7.50	46.87	-	-	1	-
AO Suji	8	4	1	14	6	4.66	56.00	-	-	5	-
MA Suji	20	13	7	68	15*	11.33	54.83	-	-	5	-
LO Tikolo	3	2	2	36	25*	-	48.00	-	-	2	-
SO Tikolo	20	19	0	569	96	29.94	66.70	-	6	5	-
AV Vadher	5	5	2	141	73*	47.00	57.78	-	2	-	-

KENYA BOWLING RECORDS

Name	Mat	O	M	R	W	Ave	Best	4w	5w	SR	Econ
RW Ali	6	41.2	3	190	10	19.00	3-17	-	-	24.8	4.59
JO Angara	4	32	1	203	5	40.60	2-50	-	-	38.4	6.34
DN Chudasama	7	-	-	-	-	-	-	-	-	-	-
SK Gupta	2	-	-	-	-	-	-	-	-	-	-
IT Iqbal	3	-	-	-	-	-	-	-	-	-	-
JK Kamande	2	18	0	89	1	89.00	1-51	-	-	108.0	4.94
AY Karim	15	106.2	10	439	8	54.87	3-7	-	-	79.7	4.12
HS Modi	18	-	-	-	-	-	-	-	-	-	-
CO Obuya	9	77.5	4	374	13	28.76	5-24	-	1	35.9	4.80
DO Obuya	4	-	-	-	-	-	-	-	-	-	-
TM Odoyo	17	120	8	569	16	35.56	4-28	1	-	45.0	4.74
EO Odumbe	6	16.5	0	95	4	23.75	2-8	-	-	25.2	5.64
MO Odumbe	19	116.5	9	567	18	31.50	4-38	1	-	38.9	4.85
PJ Ongondo	9	55.2	4	226	4	56.50	2-44	-	-	83.0	4.08
LN Onyango	1	4	0	31	0	-	-	-	-	-	7.75
KO Otieno	20	-	-	-	-	-	-	-	-	-	-
BJ Patel	6	-	-	-	-	-	-	-	-	-	-
RD Shah	14	-	-	-	-	-	-	-	-	-	-
M Sheikh	2	7	0	35	0	-	-	-	-	-	5.00
AO Suji	8	29	1	155	1	155.00	1-45	-	-	174.0	5.34
MA Suji	20	154.2	17	696	14	49.71	3-19	-	-	66.1	4.50
LO Tikolo	3	8	0	55	0	-	-	-	-	-	6.87
SO Tikolo	20	55.3	2	298	10	29.80	3-14	-	-	33.3	5.36
AV Vadher	5	-	-	-	-	-	-	-	-	-	-

CANADA
Winners: Never
Runner's Up: Never
Semi-Final Finish: Never
Participants: 1979 and 2003

They may have only played in two World Cups 24 years apart, but Canada are now likely to become regular participants, as the tournament's format continues expanding to include more teams. Despite a rich heritage in Canada, cricket has never progressed beyond the amateur level. In 2003 however, Canada fielded a team with a handful of players with professional experience overseas, to mix in with the amateurs and the result was instant credibility for the team. Still too weak to compete consistently at the highest level, Canada are nevertheless among the strongest of the weakest when they have their first-choice team available.

Best World Cup: 2003. John Davison made the world sit up and take notice with his heroic whirlwind hundred against the West Indies. Although Canada lost the match, Davison's 111 off 67 balls was one of the best innings of the tournament. Davison's individual brilliance aside, the real highpoint of the tournament was that Canada won a match, beating Bangladesh, a team with Test status. This World Cup could only be seen as an unqualified success.

Worst World Cup: 1979. Canada's debut in 1979 was nothing to write home about, with losses in all three matches played. Canada recorded the lowest score by a team in a World Cup match with their 45 all-out against England (oddly 'beating' their own world record in 2003 with 36 all-out against Sri Lanka). A bright note for Canada was the bowling of Montreal-born John Valentine, who bowled Pakistan's celebrated opener Majid Khan for 1 and then dismissed England's captain Mike Brearley LBW for 0 in Canada's next match.

CANADA RESULTS

CANADA RESULTS	M	Won	Lost	Tied	NR
v Australia	1	0	1	0	0
v Bangladesh	1	1	0	0	0
v England	1	0	1	0	0
v Kenya	1	0	1	0	0
v New Zealand	1	0	1	0	0
v Pakistan	1	0	1	0	0
v South Africa	1	0	1	0	0
v Sri Lanka	1	0	1	0	0
v West Indies	1	0	1	0	0
Total	9	1	8	0	0

Success Percentage: 11.11

CANADA BATTING RECORDS

Name	Mat	I	NO	Runs	HS	Ave	SR	100	50	Ct	St
A Bagai	6	6	1	56	28*	11.20	50.45	-	-	8	2
S Baksh	1	1	0	0	0	0.00	0.00	-	-	-	-
IS Billcliff	6	6	0	147	71	24.50	58.10	-	1	-	-
RG Callender	2	2	0	0	0	0.00	0.00	-	-	-	-
CJD Chappell	3	3	0	38	19	12.66	26.57	-	-	-	-
D Chumney	5	5	0	68	28	13.60	61.26	-	-	-	-
A Codrington	5	5	0	28	16	5.60	43.07	-	-	-	-
JM Davison	6	6	0	226	111	37.66	118.94	1	1	1	-
NA de Groot	6	6	0	44	17	7.33	34.64	-	-	-	-
FA Dennis	3	3	0	47	25	15.66	27.48	-	-	-	-
JV Harris	6	6	0	91	31	15.16	44.60	-	-	1	-
CC Henry	2	2	1	6	5	6.00	42.85	-	-	-	-
N Ifill	3	2	0	16	9	8.00	37.20	-	-	1	-
D Joseph	4	3	3	13	9*	-	54.16	-	-	-	-
I Maraj	6	6	1	98	53*	19.60	37.12	-	1	2	-
CA Marshall	2	2	0	10	8	5.00	24.39	-	-	-	-
BM Mauricette	3	3	0	20	15	6.66	29.41	-	-	-	-
A Patel	2	1	0	25	25	25.00	86.20	-	-	-	-
JM Patel	3	3	0	3	2	1.00	13.04	-	-	-	-
AM Samad	1	1	0	12	12	12.00	60.00	-	-	-	-
AF Sattaur	3	3	0	20	13	6.66	33.33	-	-	2	-
GR Sealy	3	3	0	73	45	24.33	48.99	-	-	-	-
BB Seebaran	4	3	2	4	4*	4.00	30.76	-	-	1	-
MP Stead	2	2	0	10	10	5.00	22.22	-	-	-	-
Tariq Javed	3	3	0	15	8	5.00	19.48	-	-	-	-
S Thuraisingam	3	3	0	25	13	8.33	64.10	-	-	-	-
JN Valentine	3	2	2	3	3*	-	17.64	-	-	1	-
JCB Vaughan	3	3	0	30	29	10.00	54.54	-	-	-	-

CANADA BOWLING RECORDS

Name	Mat	O	M	R	W	Ave	Best	4w	5w	SR	Econ
A Bagai	6	-	-	-	-	-	-	-	-	-	-
S Baksh	1	-	-	-	-	-	-	-	-	-	-
IS Billcliff	6	-	-	-	-	-	-	-	-	-	-
RG Callender	2	9	1	26	1	26.00	1-14	-	-	54.0	2.88
CJD Chappell	3	-	-	-	-	-	-	-	-	-	-
D Chumney	5	-	-	-	-	-	-	-	-	-	-
A Codrington	5	25	4	129	6	21.50	5-27	-	1	25.0	5.16
JM Davison	6	42	5	187	10	18.70	3-15	-	-	25.2	4.45
NA de Groot	6	13.3	0	88	3	29.33	2-45	-	-	27.0	6.51
FA Dennis	3	-	-	-	-	-	-	-	-	-	-
JV Harris	6	-	-	-	-	-	-	-	-	-	-
CC Henry	2	15	0	53	2	26.50	2-27	-	-	45.0	3.53
N Ifill	3	12	0	88	0	-	-	-	-	-	7.33
D Joseph	4	31	3	170	5	34.00	2-42	-	-	37.2	5.48
I Maraj	6	4.3	0	22	0	-	-	-	-	-	4.88
CA Marshall	2	-	-	-	-	-	-	-	-	-	-
BM Mauricette	3	-	-	-	-	-	-	-	-	-	-
A Patel	2	10	0	73	3	24.33	3-41	-	-	20.0	7.30
JM Patel	3	15.1	0	47	0	-	-	-	-	-	3.09
AM Samad	1	-	-	-	-	-	-	-	-	-	-
AF Sattaur	3	-	-	-	-	-	-	-	-	-	-
GR Sealy	3	6	0	21	0	-	-	-	-	-	3.50
BB Seebaran	4	18	0	130	1	130.00	1-61	-	-	108.0	7.22
MP Stead	2	4.5	0	24	0	-	-	-	-	-	4.96
Tariq Javed	3	-	-	-	-	-	-	-	-	-	-
S Thuraisingam	3	18.4	1	109	4	27.25	2-53	-	-	28.0	5.83
JN Valentine	3	19	5	66	3	22.00	1-18	-	-	38.0	3.47
JCB Vaughan	3	11	1	36	0	-	-	-	-	-	3.27

NETHERLANDS
Winners: Never
Runner's Up: Never
Semi-Final Finish: Never
Participants: 1996 and 2003

The Netherlands (or Holland, as their team shirts say) have taken the field in two World Cups. Considered among the stronger minnows, the Dutch have had some creditable performances, without ever threatening to upset the bigger teams. They did however look like one of the big boys during their sole win in the tournament. Namibia were clobbered by 64 runs, but more importantly the Dutch crossed the 300-run mark with the bat; Feiko Kloppenburg (121) and Klaas-Jan van Noortwijk (134) sharing a mammoth stand of 228 runs for the second wicket.

Best World Cup: 2003. The Netherlands beat Namibia to record their first win in World Cup history. They also gave eventual runner's up India a right scare, bowling them out for a mere 204 inside of 50 overs.

Worst World Cup: 1996: The Netherlands failed to win any matches, losing even to the UAE who were thought to be the weaker team. Amongst the thrashings, there was some cheer when Klaas-Jan van Noortwijk and a then 19-year old Bas Zuiderent put on a 114 run partnership for the fifth wicket against England.

NETHERLANDS RESULTS		M	Won	Lost	Tied	NR
v	Australia	1	0	1	0	0
v	England	2	0	2	0	0
v	India	1	0	1	0	0
v	Namibia	1	1	0	0	0
v	New Zealand	1	0	1	0	0
v	Pakistan	2	0	2	0	0
v	South Africa	1	0	1	0	0
v	United Arab Emirates	1	0	1	0	0
v	Zimbabwe	1	0	1	0	0
	Total	11	1	10	0	0

Success Percentage: 9.09

Klaas-Jan van Noortwijk: 322 runs at an average of 46.00 in the World Cup

NETHERLANDS BATTING RECORDS

Name	Mat	I	NO	Runs	HS	Ave	SR	100	50	Ct	St
Adeel Raja	3	2	1	2	2	2.00	13.33	-	-	1	-
GJAF Aponso	5	4	0	120	58	30.00	48.58	-	1	-	-
PJ Bakker	5	1	1	1	1*	-	25.00	-	-	-	-
PE Cantrell	5	5	0	160	47	32.00	52.11	-	-	-	-
NE Clarke	5	5	0	50	32	10.00	44.64	-	-	3	-
TBM de Leede	11	11	1	188	58*	18.80	58.93	-	1	2	-
JJ Esmeijer	4	3	1	3	3*	1.50	15.78	-	-	3	-
EL Gouka	3	2	1	19	19	19.00	52.77	-	-	-	-
F Jansen	2	0	-	-	-	-	-	-	-	1	-
JF Kloppenburg	5	5	0	158	121	31.60	65.02	1	-	1	-
RP Lefebvre	9	9	3	135	45	22.50	68.52	-	-	3	-
SW Lubbers	4	4	1	24	9	8.00	64.86	-	-	1	-
HJC Mol	4	3	0	38	23	12.66	40.42	-	-	2	-
MMC Schewe	5	4	1	49	20	16.33	72.05	-	-	2	1
E Schiferli	6	6	0	75	22	12.50	67.56	-	-	1	-
RH Scholte	3	3	0	16	8	5.33	28.57	-	-	-	-
J Smits	6	5	2	58	26	19.33	42.02	-	-	4	1
NA Statham	2	2	0	7	7	3.50	15.90	-	-	-	-
DLS van Bunge	6	5	0	135	62	27.00	55.10	-	1	2	-
KJJ van Noortwijk	9	9	2	322	134*	46.00	75.23	1	1	-	-
RF van Oosterom	2	2	2	7	5*	-	36.84	-	-	1	-
LP van Troost	6	6	1	96	26	19.20	69.06	-	-	-	-
B Zuiderent	11	11	1	126	54	12.60	49.60	-	1	9	-

NETHERLANDS BOWLING RECORDS

Name	Mat	O	M	R	W	Ave	Best	4w	5w	SR	Econ
Adeel Raja	3	22.5	0	123	6	20.50	4-42	1	-	22.8	5.38
GJAF Aponso	5	40.2	0	257	2	128.50	1-57	-	-	121.0	6.37
PJ Bakker	5	43	2	215	3	71.66	2-51	-	-	86.0	5.00
PE Cantrell	5	31	0	170	3	56.66	1-18	-	-	62.0	5.48
NE Clarke	5	-	-	-	-	-	-	-	-	-	-
TBM de Leede	11	72.5	0	432	11	39.27	4-35	1	-	39.7	5.93
JJ Esmeijer	4	31	0	154	0	-	-	-	-	-	4.96
EL Gouka	3	3.4	0	51	1	51.00	1-32	-	-	22.0	13.90
F Jansen	2	9	0	62	1	62.00	1-40	-	-	54.0	6.88
JF Kloppenburg	5	38.2	0	168	7	24.00	4-42	1	-	32.8	4.38
RP Lefebvre	9	75	6	273	7	39.00	2-38	-	-	64.2	3.64
SW Lubbers	4	36	0	187	5	37.40	3-48	-	-	43.2	5.19
HJC Mol	4	13	0	89	2	44.50	1-24	-	-	39.0	6.84
MMC Schewe	5	-	-	-	-	-	-	-	-	-	-
E Schiferli	6	49	5	261	4	65.25	2-43	-	-	73.5	5.32
RH Scholte	3	-	-	-	-	-	-	-	-	-	-
J Smits	6	-	-	-	-	-	-	-	-	-	-
NA Statham	2	-	-	-	-	-	-	-	-	-	-
DLS van Bunge	6	12	0	85	5	17.00	3-16	-	-	14.4	7.08
KJJ van Noortwijk	9	-	-	-	-	-	-	-	-	-	-
RF van Oosterom	2	-	-	-	-	-	-	-	-	-	-
LP van Troost	6	3	0	22	0	-	-	-	-	-	7.33
B Zuiderent	11	-	-	-	-	-	-	-	-	-	-

EAST AFRICA
Winners: Never
Runner's Up: Never
Semi-Final Finish: Never
Participants: 1975

East Africa appeared in the 1975 World Cup and never qualified for the tournament again. The team was a collective of players from Kenya, Uganda, Tanzania and Zambia. Kenya have gone on to forge their own path in cricket and no team by the name of East Africa is currently a member of the ICC. A notable player for East Africa was England-born Don Pringle, whose Nairobi-born son, Derek played for England in the 1987 and 1992 World Cups.

Best World Cup/Worst Cup: 1975. It was the best of times; it was the worst of times. But really, it was just the worst of times.

EAST AFRICA RESULTS

		M	Won	Lost	Tied	NR
v	England	1	0	1	0	0
v	India	1	0	1	0	0
v	New Zealand	1	0	1	0	0
	Total	3	0	3	0	0

Success Percentage: 0.00

EAST AFRICA BATTING RECORDS

Name	Mat	I	NO	Runs	HS	Ave	SR	100	50	Ct	St
Frasat Ali	3	3	0	57	45	19.00	32.38	-	-	-	-
Harilal Shah	3	3	0	6	6	2.00	10.71	-	-	-	-
Jawahir Shah	3	3	0	46	37	15.33	40.35	-	-	-	-
H McLeod	2	2	0	5	5	2.50	50.00	-	-	-	-
Mehmood Quaraishy	3	3	1	41	19	20.50	26.62	-	-	-	-
PS Mehta	1	1	0	12	12	12.00	29.26	-	-	-	-
J Nagenda	1	0	-	-	-	-	-	-	-	-	-
PG Nana	3	3	2	9	8*	9.00	20.00	-	-	2	-
DJ Pringle	2	2	0	5	3	2.50	33.33	-	-	-	-
RK Sethi	3	3	0	54	30	18.00	29.18	-	-	1	-
S Sumar	1	1	0	4	4	4.00	36.36	-	-	-	-
S Walusimbi	3	3	0	38	16	12.66	30.15	-	-	-	-
Yunus Badat	2	2	0	1	1	0.50	14.28	-	-	-	-
Zulfiqar Ali	3	3	1	39	30	19.50	51.31	-	-	1	-

EAST AFRICA BOWLING RECORDS

Name	Mat	O	M	R	W	Ave	Best	4w	5w	SR	Econ
Frasat Ali	3	24	1	107	0	-	-	-	-	-	4.45
Harilal Shah	3	-	-	-	-	-	-	-	-	-	-
Jawahir Shah	3	-	-	-	-	-	-	-	-	-	-
H McLeod	2	-	-	-	-	-	-	-	-	-	-
Mehmood Quaraishy	3	18	0	94	3	31.33	2-55	-	-	36.0	5.22

EAST AFRICA BOWLING RECORDS *continued*

Name	Mat	O	M	R	W	Ave	Best	4w	5w	SR	Econ
PS Mehta	1	-	-	-	-	-	-	-	-	-	-
J Nagenda	1	9	1	50	1	50.00	1-50	-	-	54.0	5.55
PG Nana	3	28.5	4	116	1	116.00	1-34	-	-	173.0	4.02
DJ Pringle	2	15	0	55	0	-	-	-	-	-	3.66
RK Sethi	3	20	1	100	1	100.00	1-51	-	-	120.0	5.00
S Sumar	1	-	-	-	-	-	-	-	-	-	-
S Walusimbi	3	-	-	-	-	-	-	-	-	-	-
Yunus Badat	2	-	-	-	-	-	-	-	-	-	-
Zulfiqar Ali	3	35	3	166	4	41.50	3-63	-	-	52.5	4.74

UNITED ARAB EMIRATES
Winners: Never
Runner's Up: Never
Semi Final Finish: Never
Participants: 1996

With a large number of expatriates from cricket-playing countries, the sport is extremely popular in the United Arab Emirates. No ground has hosted more ODI matches than the Sharjah Cricket Association Stadium, even though only two of those matches involved the host nation. Membership to the ICC was granted in 1990 and six short years later the UAE were playing in the World Cup. They have been unable to qualify again, but with the ICC headquarters now in Dubai, and the construction of more world-class cricket stadiums in the Emirates, the future of the sport is bright in the UAE. It is only a matter of time before they qualify again.

Best World Cup/Worst Cup: 1996. The UAE did well to win a match in their first World Cup appearance. The team enjoyed a notable profile when their Lamborghini driving captain Sultan Zarawani became something of a cult figure during the tournament, courtesy of his decision to face Allan Donald without a helmet.

EMIRATES RESULTS

		M	Won	Lost	Tied	NR
v	England	1	0	1	0	0
v	Netherlands	1	1	0	0	0
v	New Zealand	1	0	1	0	0
v	Pakistan	1	0	1	0	0
v	South Africa	1	0	1	0	0
	Total	5	1	4	0	0

Success percentage: 20.00

EMIRATES BATTING RECORDS

Name	Mat	I	NO	Runs	HS	Ave	SR	100	50	Ct	St
Arshad Laeeq	4	4	1	66	43*	22.00	47.14	-	-	-	-
Azhar Saeed	5	5	0	58	32	11.60	33.14	-	-	2	-
SF Dukanwala	5	4	2	84	40*	42.00	60.43	-	-	2	-
Imtiaz Abbasi	5	4	3	4	2*	4.00	18.18	-	-	2	2
Mazhar Hussain	5	5	0	99	33	19.80	52.38	-	-	1	-
V Mehra	4	4	1	44	29*	14.66	39.28	-	-	1	-
Mohammad Aslam	4	4	0	38	23	9.50	52.05	-	-	-	-
Mohammad Ishaq	3	3	1	71	51*	35.50	84.52	-	1	1	-
G Mylvaganam	3	3	0	36	23	12.00	39.13	-	-	1	-
Saeed-al-Saffar	1	0	-	-	-	-	-	-	-	1	-
Saleem Raza	4	4	0	137	84	34.25	100.73	-	1	-	-
JA Samarasekera	5	4	1	90	47*	30.00	68.18	-	-	-	-
Shehzad Altaf	2	0	-	-	-	-	-	-	-	-	-
Sultan Zarawani	5	4	0	16	13	4.00	44.44	-	-	1	-

EMIRATES BOWLING RECORDS

Name	Mat	O	M	R	W	Ave	Best	4w	5w	SR	Econ
Arshad Laeeq	4	19	0	117	1	117.00	1-25	-	-	114.0	6.15
Azhar Saeed	5	31	1	157	6	26.16	3-45	-	-	31.0	5.06
SF Dukanwala	5	33	1	153	6	25.50	5-29	-	1	33.0	4.63
Imtiaz Abbasi	5	-	-	-	-	-	-	-	-	-	-
Mazhar Hussain	5	8	0	60	0	-	-	-	-	-	7.50
V Mehra	4	-	-	-	-	-	-	-	-	-	-
Mohammad Aslam	4	-	-	-	-	-	-	-	-	-	-
Mohammad Ishaq	3	-	-	-	-	-	-	-	-	-	-
G Mylvaganam	3	-	-	-	-	-	-	-	-	-	-
Saeed-al-Saffar	1	3	0	25	0	-	-	-	-	-	8.33
Saleem Raza	4	22	1	108	1	108.00	1-48	-	-	132.0	4.90
JA Samarasekera	5	34	4	157	3	52.33	1-17	-	-	68.0	4.61
Shehzad Altaf	2	13	3	37	1	37.00	1-15	-	-	78.0	2.84
Sultan Zarawani	5	37	0	209	4	52.25	2-49	-	-	55.5	5.64

SCOTLAND
Winners: Never
Runner's Up: Never
Semi-Final Finish: Never
Participants: 1999

Scotland's sole appearance in the World Cup saw them struggle in a pool that also included Australia, Pakistan, New Zealand and the West Indies. Their only realistic chance of winning was against Bangladesh and that went begging. The batting of all-rounder Gavin Hamilton was a bright spot for Scotland, but virtually every other step of the way the team looked like no more than a collection of talented weekend cricketers, utterly out of their depth.

Best World Cup/Worst Cup: 1999. Besides Gavin Hamilton's two half-centuries, the best thing about Scotland's campaign was that they had the best-looking uniforms. The worst thing of course, being their five losses in a row.

Scotland's Gavin Hamilton during the 1999 World Cup: Unhappy despite scoring two half-centuries and having a snappy uniform.

SCOTLAND RESULTS

		M	Won	Lost	Tied	NR
v	Australia	1	0	1	0	0
v	Bangladesh	1	0	1	0	0
v	New Zealand	1	0	1	0	0
v	Pakistan	1	0	1	0	0
v	West Indies	1	0	1	0	0
	Total	5	0	5	0	0

Success Percentage: 0.00

SCOTLAND BATTING RECORDS

Name	Mat	I	NO	Runs	HS	Ave	SR	100	50	Ct	St
MJD Allingham	3	3	0	11	6	3.66	11.45	-	-	1	-
Asim Butt	5	4	0	23	11	5.75	82.14	-	-	-	-
JAR Blain	5	5	1	15	9	3.75	30.00	-	-	1	-
JE Brinkley	5	5	0	52	23	10.40	44.06	-	-	1	-
AG Davies	5	5	1	83	32	20.75	53.89	-	-	2	1
NR Dyer	5	4	3	3	2*	3.00	21.42	-	-	2	-
GM Hamilton	5	5	1	217	76	54.25	68.67	-	2	1	-
BMW Patterson	3	3	0	10	10	3.33	23.25	-	-	-	-
IL Philip	3	3	0	20	17	6.66	22.47	-	-	4	-
G Salmond	5	5	0	57	31	11.40	52.29	-	-	1	-
MJ Smith	5	5	0	19	13	3.80	22.35	-	-	-	-
IM Stanger	4	4	0	47	27	11.75	32.63	-	-	2	-
JG Williamson	2	2	0	11	10	5.50	31.42	-	-	-	-

SCOTLAND BOWLING RECORDS

Name	Mat	O	M	R	W	Ave	Best	4w	5w	SR	Econ
MJD Allingham	3	-	-	-	-	-	-	-	-	-	-
Asim Butt	5	37	6	148	4	37.00	2-24	-	-	55.5	4.00
JAR Blain	5	37.1	1	210	10	21.00	4-37	1	-	22.3	5.65
JE Brinkley	5	28	0	117	2	58.50	1-29	-	-	84.0	4.17
AG Davies	5	-	-	-	-	-	-	-	-	-	-
NR Dyer	5	26	2	117	5	23.40	2-26	-	-	31.2	4.50
GM Hamilton	5	35.4	4	149	3	49.66	2-36	-	-	71.3	4.17
BMW Patterson	3	-	-	-	-	-	-	-	-	-	-
IL Philip	3	-	-	-	-	-	-	-	-	-	-
G Salmond	5	-	-	-	-	-	-	-	-	-	-
MJ Smith	5	-	-	-	-	-	-	-	-	-	-
IM Stanger	4	9	0	56	0	-	-	-	-	-	6.22
JG Williamson	2	-	-	-	-	-	-	-	-	-	-

NAMIBIA
Winners: Never
Runner's Up: Never
Semi-Final Finish: Never
Participants: 2003

An ICC associate member only since 1992, Namibia did well to qualify for the 2003 World Cup. As expected, the Namibians lost their six matches, but throughout the tournament the team looked to be having the time of their lives. Jan Berrie-Burger made a scintillating 85 from 86 balls against England and the team generally impressed observers with their athleticism in the field.

Best World Cup/Worst Cup: 2003, with the glass being half full.

NAMIBIA RSESULTS		M	Won	Lost	Tied	NR
v	Australia	1	0	1	0	0
v	England	1	0	1	0	0
v	India	1	0	1	0	0
v	Netherlands	1	0	1	0	0
v	Pakistan	1	0	1	0	0
v	Zimbabwe	1	0	1	0	0
	Total	6	0	6	0	0

Success Percentage: 0.00

NAMIBIA BATTING RECORDS

Name	Mat	I	NO	Runs	HS	Ave	SR	100	50	Ct	St
AJ Burger	6	6	0	199	85	33.16	100.50	-	1	-	-
LJ Burger	6	6	1	11	5	2.20	17.74	-	-	6	-
SF Burger	2	2	0	11	6	5.50	55.00	-	-	1	-
M Karg	3	2	0	45	41	22.50	69.23	-	-	1	-
D Keulder	6	6	0	132	52	22.00	60.00	-	1	3	-
BL Kotze	5	4	1	27	24*	9.00	52.94	-	-	1	-
DB Kotze	6	6	1	82	27	16.40	60.74	-	-	3	-
JL Louw	1	0	-	-	-	-	-	-	-	1	-
BG Murgatroyd	6	6	0	90	52	15.00	62.06	-	1	-	-
G Snyman	5	4	0	5	5	1.25	55.55	-	-	-	-
SJ Swanepoel	5	5	0	43	23	8.60	45.74	-	-	-	-
BO van Rooi	3	3	2	26	17	26.00	68.42	-	-	-	-
M van Schoor	5	5	1	58	24	14.50	52.25	-	-	4	-
RJ van Vuuren	5	5	2	26	14	8.66	68.42	-	-	-	-
R Walters	2	2	0	0	0	0.00	0.00	-	-	-	-

Namibia's Rudi van Vuuren does the bhangra.

NAMIBIA BOWLING RECORDS

Name	Mat	O	M	R	W	Ave	Best	4w	5w	SR	Econ
AJ Burger	6	16	0	104	3	34.66	1-18	-	-	32.0	6.50
LJ Burger	6	55	3	297	6	49.50	3-39	-	-	55.0	5.40
SF Burger	2	11	0	67	0	-	-	-	-	-	6.09
M Karg	3	-	-	-	-	-	-	-	-	-	-
D Keulder	6	-	-	-	-	-	-	-	-	-	-
BL Kotze	5	43	2	276	3	92.00	2-51	-	-	86.0	6.41
DB Kotze	6	47	0	256	2	128.00	1-32	-	-	141.0	5.44
JL Louw	1	10	0	60	1	60.00	1-60	-	-	60.0	6.00
BG Murgatroyd	6	-	-	-	-	-	-	-	-	-	-
G Snyman	5	48	0	281	6	46.83	3-69	-	-	48.0	5.85
SJ Swanepoel	5	-	-	-	-	-	-	-	-	-	-
BO van Rooi	3	20	0	119	1	119.00	1-24	-	-	120.0	5.95
M van Schoor	5	-	-	-	-	-	-	-	-	-	-
RJ van Vuuren	5	50	5	298	8	37.25	5-43	-	1	37.5	5.96
R Walters	2	-	-	-	-	-	-	-	-	-	-

Pakistan's Wasim Akram is the most successful bowler in World Cup history; pictured here after capturing his 500th wicket in ODI cricket during Pakistan's match against the Netherlands in the 2003 World Cup.